Th<
Ya<

ALSO BY JIM SARGENT

We Were the All-American Girls: Interviews with
Players of the AAGPBL, 1943–1954 (McFarland, 2013)

JIM SARGENT and ROBERT M. GORMAN

The South Bend Blue Sox: A History of the All-American
Girls Professional Baseball League Team and Its Players,
1943–1954 (McFarland, 2012)

The Tigers and Yankees in '61

*A Pennant Race for the Ages,
the Babe's Record Broken
and Stormin' Norman's
Greatest Season*

JIM SARGENT

Foreword by Jake Wood

McFarland & Company, Inc., Publishers
Jefferson, North Carolina

LIBRARY OF CONGRESS CATALOGUING-IN-PUBLICATION DATA

Names: Sargent, Jim, 1941– author.
Title: The Tigers and Yankees in '61 : a pennant race for the ages,
    the Babe's record broken and Stormin' Norman's greatest season /
    Jim Sargent ; foreword by Jake Wood.
Description: Jefferson, North Carolina : McFarland & Company, Inc.,
    Publishers, 2016. | Includes bibliographical references and index.
Identifiers: LCCN 2016014871 | ISBN 9780786498628 (softcover :
    acid free paper) ∞
Subjects: LCSH: Baseball—United States—History—20th century. |
    Detroit Tigers (Baseball team)—History—20th century. | New York
    Yankees (Baseball team)—History—20th century.
Classification: LCC GV863.A1 S317 2016 | DDC 796.357/640973—dc23
LC record available at https://lccn.loc.gov/2016014871

BRITISH LIBRARY CATALOGUING DATA ARE AVAILABLE

ISBN (print) 978-0-7864-9862-8
ISBN (ebook) 978-1-4766-2311-5

Front cover: New York Yankees outfielder Roger Maris hits
an extra-inning home run against Detroit at Tiger Stadium
on September 18, 1961 (*Detroit Free Press*)

Printed in the United States of America

*McFarland & Company, Inc., Publishers
    Box 611, Jefferson, North Carolina 28640
    www.mcfarlandpub.com*

Table of Contents

Foreword by Jake Wood

In 1937 there were no black players in major league baseball. What are the odds that a son born to Jacob and Roberta Wood on June 22, 1937, in Elizabeth, New Jersey, would become part of a Detroit Tigers team in 1961 that would win 101 games? Unfortunately, those Tigers on which I played did not win the American League pennant, because the New York Yankees won 109 games.

It all began on the sandlots, the playgrounds, and the parks in Union County, New Jersey. After four years of minor league baseball in places such as Erie, Pennsylvania, Durham, North Carolina, Idaho Falls, Idaho, Fox Cities, Wisconsin, Knoxville, Tennessee, and Denver, Colorado, I finally made it to Detroit.

Could these places, teammates, and experiences adequately prepare a person for the emotional roller coaster that would ensue during a 162-game major league season?

What you have to figure out is how you approach those veterans on the Tigers team that already had similar experiences.

The elation one feels getting prepared to participate in your first major league game is hard to express. Yet deep down inside, you feel as though something was missing. You feel a kind of void that can't be filled by baseball.

Who were some of the individuals that made this team's accomplishments possible?

Al Kaline (the Silent Assassin): Al didn't say much, but he displayed a fierce competitiveness on the field.

Rocky Colavito (The Rock): Rocky was solid in his mannerisms. You couldn't tell if he went 4-for-4, or 0-for-4 on any given day.

Norm Cash (Stormin' Norman): He was consistent throughout the season. Hitting seemed easy to Norm.

Frank Lary (Taters): A fierce competitor on the field, a jokester off it.

Steve Boros (a gentleman's gentleman): One of the finest persons you would ever want to be associated with on and off the field.

Billy Bruton (Gandhi): We all believed he was much older than the records showed.

Chico Fernandez (Ernie): When Chico started hitting home runs, he became the "Ernie Banks" of Detroit.

Hank Aguirre (Mex): All business on the mound, loose and funny off it.

Don Mossi (Moss): A good guy who always appeared to be stoic.

Charlie Maxwell (Paw Paw): Every Sunday you could count on Charlie to hit a home run.

Dick Brown (Brownie): A model teammate who treated you with respect, regardless of your status on the team.

Some of the highlights I enjoyed in 1961, on the high side of the emotional coin:

Hitting a home run against the Cleveland Indians on Opening Day, April 11.

Having my entire family and my friends from home come to see me during the first game the Tigers played at Yankee Stadium.

Scoring from second base on a sacrifice fly hit by Charlie Maxwell against the Cleveland Indians.

Going 5-for-5 in a game against the Chicago White Sox.

Hitting a grand slam home run against the Washington Senators.

On the flip side of the emotional coin, you expect negative comments on the road from fans, and those comments help motivate you. When you hear vile, negative comments expressed by the home crowd at Tiger Stadium, it causes emotional turbulence.

When the strikeouts begin to pile up, you find an ironing board (representing a baseball bat) in your locker, and you feel psychologically devastated.

After making an error, you find a large basket in your locker (representing a ball glove), and you feel alone and isolated.

If looks could kill, I died many a day in 1961. After many years, I discovered that having a relationship with God is the only way to fill the void that existed during my baseball career. God made me feel at ease.

After all is said and done, after experiencing all of the physical, the emotional, and the mental ups and downs, it is with a grateful heart that I thank God for the baseball season of 1961.

Jake Wood was signed by Detroit in 1956 and, after four solid minor league seasons, worked his way into the Tigers' everyday lineup in 1961, becoming the first African American starter signed by the franchise. That season the speedy second baseman stole 30 bases and led the American League with 14 triples. He would go on to hit .250 over seven big league seasons, spending all but one in Detroit.

Preface

The 1961 season was a particularly memorable one for Detroit's most famous sports team. The Tigers battled the perennial champion New York Yankees for the pennant all summer long. The climax came in a fateful three-game series in the Bronx over the Labor Day weekend, when the Yankees swept the Tigers, launched a 13-game winning streak, rolled to the American League pennant, and captured the World Series over the Cincinnati Reds, winners of the National League's pennant.

In those glory days, like many other baseball fans, I read about my favorites in the newspapers, in my case the *Flint Journal*. I also listened to the Tigers on the radio, saw them play on television once in a while, and traveled to the Motor City with friends a handful of times to catch the excitement of a big league game. The double-decked, steel-beamed, concrete stadium at "The Corner" of Michigan and Trumbull Avenues had what seemed like the greenest grass in the world to go with the green walls and green seats. The fan-friendly old ballpark seated nearly 52,000, and the facility was shared by the NFL's Lions, starting in September. The price of admission was affordable, $2.00 for reserved and $3.00 for box seats in 1961. You could drive the 70 miles from Flint to the stadium in an hour and a half, even if traffic was heavy on the John Lodge Expressway.

I started to write this book with a memory of seeing Norm Cash hit a baseball out of Tiger Stadium, a tremendous drive that carried over the right field roof on June 11, 1961. I will never forget seeing that Tigers game, a memory frozen in time, and watching Cash's blast, but I figured out the date by using Baseball-reference.com. In writing this book I highlight the players and games of two teams rather than one. Why? The New York side of this story, after all, has been well documented by a number of books. The Tigers' story has never been told, except briefly in two biographies of Kaline and one of Cash, and even in the articles and books on the 1961 Yankees, the pennant race itself is not explored in any depth. I wanted to learn much more about the players and games on both sides that made the season so special.

Baseball is a game mainly played by kids. Many of us who love the game grew up learning to play ball, enjoying varying degrees of success with many guys on a number of teams, and we still fondly recall some of those good friends and highlight experiences.

I first remember playing baseball during recess in the fourth grade at Tanner Elementary School in the spring of 1950, and later, in higher grades, we played on the playground behind Kearsley High, located on Richfield Road near the corner of Genesee Road. Even later, I played for the school's junior varsity and varsity teams, on summer teams at Kearsley Park in Flint in leagues for boys ages 13–14 and 15–16, and for a couple of summers after high school on a semipro team in Montrose, thirty miles northwest of Flint. In later years, I spent a good deal of time playing fast-pitch, and after I was older, slow-pitch softball in too many leagues to remember. Nowadays girls play baseball too. Before the 1970s, however, baseball was largely a game played by boys, some of whom proved good enough to rise to pro ball, and some even to the major leagues. They are the big boys of summer that we remember, just as we remember our own experiences.

Yankee manager Ralph Houk, writing in *Season of Glory* (1988) about major leaguers in the 1961 season, said, "They're still little boys. They love to win and they love to joke, and that's why they haven't changed as much as you read they have." The Major, or "Maj," as Houk was known from his Army experience during World War II, continued, "Sure, they make all this money, but once they walk into that clubhouse and put on that uniform, they're little boys again. They want to look good in front of people. They want to do well. They're competitive, or they wouldn't be good athletes."

Houk's comments ring true. They remind me of a picture above a story on the sports pages of the *Roanoke Times* around 1981, when I was playing slow-pitch on a city league team called the Wild Dogs. The picture above the story showed three smiling guys in their 40s walking toward a ball field and carrying their equipment, and the caption said, "Boys Once More." Those guys loved the game and the camaraderie that major leaguer Jim Bouton wrote about in his 1970 book, *Ball Four*. In his conclusion, Bouton wryly observed, "You see, you spend a good piece of your life gripping a baseball and in the end it turns out that it was the other way around all the time."

This book is about big boys playing ball at the major league level in 1961. During the virtual explosion of media attention captured by the exciting home run race between Roger Maris and Mickey Mantle, and to a lesser extent the thrilling feats of Detroit's Norm Cash, Rocky Colavito, Al Kaline, Frank Lary, and more, the teams and many of the players were described, often glamorized, and sometimes criticized, especially Maris, by writers who were earning a living by trying to be the first to convey what Jim Bouton later expressed so well.

As the nation and the world came to be more and more media-driven in the 1960s, baseball was fueled more and more by those who wanted to "market" the game. The bottom line was that teams and players earned more money and reaped more rewards. Fortunately for the reader, *The Tigers and Yankees in '61* covers the first of the real media-hyped seasons, so maybe we can have fun by looking back at what those teams and those players achieved as America entered a new age of televised sports during the first year of John F. Kennedy's Presidency.

When you write a book, you get a lot of help from friends and those who become new friends, because nobody completes such a daunting task on their own. I would like to acknowledge the help of many friends, starting with Karen Bergeron, of Harrison Township, Michigan, an excellent researcher who dug out most of the stories I used from the Detroit newspapers, notably the *Free Press*. My friend David Hillman, retired as Director of Library Services at Virginia Western Community College in Roanoke, proofed the manuscript more than once, and David offered countless useful suggestions for improvement. Clifford Blau, of White Plains, New York, is a member of SABR, the Society for American Baseball Research, and he did another excellent job for me as a fact-checker. I also received a number of player files and pictures from the Library at the National Baseball Hall of Fame, thanks to staff members like Matt Rothenberg and John Horne, and I obtained other pictures through Nathan Kelber at the Detroit Historical Society. My wife Betty read many pages of different chapters, and she encouraged me throughout the complex process of turning an endless series of thoughts and a pile of research into a book. Several friends read different chapters and offered comments, and while they are too numerous to name, I appreciate all of them and their insights.

Some of the book's pictures were provided by the Baseball Hall of Fame and others by the Detroit Historical Society, and those are credited accordingly. Author Irwin Cohen contributed a couple of his pictures. Several images came from my own collection of baseball pictures, particularly covering the Tigers.

In the end, this book is my responsibility, and whatever mistakes made are mine. While authors strive to write in accurate, readable, and, hopefully, entertaining fashion, I suspect nobody is ever totally satisfied with his or her work. Still, if Robert L. Sargent, Senior, who wrote three editions of a textbook about his passion, *Automobile Sheet Metal Repair*, was still alive, I think Dad would be impressed.

To my friends as well as those who contacted me about *Yesterday's Tiger*

Heroes, I value your insights and your support. I hope you find *Tigers and Yankees in '61* an even better book. Once again I had a good time creating it and writing it, kind of like the 15-year-old boy who learned to hit a curve ball, thanks to Kearsley coach Don Spencer, and connected for his first home run in a game against Hirsch Jewelers at Kearsley Park in Flint during the long ago summer of 1956. Maybe that ball is still rolling.

1

The Tigers, the Yankees,
and the Pennant Race of 1961

The first home run hit out of Detroit's renamed Tiger Stadium was a memorable event in 1961, and it occurred during that season's pennant race. On June 11, a bright Sunday afternoon, in the sixth inning of the first game of a doubleheader, Norm Cash, after his customary stroll to home plate while swirling two bats over his head, stepped in against Joe McClain of the expansion Washington Senators. McClain, pitching carefully to the muscular slugger, fell behind with a 3–1 count. Getting his sign, the big right-hander wound up and broke a curve high and just inside to the left-handed-hitting Cash. Seeing the ball as quickly as it left the pitcher's hand, one of his special talents, Detroit's first baseman, who was accustomed to the American League umpires calling a "high" strike zone, smashed the pitch, driving it high and deep to right field.

Exhilarated, Cash, the league's hottest hitter, dropped his bat and turned to run, his eyes glued to the soaring baseball, a moonshot over the 325-foot marker about ten feet inside the foul line, that seemed headed for Michigan's Upper Peninsula. The ball quickly disappeared from sight beyond the gray-walled stadium's 94-foot-high roof, finally bouncing in the middle of Trumbull Avenue and hitting a building across the street. The scene lasted only a few seconds, but for fans who saw the first out-of-the-stadium home run hit by a Tiger, it was one of those indelible memories that live in the back of your mind. That afternoon I had a reserved seat in back of third base, but I walked along the concourse surrounding the field behind the first few rows of lower deck box seats to watch Cash hit. After his longball, Cash, full of boyish enthusiasm, trotted happily around the bases, clapping for himself and grinning as he crossed home plate.

Unfazed, McClain, a six-foot Southerner from Johnson City, Tennessee, who was selected by the new Washington franchise in the minor league phase of the 1960 expansion draft, persevered and won, 7–4, yielding two singles and four solo home runs in his seven-plus innings. McClain

Tiger Stadium as seen from the air looking toward the east in the 1960s. The third base side of the stadium is in the lower front edge of the picture, Michigan Avenue runs toward downtown Detroit on the first base edge of the ballpark, and Trumbull Avenue intersects Michigan Avenue at "The Corner" behind the right field wall. Norm Cash's out-of-the-park home run on June 11 finally landed on Trumbull Avenue (Detroit Historical Society).

recorded his sixth victory, saved by six straight outs of relief by John Gabler, but Cash's long blast was the big news in Joe Falls' story in the *Detroit Free Press*. Ted Williams was the first hitter to clear the stadium's right field roof with a home run on May 4, 1939, and Mickey Mantle achieved the feat three times, all batting left-handed. Mantle hit those homers on June 18, 1956, September 17, 1958, and September 10, 1960, with the first and third clouts coming off fastballs from Detroit's Paul Foytack. No batter had yet cleared the roof in left field at Briggs or Tiger Stadium.

Surprisingly, Cash's longest home run to date came off a breaking pitch by McClain. "If it had been a fast ball, it'd still be rolling," quipped Tigers manager Bob Scheffing. Joe Martin, a taxi driver, was standing next to his cab on Trumbull Avenue, and he spotted the ball and retrieved it. After the game, he went to the Tigers' clubhouse and offered the ball to Cash as a memento of the event. In return, Martin was given a new ball autographed by three of Detroit's biggest stars, Cash, Rocky Colavito, and Al Kaline.[1]

Home runs were baseball's rage in 1961. Colavito, Detroit's left fielder and a powerful right-handed hitter, slugged his 17th homer in the bottom of the fourth frame, just a minute or two before Cash connected for his 15th circuit clout. Cash's number 16 in the sixth left the stadium, and in the eighth, Al Kaline led off with his fifth home run, a blow that ended McClain's day. Detroit's tall, stocky, left-handed Hal Woodeshick, who gave up five runs on seven hits, took the loss, and the Senators' triumph dropped the second-place Tigers' record to 36–21, 1.5 games behind the league-leading Cleveland Indians. At that point the perennial pennant-winning New York Yankees were in third place, two games behind Cleveland.

In the nightcap, Cash, who had socked two home runs in his four trips in Sunday's first game, rapped four hits in five at-bats, including another homer, to lead the Tigers to a 7–6, 11-inning win. Kaline belted his sixth four-bagger to open the scoring off right-hander Tom Sturdivant in the third inning, but after six innings the Senators built a 6–4 lead with six unearned runs off Bob Bruce, a big right-hander, and Terry Fox, Detroit's top reliever. In the seventh, Cash and Steve Boros, the young third baseman from Flint, Michigan, connected for bases-empty homers to tie the game at 6–6. Neither team could score again until the 11th, when Kaline worked ex–Tigers righty Dave Sisler for a lead-off walk, Charlie Maxwell flew out, and Colavito, batting cleanup, walked. Cash chopped an infield hit down the third-base line to load the bases, and Boros drilled a single to left for the winning run, giving the Tigers a split in the doubleheader. Cash, later laughing in the clubhouse, collected six hits in nine trips for the day, boosting his average to .370. The drawling Texan's hot afternoon left him one point behind Cleveland's Jim Piersall and 19 points ahead of New York's Elston Howard in the American League batting race.

Norm Cash, the Tigers' first baseman obtained in a trade with Cleveland on April 12, 1960, enjoyed a career year by June of 1961. "Stormin' Norman," as fans called him, led the American League with a .361 average, slugging 41 home runs and driving in 132 runs (National Baseball Hall of Fame, Cooperstown, New York).

Rocky Colavito, who belted 45 home runs and drove home 140 runs for the Tigers in 1961, liked to start each at-bat by pointing his bat at the pitcher (photograph by Irwin Cohen).

The *Free Press'* Watson Spoelstra, who also wrote for baseball's weekly *The Sporting News*, referred to Detroit being the nation's leading producer of automobiles and auto components by saying the doubleheader showed the Tigers were fueled by a twin-engine job, "Rock and Sock." The Rock was Colavito, who had connected for 42 home runs for Cleveland in 1959, tying for the American League lead with Harmon Killebrew, who enjoyed his breakout 42-homer season with the old Washington Senators (now the Minnesota Twins). Colavito hit 35 circuit clouts for Detroit in 1960, making him a proven longball threat. The Sock was Cash, "the most exciting slugger in the big leagues." After nine weeks of the season, each Bengal belter had 17 homers.

This was the second Rock-and-Sock performance in two days. Facing the Indians' third-year right-hander Gary Bell on Saturday in the seventh inning on Saturday, Colavito homered to left field, and Cash followed with a home run into the right field stands. The two clouts gave lanky, right-handed sidearmer Jim Bunning, who could be overpowering, a 2–0 victory, once righty reliever Bill Fischer, who grew up in Wausau, Wisconsin, retired the final Indians batter. Starting on April 29, the Tigers led the league for 38 straight days. However, the improving Indians grabbed first place with their eighth straight win on June 6, a 14–3 romp over sixth-place Washington. When Cleveland came to Detroit on June 8, the Tigers split four games, winning the second and fourth tilts. Detroit's second win, fueled by Colavito's and Cash's home runs, showed the Tigers had, according to Spoelstra, "the capacity to bounce back against the best."[2]

Joe Falls, the witty, forthright *Free Press* columnist who lived three houses down from Norm Cash and his wife Myrta in suburban Nankin Township (which today is Westland), 16 miles west of downtown Detroit, commented on the disruption Cash's celebrity status was causing in the neighborhood. Norm and Myrta were following a typical baseball practice by renting the house of a ballplayer who once played for Detroit, Billy Hoeft, who pitched for the Tigers from 1952 until he was traded to the Red Sox in 1959. Few players buy a house in a new major league city until they have a good chance to stay with a ball club.

Life in Nankin Township wasn't quite the same as before Cash arrived. As many as a dozen kids might be playing catch in Cash's front yard, waiting to see the first baseman as he backed his car out of the driveway to head for Tiger Stadium. They hoped he would notice them and wave. Once Falls was the "big guy" in the neighborhood, but no more. His wife used to say something like, "Nice story today, Hon." Now it was, "Gee, that Cash is really something, isn't he?"

Falls arranged to eat breakfast with his Tiger neighbor on Monday, June 12, the day after Detroit split the Washington doubleheader and Cash homered three times. Falls found plenty of disruption in the Cash household. The telephone was always ringing, and so was the doorbell. Many people called or came to the house, wanting Cash to buy things or sell things. Most just wanted to talk, like New York writer Joe Williams, who was in town to cover golf's U.S. Open at the exclusive Oakland Hills Country Club, but decided to write a story on "baseball's hottest hitter." Cash, exhausted, didn't arrive home from the Sunday twin bill until 10 p.m. but he stayed up late to talk baseball with Williams. The following day, when the Tigers were scheduled to board a chartered flight to Chicago, Cash agreed to have late breakfast with Falls.

Cash claimed to be as surprised as anyone about why he was hitting so well. In a day and age when you could meet and know athletes as people, the down-home, likeable Cash, blessed with an easy grin, kept chatting and eating with his neighbor, the well-known *Free Press* writer.[3]

In his first full season with Detroit, 1960, the first baseman learned to hit all kinds of breaking balls. Jim Bunning answered the same question about Cash during spring training of 1962 for *Sport*. "Up till August of 1960," Bunning observed, "Norm was strictly a low, fastball hitter. Then he started hitting the curve ball, the off-speed pitch. Last year he was hitting everything."[4]

Baseball players have their camaraderie sealed by being members of a very elite fraternity, one that requires a strong personality, exceptional talent, the opportunity to earn a roster spot—and hopefully a regular position—with a good team, the right mix of players and skills on that team, and an insightful, experienced manager who can meld the skills of those standout athletes into a winner. Cash was living that once-in-a-lifetime baseball dream in Detroit, and when the chance came to talk with a friendly writer, like most players, he was happy to oblige. After all, even major leaguers never knew when good times might end, so there is no time like the present.

Most writers, following the Grantland Rice school of journalism by elevating sports stars into heroes and role models for kids and adults, also cleaned up the casual comments of athletes, many of whom were not well-educated, and most of whom spiced their remarks with expletives. Later, by the 1970s, most writers were using real quotes to personify heroes.[5]

In any event, baseball's conservative weekly, *The Sporting News*, complained that modern-day players were earning more in a year than many past stars made in a career. In addition, "fringe benefits" for guys like Cash included payments made for extolling the virtues of everything from razor blades and hair tonic to fine clothes and sports cars. "Any player worth his salt or has had a good season," the editors stated, "owns a restaurant or a bowling alley or writes a book. If he stays five years in the majors, he has earned a pension." Thus, baseball's "Bible" (as the weekly used to be called) asked, "Doesn't anybody just play ball any more?"[6] The national pastime had always been a big business as well as a ball game, even if *The Sporting News* wanted to pretend otherwise.

In that sporting business, Cash was enjoying what became a career year, but many other hitters hiked their averages for a variety of reasons in the AL's first expansion season. A small-college football star who never played baseball in high school, Cash was signed as an amateur free agent by the White Sox on May 21, 1955 (baseball's amateur draft didn't begin until 1965). Given a major league contract (meaning he was guaranteed the major league minimum salary), he worked his way up in Chicago's minor league system. He got into 13 mid-season games with the Chisox in 1958, hit .240 with four home runs in 58 games in 1959, and went hitless in four at-bats as Chicago lost the 1959 World Series in six games to the Los Angeles Dodgers. The lefty, married in 1954 and living in the off-season with the family of his wife, Myrta Harper, used his World Series check of $7,000 to buy cattle for his father-in-law's ranch near Eldorado, Texas.

Two months later, Cash was dealt to the Cleveland Indians in a multi-player trade that brought veteran outfielder Minnie Minoso back to Chicago. On April 12, 1960, just before spring training ended, Cleveland traded Cash to Detroit for infielder Steve Demeter. "Stormin' Norman," as local writers were calling the new Tigers hero, slugged 41 home runs and produced 132 RBI in 1961, but in the end, the Yankees outlasted the Tigers to finish first in the American League.

In June, as the pennant race between the Tigers and the Yankees heated up, baseball's headlines and stories increasingly hyped home runs, notably the race between New York's slugging duo of Roger Maris and Mickey Mantle, the "M&M Boys," who finished with 61 and 54 four-baggers, respectively, making '61 the "Year of the Home Run." The Tigers, riding Cash's greatest season, also featured the booming bat of Rocky Colavito, who enjoyed a career year by averaging .290, socking 45 home runs, and leading the team with 140 RBI. Just ahead of Detroit's "C&C Boys," Baltimore's Jim Gentile and Minnesota's Harmon Killebrew each hit 46 home runs.

Gentile, the Orioles' longball-hitting first baseman, was a left-handed slugger obtained in a trade with the Los Angeles Dodgers on October 19, 1959. The temperamental San Francisco native had languished, despite his prolific slugging, for seven seasons in the minors. He was still at the Triple-A level and behind the Dodgers' Gil Hodges and Norm Larker, before Paul Richards engineered his trade to the O's. Given the opportunity in Baltimore, "Diamond Jim," an immaculately groomed, finely dressed, Western-looking hero who yearned for a chance to prove his worth, enjoyed his best-ever season in 1961, hitting .302 with 46 home runs and 141 RBI. The hard-hitting Gentile, who had learned to control his temper, hit five grand slams, making him the first American Leaguer to achieve that one-season feat. Further, his 141 RBI tied him for first in the AL with Roger Maris, although that fact was not discovered until 2011 by a SABR researcher.[7] Such impressive figures helped Gentile, the 6'3", 210-pound, long-legged first sacker who had the peculiar ability to do the splits in order to catch an infielder's throw, rank third in the league's MVP voting. Maris and Mantle outpolled him, and Cash followed.[8]

Killebrew, the Twins' six-foot, 195-pound strongman from Payette, Idaho, was also a feared slugger, and in 1961 he enjoyed a huge season, averaging .288 with 46 home runs and 122 RBI. Gentle and kind, he was nicknamed "Killer" because of his sky-high, tape-measure home runs. In fact, Killebrew, stocky, muscular, and quick-handed, was a soft-spoken gentleman on and off the field, and he treated everyone from the greenest rookies to his best friends with great respect. Like Gentile, Killebrew, with his strong hands and wrists and his keen vision of the strike zone, was just coming into his own. Killebrew made the All-Star team as a first baseman, a third baseman, and an outfielder. The popular slugger hit 40 or more homers eight times from 1959 to 1970, which won him induction into the Baseball Hall of Fame in 1984.[9]

Also on June 11, 1961, the Yankees, like the Tigers, hosted an expansion team for a twin bill, but the Bronx Bombers swept both games from the Los Angeles Angels, 2–1 behind stalwart Ralph Terry, and 5–1 behind rookie Rollie Sheldon. In the opener, Maris and Mantle each singled one time in four trips, but the winning run came on Yogi Berra's bases-empty homer in the seventh, his second solo blast of the day. In the nightcap, Mantle powered his 18th home run, a three-run blast off ex–Yankee Eli Grba in the first inning, and Maris belted his 19th and 20th homers, his solo clout in the seventh giving Sheldon his final margin of victory.

Luis Arroyo, the stocky Puerto Rican left-hander who enjoyed a career year coming out of the bullpen and stifling batters with a nasty screwball that "dropped off the table" (said teammate Joe DeMaestri),[10] saved Sheldon after he ran into trouble in the ninth inning. Arroyo learned the pitch in winter ball in 1959–1960 from Al Hollingsworth, one of the coaches at San Juan. He improved on the pitch in 1960. He was almost traded by the Yankees after the season. Instead, Ralph Houk became the new manager, and Arroyo, given the opportunity, became the best reliever in baseball in 1961, going 15–5 in 65 relief appearances with a league-best 29 saves. He threw variations of the "scroogie" that broke either way, often causing batters to hit ground balls. Considering the Yankees' talent-heavy roster, the critical edge was the clutch hurling of Arroyo. Explaining in thickly accented English, he said he gripped the screwball between the seams with his first two fingers, and twisted his wrist "opposite way from my curve ball."[11]

Detroit's best fireman was Terry Fox, a talented, savvy, rookie right-hander from Chicago who racked up a 5–2 record while recording 12 saves. In 1961 the Tigers used more of what today is called a bullpen-by-committee approach, because no one reliever, except Fox, came through consistently.

Arroyo, despite his game-changing performances, could hardly generate the charisma, star power, and excitement brought to the ballpark by the glamorous Mantle, who had enjoyed a Triple Crown season in 1956 with a .353 average, 52 homers, and 130 RBI, or the under-appreciated Maris, the slugging outfielder who came to New York in a multi-player trade with Kansas City on December 11, 1959. In his first season wearing the famed pinstripes in the media capital of the world, Maris won the MVP Award by averaging .283 with 39 home runs and a league-best 112 RBI, helping lift the Yankees to the ball club's tenth pennant since 1949. Still, Maris tailed off late in the season. After connecting for two home runs in New York's

16–4 rout of Kansas City on August 6, he hit no more homers in August and just four in September.

Strange as it may appear today, Maris wasn't seen as a "real" Yankee by many of New York's diehard rooters. Instead, he started his career in Cleveland's minor league system. The crew-cut, pale-eyed, hard-hitting slugger, who could be as straightforward or brusque with writers as Mantle could be indirect or charming, kept hearing boos. After winning a second straight MVP Award with his 61-homer season of 1961, Maris followed up with a disappointing (for him) .256 average, 33 home runs, and 100 RBI in 1962. Such statistics were scorned by lesser mortals than the reluctant hero who, dealing with the endless questions from the crowd of irreverent reporters around his clubhouse cubicle after mid–July, had broken Babe Ruth's home run record of 60 in 1961.

Maris deserved better, but Mantle was the popular switch-hitting slugger that most fans were pulling for to break the Babe's supposedly sacrosanct mark. "The Mick," who came out of the depressed lead and zinc mining town of Commerce, Oklahoma, was able to hit a baseball farther than anyone within memory, except possibly Ruth himself. The owner of a ferocious swing, Mantle took a cut that either missed completely or hit the ball harder than others, often driving the horsehide toward the roof of the stadium. A blond, boyish, smiling hero who was often sullen during earlier seasons, he remained the renowned slugger who kept the spectators' eyes fastened on him whenever he walked up to the plate. Tension and excitement would rise because spectators

Roger Maris shakes hands with Mickey Mantle (#7), who is on deck, as the slugger crosses home plate after hitting home run number 46, a bases-empty blast off Juan Pizarro at Yankee Stadium in a 2–1 loss to the White Sox on August 15, 1961. The Yankees' batboy is in the foreground (National Baseball Hall of Fame, Cooperstown, New York).

didn't know if he would strike out, draw a base on balls, drive a base hit over the infield, or crush a home run, but his swings drew appreciative noise from many fans.

Mantle epitomized professional baseball in the 1950s. Supremely talented, inordinately strong, ready to party, and quick to grin, he was a cowboy in the outfield, swinging a bat instead of drawing a gun, a boy wearing a man's uniform, a flawed superstar who often played hurt. His legend, stoked by his hitting feats and his macho behavior, continued to grow in the 1960s. He was the highest-paid Yankee, earning $70,000 in salary by 1961, but he easily surpassed his salary with income pocketed from endorsements and other perks of his fame. Mantle, all 5'11" and 195 pounds of him, was the biggest star on baseball's biggest winner, and in 1961 he proved it again, averaging .317 with 54 home runs, before he suffered a hip abscess with two weeks to go. Even though Mantle, like Maris, came back in 1962 with a lesser season, hitting .321 with 30 homers and 89 RBI, he was the Mick and, unlike "Rajah," his sins were forgiven.

At a time when professional athletes were perceived as celebrities, Maris, who disliked the bright media spotlight, hit the major league-record 61 home runs under the worst pressure imaginable, so much so that the 6'0", 195-pound left-handed batter lost some of his hair, most of his privacy, and likely more sleep than any other ballplayer in America. Utilizing his smooth, upward swing, called a "home run stroke" by pitcher Camilo Pascual, Maris usually hit home runs in streaks, starting with nine in one 13-game stretch in May.

Maris and Mantle, teammates and friends, were waging a friendly, intense competition for the league's home run lead, and on June 11, Maris' circuit clout number 20 put him ahead of Mantle's 18. The former Fargo, North Dakota, gridiron great was also ahead of the 17 homers by Norm Cash and Rocky Colavito, 14 by Jim Gentile, and 13 by Harmon Killebrew. For the season, Maris batted a less-than-stellar .269, much to the satisfaction of his detractors, but along with 61 round-trippers, he totaled a league-best 141 RBI (he had 142 in 1961), the same as Gentile's 141 and one more than Colavito's 140. In the end, no other player, not even Mantle, came close to the press scrutiny that Maris was forced to endure. New York had more than a dozen daily newspapers that usually sent reporters to the ballpark and on the road, hoping for a new tidbit of baseball lore about Maris, his home runs, his family, anything.

Despite the Mantle–Maris home run race, continued from the 1960 season when Mantle hit 40 and Maris finished with 39 four-baggers, Maris proved in the twin bill at Yankee Stadium on June 11, 1961, why he was an excellent outfielder as well as a stellar slugger. The Bronx Bombers had won eight of their last nine games, and they took two more from the Angels. Maris made two of the greatest catches of his career in the first game, robbing ex–Yankee Ken Hunt of a home run that would have tied the score in the seventh inning. New York's right fielder leaped high to snag the ball, falling into the lap of a female fan in the front row. In the ninth, he reached over the bullpen fence in right center to take a homer away from powerful Ted Kluszewski.

Maris' defensive gems were critical to New York's 2–1 win, but the cameras didn't catch either gem and reporters didn't ask about the catches. In the nightcap, Maris hit round-tripper number 19 off a hanging curve thrown by onetime apartment-mate Eli Grba, and he hit number 20 off former Yankee Johnny James on a sinker that didn't sink. Maris, who didn't like twin bills, later called the Yankees' double defeat of the Angels "one of the greatest doubleheaders of my life."[12]

By mid–June, Maris and Mantle both noticed more writers than usual gathered around their lockers after a game. "The very true fact," manager Ralph Houk recalled, "is that they were just trying to win the pennant, but the writers would come in and all they wanted to talk about was home runs."[13]

In other words, while the world wondered whether war would break out between the U.S. and the Soviet Union over Berlin, Germany, a conflict that resulted in the Communists building the Berlin Wall in mid–August 1961, to seal off West Berlin from East Berlin, the world of baseball was enthralled by home runs. In that famed season more home runs were hit by one man, Maris, one team, the Yankees (240), one major league, the American (1,534), and both major leagues (2,730), than ever before. Further, the Yankees became the first team to have two players hit more than 50 homers, Maris and Mantle. For the first time six players hit more than 40 homers—Maris, Mantle, Gentile, Killebrew, Colavito, and Cash. Also for the first time, 41 major leaguers hit more than 20 homers. The Yankees who hit more than 20 homers, aside from Maris and Mantle, were Bill Skowron, 28, Yogi Berra, 22, and Elston Howard and John Blanchard, 21 each. Blanchard hit homers in four straight at-bats in July, the first two as a pinch-hitter.

Everyone, it seemed, was going for four-baggers. Of New York's eight regular position players, only infielders, second baseman Bobby Richardson (three), shortstop Tony Kubek (eight), and third baseman Clete Boyer (11) didn't reach 20 home runs. Except for Colavito and Cash, no Tiger hit *more* than 20 home runs, but other Bengals with ten or more homers were Kaline, 19, Bill Bruton, 17, Dick Brown, 16, and Jake Wood, 11. Of Detroit's regular position players, only infielders Steve Boros (five) and Chico Fernandez (three) failed to reach double digits in homers. Remarkably, the Yankees hit 240 home runs, 60 more than the Tigers' 180.

Home runs make money, and Arnold Hano, who grew up in New York City, worked as editor of Bantam Books, and later became a freelance writer living in Laguna Beach, California, pointed out that Babe Ruth was the first to proclaim that truth. Rocky Colavito was criticized for trying to hit home runs for the Indians, and Frank Lane finally traded him to the Tigers. Now Detroiters claimed that Colavito was a team player. The Detroit papers memorialized Colavito's one bunt in 1961 as proof he was out for the team. Supposedly, no home run hitter swings hard. They all simply try to meet the ball. Eddie Mathews of Milwaukee claimed the Braves played better when he didn't go for home runs. Cash said he "enjoys making a good fielding play more than creaming a baseball." And, Hano added sarcastically, "I don't want to write a best-seller."

Baseball was about home runs, and never more so than 1961. Ralph Kiner, the seven-time home run king of the Pittsburgh Pirates, said, "Home-run hitters drive Cadillacs." In a brief homer-hitting contest in North Carolina following the 1961 World Series, Maris earned $16,000 and fellow sluggers Jim Gentile and Harmon Killebrew picked up $4,000 apiece.[14] As the man said, that's nice work if you can get it.

Regardless, sportswriters who follow each major league team always find dozens of stories to write, and in 1961, the Tigers, the team the Bronx Bombers trailed for most of the season's first three months, generated a wide spectrum of game stories, profiles of players, and feature articles about Michigan's greatest sports team. Detroit, however, had two major daily newspapers, the *Free Press* and the *News*, compared to more than a dozen dailies operating in New York City. As a result, the Yankees' 1961 pennant drive was widely chronicled, and most of the players were often interviewed, but the same was less true of the Tigers' first pennant contender since 1950, except for Al Kaline, who was enjoying one of the better seasons of a 22-year career that led to his enshrinement in the National Baseball Hall of Fame in 1980.

The pinstriped Bombers were the best team in baseball, but in 1961 the Tigers were just as good until September, when Detroit, sporting a record of 86–47 and trailing the Yankees by 1.5 games, flew into New York to play a crucial three-game series over the Labor Day weekend. New managers led each team. Ralph Houk had taken over the position held since 1949 by Casey Stengel, who piloted the Yankees to their tenth pennant in 12 seasons in 1960, but New York fell to the Pittsburgh Pirates on Bill Mazeroski's home run in the seventh game of the World Series. Whether the 70-year-old Stengel was "too old" suddenly seemed to matter, and the front office promoted heir-apparent Ralph Houk to manager, rather than risk losing him to another team.

On the other hand, the Tigers had finished as high as fourth place only twice since 1950. Worse, Detroit, although trading for talented players like Colavito and Cash, fell to sixth place in 1960. Bob Scheffing, a former coach in both major leagues who had managed the Cubs, was hired to replace Joe Gordon, who came to Detroit from Cleveland in a weird trade for managers on August 3, 1960, when Detroit's Jimmy Dykes was dealt to the Indians.

Scheffing, big, affable, and outgoing, hoped to inspire his team to rise above mediocrity and challenge for the pennant, and he saw one major key to those aspirations in the talented Cash, who looked good in spring training. A hands-off manager, Scheffing spent a good deal of time over the winter reading statistics about his players, and in spring training he got to know them. The new pilot was encouraged, and he believed big things were in store for Detroit.

One day before practice in Lakeland, Scheffing watched the newsreel photographers snap their usual round of pictures and film clips of each player. When the camera crew was packing to leave, the manager pointed out that they forgot one man: Norm Cash. One said, "Who's he?" Scheffing replied, in an oft-quoted statement, "Well, he might just turn out to be the batting champion of the American League."[15]

Comparisons between the lineups of famous Yankees and not-so-famous Tigers abound, starting with each team's superstar outfielder, Mickey Mantle and Al Kaline. The league's most feared slugger, Mantle, hitting cleanup under Ralph Houk, reached his personal peak with 54 homers in 1961, while producing 128 RBI and a league-leading slugging percentage of .687. Kaline, who batted .324 en route to a lifetime average of .297, hit 19 home runs in 1961 (his peak was 29 in 1962 and 1966), drove in 82 runs, and posted a more modest slugging mark of .515, batting mostly in the third spot in the order. Detroit's RBI leaders were Colavito, hitting fourth, and Cash, hitting fifth, who drove home 272 runs between them. The Bengal blasters knocked in three more runs than the combined total of Maris and Mantle. But the Yankees' longball stars combined for 115 home runs, while Colavito and Cash thrilled Tigers fans with their total of 86.

Kaline led the league in doubles in 1961 with 41, and just as Houk designated Mantle as the Yankees' on-field leader through his actions, Kaline was the Bengals' diamond leader by example. While Mantle made his share of fine plays in the outfield, Kaline's career was filled with sensational catches, not the least of which was one he made in Yankee Stadium in the second game of a doubleheader on July 18, 1956, to rob Mantle of a three-run home run and protect a 4–3 win for ace Frank Lary. The fleet Kaline, the longtime hero of thousands of fans in and around the Motor City, would never reach 30 homers in a season, but his excellent all-around play made him an 18-time All-Star and a ten-time Gold Glover.[16]

Baseball in the 1960s heralded changes in the national pastime. Unlike the 24–7 media-hyped world of today, fans at the time were reading about their favorite teams in the daily newspapers, listening to them on the radio, occasionally seeing games on TV, and seeing a few games each summer at the ballpark. In the 1960s, writers and fans treated sports stars like celebrities, many of whom expected to get paid for making public appearances or what was later called "giving back" to the community. Also, spectators in two new American League cities, Minnesota and Los Angeles, were excited in 1961 about their new hometown heroes. As August turned into September, the nights grew cooler and the leaves began showing the autumn's brilliant colors, Maris and Mantle continued their relentless chase of Ruth's hallowed record. While Detroit battled New York for first place, Rocky Colavito and Norm Cash staged their own exciting home run duel.

As Tigers players and personnel boarded a plane out of Detroit's Metro Airport on August 31 for their rendezvous with destiny at Yankee Stadium, President John F. Kennedy was leading the nation toward a New Frontier, including a nuclear test ban treaty and a Peace Corps abroad and improved civil rights laws and expanded Social Security at home. Still, newspapers and magazines were filled with the specter of nuclear war as the United States held to a precarious balance of power with the Soviet Union. Cold War rhetoric between the U.S. and the USSR continued over Cuba and the failed Bay of Pig invasion, the Kennedy–Khrushchev summit at Vienna on June 4, and the crisis over the Western Allies' determination to defend West Berlin, which led to East German forces building the Berlin Wall starting in the pre-dawn hours of August 13. Three weeks earlier, after considering various military options, the President asked Congress for $3.2 billion to strengthen the armed forces, promising a request would follow for increasing the size of the Army and Navy by more than a quarter of a million men.[17]

As public schools prepared to open following Labor Day, many people wondered about the East-West conflict and whether a nuclear fallout shelter would help their family in case of a Russian attack. In matters affecting thousands of workers in Michigan and elsewhere, the "Big Four" auto makers—General Motors, Ford, Chrysler, and American Motors—kept negotiating to avoid a crippling strike, especially with GM showing a one-third increase in net profits for the year's second quarter, thanks in part to the rise in sales of compact cars. By June 30, 1961, GM's employment across America reached 294,000, and the worker's weekly pay averaged $122.[18]

Detroit and America were prospering, but the times, Bob Dylan later sang, they were a-changing. Thinking about the upcoming series in New York as they flew through the night skies, the Tigers hoped the Yankees' dominance in baseball was changing too.

2

Bob Scheffing, Ralph Houk, and the Spring of 1961

New Managers

Spring training in 1961 was the most important one yet for Detroit's Bob Scheffing and New York's Ralph Houk, a pair of new managers who each had considerable baseball experience. Scheffing, a 6'2" catcher from Overland, Missouri, served three years with the Navy during World War II, after he played the first two of his eight major league seasons in 1941 and 1942. Enjoying his best year in 1948, the 34-year-old receiver averaged .300 as part of the Chicago Cubs' catching platoon with young Rube Walker, a left-handed batter. Scheffing, a devout Catholic who wore a cross on a chain around his neck that, he said, saved his life several times during the war, was an experienced handler of pitchers and a lifetime .263 hitter. After retiring as a player, he coached for the St. Louis Browns in 1952–1953 and with the Cubs in 1954 and for the early part of the next season. On May 25, 1955, he became manager of the Los Angeles Angels of the Pacific Coast League, and he led the Angels to the PCL title in 1956.

Promoted to the Windy City in 1957, Scheffing managed the Cubs to a pair of fifth-place finishes in his last two of three seasons at Chicago's helm. Resigning after the 1959 season, the former catcher coached one year for the Milwaukee Braves, serving under manager Chuck Dressen. Hired by the Tigers on November 20, 1960, Scheffing was bright, down-to-earth, and good-natured. He studied the records of his players that winter, and once spring training opened at Henley Field in Lakeland, he spent much of his time getting to know his players.

Houk, from Lawrence, Kansas, was also a big former catcher who worked well with people, and like Scheffing, he served in World War II, but not on the sea. Houk was an Army Ranger who fought, among other places, at the Battle of the Bulge in December 1944 and January 1945. He rose to the rank of major, which later became his baseball nickname. A right-handed batter like Scheffing, Houk was a third-string catcher behind Yogi Berra during his playing days with the Yankees from 1947–1954. Houk was named the team's bullpen coach in his last season, and he learned the ropes of coaching and managing. The Yankees sent him to Denver in 1955, where the air is thinner and home runs fly more often. Houk piloted the Bears of the American Association for three seasons. Returning to the Bronx in 1958, he served as Casey Stengel's first base coach through the 1960 World Series, lost by the Yankees to the Pittsburgh Pirates.

Two days after the '60 fall classic ended, Houk was available and eager when co-owner Dan Topping announced that Stengel was retiring due to his age, 70, but Stengel told reporters he was fired. Houk was named manager, but it wasn't a surprise. When Stengel had gone into Lenox Hill Hospital for two weeks in June 1960 with a bladder infection, Houk, rather than coach Frank Crosetti, was picked to run the team. Concluded Tony Kubek in his insightful 1987 book, *Sixty-One*, "The team went 6–6 without Casey, but the Yankees front office saw that Houk was willing to use the young players," for example, Clete Boyer at third, and give more playing time to John Blanchard as catcher and Hector Lopez in left field.[1] Having spent his career with the Yankees, the Major knew the players, and he didn't needle his men in the press, like Stengel often did. Houk, like Scheffing, worked well with young as well as veteran players.

Scheffing and Houk both had much to learn, because the American League made big changes over the off-season. On October 17, 1960, National League owners voted to expand to ten teams in 1962, adding one new team in New York and the other in Houston. American League owners, not to be outdone, met in New York nine days later and voted to expand in 1961, beating the NL to the punch. Harry Sisson, Detroit's executive vice president, represented the Tigers, since majority owner John E. Fetzer was ill. The meeting achieved several goals. First, the Washington Senators were relocated to the urban center of Minneapolis–St. Paul, where they became the Minnesota Twins. Second, new teams were added in Washington, D.C., and Los Angeles, named the Senators and the Angels, respectively. Also, the expansion teams would obtain players (at a cost of $75,000 each) from other AL ball clubs, with the eight established teams each naming 15 players from the 40-man roster that could be picked. Finally, in order to accommodate ten teams, the schedule was expanded to 162 games from the traditional 154-game season. Each team played every other team 18 times, instead of the 22 they played in past decades.[2]

The Tigers were making changes to the front office and to Detroit's ballpark, Briggs Stadium. After the sixth-place finish of 1960, John Fetzer, leader of the syndicate that purchased the ball club in 1956 from the family of the deceased Walter O. Briggs, Senior, decided to revamp the organizational structure. On October 11, 1960, Fetzer, a multi-millionaire in the broadcasting business in Michigan, bought the controlling interest in the Tigers and made himself team president. One week later Bill DeWitt, the club's president, was offered an assistant's title. Instead, DeWitt, a supreme egoist who loved to trade players, departed to become president of the Cincinnati Reds. Fetzer's front office shuffle left him with three key aides. Harry Sisson, the longtime club secretary and vice president, was put in charge of financial matters. Rick Ferrell, a standout catcher for 18 years who became a Tigers coach in 1950, had started directing the farm system in 1958. After John McHale resigned in early 1959, Ferrell became acting general manager, and, on April 10, 1959, the Tigers' general manager. When Fetzer reorganized, Ferrell also became his special assistant and director of major league personnel. Jim Campbell, who had started as a minor league executive in 1949, helped create the Tigertown minor league complex in 1953 and became a scout in 1960, was named director of the farm system.[3]

After a screening process that ended before Thanksgiving, Ferrell hired Scheffing, 47, along with coaches Don Heffner and Phil Cavarretta. Tom Ferrick, the pitching coach in 1960, was retained. Ending any remaining influence of the Briggs family on December 29, 1960, Fetzer renamed the ballpark Tiger Stadium, since, after all, the facility represented the team, not the owner.[4]

Diversity on the Diamond

Bob Scheffing wanted to rebuild the Tigers at certain positions. Having arrived from a one-season stint coaching the Braves, the Bengals' pilot knew the front office personnel in Milwaukee. John McHale, the Braves' general manager, was a former Tiger during the 1940s, director of Detroit's farm system from 1949 to 1957, and the Bengals' GM until he left for the same position with Milwaukee in January 1959. Scheffing used his inside knowledge of the Braves to inspire an important trade. On December 7, 1960, Detroit gave up steady second baseman Frank Bolling and a player to be named later (outfielder Neil Chrisley) in return for fleet center fielder Billy Bruton, one of the National League's first-rate black stars, catcher Dick Brown, a right-handed batter who had been purchased from the Chicago White Sox nine days earlier, light-hitting Chuck Cottier, a versatile infielder, and right-hander Terry Fox, who had no decisions and a 4.32 ERA in five games as a rookie for the Braves in 1960.

Scheffing had several goals. At second base he hoped to use Jake Wood, a fast, quick-handed, hard-hitting young black star who had averaged .305 at Denver in 1960. Bruton, a savvy, speedy, heads-up batter and base runner, would patrol center field, fixing a weakness in Detroit's outfield created after dependable Bill Tuttle was traded to Kansas City following the 1957 season. Al Kaline, who had played center at different times, including much of the 1960 season, felt more at home in right field. Acquiring Bruton and calling up Wood, who replaced Bolling, meant the Tigers could start two African Americans who would room together on the road, thus improving the lineup while solving a social problem, since few whites wanted to share lodgings with black players, and vice versa. Bruton, 35, and Wood, 24, roomed together in 1961 and 1962. Asked if Bruton was a good guy, Wood said, "Oh, yeah." He added, "I wish Billy Bruton was an infielder. Maybe he could have taught me something. But he was an outfielder."[5]

Bruton and Wood improved the Tigers on and off the diamond. Of the 14 major league teams training in Florida in 1961, Detroit was the slowest to elevate African American players to respectable status. As historian Patrick Harrigan wrote, Bruton helped push the Tigers in that direction.[6]

Detroit's first nonwhite player was Ozzie Virgil, who was obtained in a trade from the San Francisco Giants on January 28, 1958. Before Virgil pulled on the white flannels trimmed in navy blue and adorned with the Old English *D*, the Tigers recruited dozens of black minor league players, starting in 1953 with Claude Agee, a 5'10" outfielder from Monongahela,

Pennsylvania, and Art Williams, a 6'2" right-hander from Camden, Arkansas. Wood, from Elizabeth, New Jersey, became the first black prospect originally signed by the Tigers to work his way through the organization's farm system, starting in 1957 with Erie of the New York–Pennsylvania League, and play for the Tigers. Wood debuted on Opening Day, April 11, 1961. Wycliffe

Jake Wood, from Elizabeth, New Jersey, experienced struggles that were not unusual for a rookie in the major leagues in 1961. In addition, Wood heard numerous "vile, negative comments" from fans on the road and also at Detroit's home games (author's collection).

Jackie Robinson, the heroic major leaguer and later Hall of Famer who was famous for breaking the "color barrier" with the Brooklyn Dodgers in 1947, encouraged other rising black stars. Robinson is pictured in Lakeland in 1960 with three Tigers, Jim Proctor (left), who pitched in two games for the Tigers in 1959, outfielder Bubba Morton, who debuted with Detroit in 1961, and infielder Ozzie Virgil (right), who first integrated the Tigers in 1958 (author's collection).

"Bubba" Morton, from Washington, D.C., became the second black prospect to sign with Detroit and play his way to the Motor City. Morton also debuted in 1961, eight days after Wood.

Jackie Robinson broke baseball's "color barrier" in 1947, and Larry Doby was the second black player to reach the majors, debuting with Cleveland on July 5, 1947. After 12 stellar seasons, Doby was traded to the Tigers on March 21, 1959. The veteran slugger, enshrined in the Baseball Hall of Fame in 1998, was nearing the end of his career, and he hit just .218 in 18 games before Detroit put him on waivers on May 13. Regardless, Doby made a mark with the Tigers, including in segregated Lakeland. That spring he took the lead in demanding that the team furnish a car for the black players—himself, Ozzie Virgil, and Jim Proctor—to ride to away games, because most Florida restaurants wouldn't serve black customers.[7] Later, Doby, the American League's home run king in 1952 and 1954, finished his career with the White Sox, playing his last game on July 26, 1959. Overall during his final season, the onetime Negro Leaguer averaged .230 in 39 games, but he connected for no home runs (Doby hit 253 homers in his 13-year career).

Jim Proctor, a right-hander from Brandywine, Maryland, was Detroit's third black player. Signed and then released by the Milwaukee Braves' organization after five games in 1955, the 5'11", 165-pound sidearmer, talented, bright, and proud, worked his way up the Tigers' system, beginning with Augusta of the Class A South Atlantic (Sally) League in 1956. In 1957, after starting the year at Augusta and posting a 7–2 mark, he was promoted to Triple-A Charleston, where he went 7–6 in 31 appearances. Proctor, who relied on the fastball, hurt his arm while pitching 11 innings against Wichita on Sunday, July 21, taking an 8–6 defeat. He spent most of the rest of the season and all of 1958 getting arm treatment, but he never fully recovered. "They didn't hesitate to treat," Proctor recalled in 2013, "but nobody knew what to do at that time."

Ballplayers try to play through most injuries, and Proctor was no exception. In 1959, along with Doby and Virgil, Proctor was invited to train with the Tigers in Lakeland. Farmed out, he fashioned a 15–5 record and a 2.19 ERA with Knoxville of the Sally League. His standout performance and work ethic got him called up to Detroit in mid–September. Proctor made two relief appearances for the Tigers, on September 14 and 26. Taking the loss in his second outing, he failed to impress the front office. After training again with Detroit in 1960, the outspoken hurler was sent to Victoria of the Double-A Texas League. He led the circuit in pitching with a 15–8 record, but the Tigers released him after the season. Disappointed, Proctor kept performing while hoping for another chance at the majors, but by mid–1963 he was out of baseball.[8]

The Boston Red Sox were the final major league team to integrate when Pumpsie Green debuted on the road at Comiskey Park on July 21, 1959. When the 1950s ended, 125 black players had reached the majors, ranging from famous heroes like Jackie Robinson, Larry Doby, Roy Campanella, Don Newcombe, Willie Mays, Hank Aaron, and Frank Robinson to short-timers such as Bob Wilson, who played three games for the Los Angeles Dodgers in 1958, and Milt Smith, a reserve infielder for the Cincinnati Reds in 1955. Only Virgil, Doby, and Proctor had worn the Tigers uniform, but baseball's door was open for black players in the 1960s.[9]

Billy Bruton, Jake Wood, Chico Fernandez, Bubba Morton, and Ozzie Virgil helped the Tigers in 1961. Away from Tiger Stadium, however, these players had little to do with white teammates, and vice versa. "We had an apartment near Livernois Avenue," Wood remembered in 2014, "and quite naturally, they were all African Americans that lived around us. My interaction with my teammates off the field was limited, or nonexistent. My interaction with persons from other cultures was nonexistent, like theirs was."[10]

Bruton had the same experience, but unlike most big leaguers, he talked about it for publication with Bill Furlong, a writer for *Sport* magazine. A slender, athletic man with thin hair, a lined face, and a pleasant but forthright personality, Bruton was born in Panola, Alabama, on December 22, 1925, but when he signed with the Boston Braves in 1950, he listed his birth year as 1929.[11] Instead of being 20, he was 24, but feared he wouldn't get a chance at his real age. Bruton worked his way through the Braves' system and debuted with Boston on April 13, 1953, soon establishing himself as the team's standout center fielder. A lifetime .273 hitter over 12 seasons, he needed surgery to repair his injured right knee following the 1957 campaign.

Regardless, Bruton again proved to be one of the best center fielders in the game. By the time he was traded to Detroit on December 7, 1960, he was well established as a community leader in Milwaukee, where he was widely accepted as a first-rate person. The Wisconsin legislature passed a resolution commending Bruton and asking him to keep his home in Milwaukee, and he did not move his family to Detroit. For a story that *Sport* published in 1962, Bruton explained the unspoken second-class treatment that black athletes usually received. "They still don't think we're human," he said about those who rejected him for being a Negro. "They don't want to rent motel rooms. They'll tell me they have no room. Then if they recognize me as a ballplayer, they'll let me have it. But I walk out. I don't want it if they're offering it only to a ballplayer."[12]

The Yankees first called up a black player in 1955, catcher-outfielder Elston Howard. New York had purchased Vic Power's contract from Drummondville, Quebec, of the Provincial League, before the 1951 season. Power, however, was considered flashy, outspoken, and unorthodox by the team's front office, partly because he dated white girls. New York traded the Puerto Rican first sacker to the Philadelphia A's in a multi-player deal on December 16, 1953, even though Power, playing for the Kansas City Blues, the Yankees' top farm club, averaged .349 and led the American Association in batting average in 1953.[13] The Yankees, criticized publicly for failing to bring up Power or Howard, replied, in effect, that they were waiting for the "right" man.[14]

Howard was a skilled catcher, but he was versatile enough to play the outfield, so he was used as an outfielder. His path to the starting lineup was blocked for years by Yogi Berra, who won the American League MVP award in 1951, 1954, and 1955. Howard, 26 years old when he broke in during spring training with the Yankees in 1955, made a good start that summer by hitting .290 in 97 games. He first played over 100 games in 1957 (110), but he didn't catch more than 100 games (111) until 1961, the year Ralph Houk took over as manager and named Howard as the regular receiver. Berra accepted going to left field, because Houk talked with Yogi and said the move was best for the team.[15] Berra, like Mantle, was a Yankee forever.

Howard suffered the usual indignities of colored athletes of the era, living during the spring in a black rooming house run by the Williams family in St. Petersburg, instead of at the team's lodgings, the swank Soreno Hotel. Florida was one of the most segregated states at the time. Yankees shortstop Tony Kubek, an eager-beaver, stringbean type of hustling athlete sporting the era's ever popular flattop, explained in *Sixty-One* that the guys knew "Ellie" at the ballpark and on the team bus, but he didn't recall any Yankees inviting Howard to dinner in 1961. The civil rights movement helped make major changes in the 1960s, notably with the Civil Rights Act of 1964. "Whether we want to admit it or not," Howard's widow Arlene recalled in the mid–1980s, "until then [1964] discrimination was the law of the land. Elston knew it. I knew it. Every black person in Florida lived with it."[16]

Norm Cash, Al Kaline, and Bob Scheffing in Lakeland

Bob Scheffing traveled to Lakeland to be ready for the Tigers' two-week advance training camp, slated to open on Friday, February 10. The "rookie camp" was designed to give promising younger players and minor leaguers additional training and practice. The Tigers' big league training was held at Henley Field beginning on February 28, but the younger players worked out at Tigertown, a large complex located less than one mile away. First opened in the spring of 1953, Tigertown featured four diamonds centered at a single point, a practice infield, batting cages, pitching mounds, and a variety of training devices. The facility also had a field house, once an airplane hangar, with a dirt floor and excellent lighting for indoor practice. The young Tigers stayed in the remodeled lodging-recreation building, formerly used as a barracks for the Lodwick Flight School, that now could house and feed up to 350 players.

Norm Cash came to sunny Lakeland for the first time in the spring 1961. Soon after he arrived, Scheffing gave him a shot at first base, saying, "I think your hitting will hold up, but you've got to improve your fielding."

Bob Scheffing, Detroit's new manager in 1961, showed the personal skills and baseball knowledge necessary to inspire the Tigers to rise above mediocrity and win 101 games (National Baseball Hall of Fame, Cooperstown, New York).

Scheffing turned Cash over to coach Phil Cavarretta, the former Cubs first sacker. Every day Cavarretta hit Cash dozens of ground balls, working him until he was dripping in sweat. The coach pointed out changes the first baseman needed to make. For example, Cash was committing himself too quickly on ground balls, and his momentum made it so he could go in only one direction. If he misjudged a grounder, he couldn't adjust well. Cavarretta hit Cash every kind of ground ball for at least one hour per day. Among other moves, Cash learned to step forward and play one-bounce grounders on the short hop, rather than back up and let the ball "play him."

Cash worked hard, kept improving, and believed more in himself. One day as Cavarretta was throwing balls in the dirt at first base, he pointed out two mistakes: "You're swiping at them with your glove and you're lifting your head, taking your eye off the ball. Cut out the swiping motion and keep your head down." Cavarretta worked with Cash on using both hands on a play, whenever possible. Cash not only improved his fielding, but he also took batting practice with the regulars, thus boosting his confidence and morale. When exhibitions started, Scheffing named Cash as the team's regular at first base. "Cash is my first baseman until someone can prove otherwise," the manager told writers like Hal Butler.[17] Norm remained the regular until 1974.

Being a regular rather than riding the bench and playing part-time is important to any player's confidence, and Cash felt the change. By the time the Bengals traveled to Detroit to open the season, he felt renewed, like an insider. Happier, he developed a more positive attitude than did the outsider who played in 1960 on a platoon basis at first base with right-handed batting Steve Bilko, the big slugger who hit 55 homers for the Angels of the Pacific Coast League in 1956.

Scheffing also had to deal with AL expansion, meeting and evaluating the players, and getting to know the writers. He toured Michigan and northern Ohio for several days in mid–January 1961, speaking to representatives of the press, radio, and TV, and answering questions such as, "What are you going to do with Maxwell?" "Ol' Paw Paw," the favored nickname of the slugging hero from southwestern Michigan, saw his average decline to .237 in 1960. Maxwell, soon to turn 34, played 134 games, belted 24 home runs, and drove in 81 runs, enjoying his fifth straight season as the Tigers' regular left fielder. This spring, with Bruton in center field, Kaline returning to right, and one-time home run king Rocky Colavito taking over left field, Maxwell was a reserve.

Scheffing, thoughtful, friendly, and shrewd with public relations, said Maxwell would be used frequently, especially on weekends, as he had a knack for hitting homers on Sunday. As a taste of the future, however, the new pilot said he liked having a good bat like Maxwell's "on the bench." Scheffing added, "He's a good hitter, a clutch hitter. His talents won't be wasted."[18]

Before daily training sessions opened, Scheffing talked with Kaline, who endured an off-year (for him) in 1960, averaging .278 with 15 home runs and 68 RBI. It was his least productive year since his first full season in 1954 (.276, four homers, 43 RBI). Scheffing asked him to be the inspirational leader. Kaline, a naturally reticent person but an organization man, was reluctant at first. He felt bad about what he told his wife Louise was a "terrible season," one in which he suffered from an injured left knee and, doctors eventually figured out, low blood pressure.[19]

Scheffing, however, explained that statistics had nothing to do with it. Kaline was actually the key man for Detroit, whether *he* thought so or not. Starting his ninth year, Kaline was looked up to by the other players. He was the Tigers' biggest star and the team's greatest hero, a stature he earned when he won the AL batting championship in 1955.

"You have to show them how to play this game not only by example," Scheffing said, "but by your willingness to help them with their problems." Younger players already used Kaline's performance on the field as their example. During one interview over the winter of 1960–1961, Kaline admitted he was the Tigers' "lead bat," even though Colavito hit more home runs.[20]

Kaline was the King Tiger in Detroit, and he promised Scheffing to give his best. In St. Pete, Ralph Houk was having a similar conversation with Mickey Mantle, surely the Yankees' "lead bat." All the other Yankees saw the charismatic Mantle as the biggest star, the greatest hero.

Spring in St. Petersburg

Ralph Houk had participated in many spring training camps in St. Petersburg, starting as a Yankee player after World War II. New York trained at what was renamed Miller Huggins Park (1930), but they played games at Waterfront Park and, starting in 1947, downtown at the newly constructed Al Lang Field. Beginning in 1938, the Yankees shared the local field with the St. Louis Cardinals, and that was a point of contention with New York's co-owners, Dan Topping and Del Webb. The usual housing practice for teams like the Yankees was that established major leaguers shared a room with another teammate, usually a friend, but rookies usually bunked three or four to a room, because the team didn't know how long they would last. "I had three or four," recalled Rollie Sheldon about life at the Soreno Hotel. "Most were guys from Class D like myself. Some of the guys would get cut, and others would move in."[21] Spring was an unsettling time for rookies trying to make a major league roster.

The Yankees had another problem after the arrival of Elston Howard in 1955, because the Soreno Hotel refused to accept non-whites. In 1961, however, Ralph Wimbush, the local NAACP leader, published a statement in the *St. Petersburg Times* saying he would no longer help black players find places to live away from the team's hotel, and he publicized the second-class treatment that all blacks endured in Florida.[22] The Yankees' front office took notice, after having forced Howard to find his own accommodations since 1955. Hardly a coincidence, Topping, talking to writers a few days later, said the organization was considering a move to Fort Lauderdale in 1962. Along with a larger stadium, the city, according to *The Sporting News*, offered the Yankees exclusive use during spring training of "a motel in which the Negro players would be welcome."[23] The move to Broward County and Prospect Field was confirmed at an official dinner in Fort Lauderdale on March 23, 1961.[24] The times were changing.

After the blond-headed

Ralph Houk, the Yankees' rookie manager, answers questions in the dugout during spring training. Houk handled players and game situations with the utmost skill and savvy (National Baseball Hall of Fame, Cooperstown, New York).

Houk, 41, arrived for spring training, writers noticed a new upbeat spirit among the players. First of all, the Major spoke in plain English, whereas Casey Stengel had talked in mumbo-jumbo diction that was often termed "Stengelese."[25] In the first week of March, Houk announced that Bobby Richardson and Tony Kubek would be the second base–shortstop combination, as they had been for Houk at Denver, and Clete Boyer would be his third baseman. If Hector Lopez and Yogi Berra could hit well enough to platoon in left field, Elston Howard and John Blanchard would do the catching. Mantle and Maris, of course, were the big sluggers in center and right field, respectively, with Bill Skowron at first base. Further, Houk figured his starting pitchers would work every fourth day, not every fifth day, and he declared the Yankees would win the pennant. At first Houk's main starting pitchers were Whitey Ford, Art Ditmar, Ralph Terry, Bob Turley, Jim Coates, Bill Stafford, and, for relief, Ryne Duren (soon traded) and Luis Arroyo. Right-hander Rollie Sheldon was the rookie hurler with the best chance to stick, and new coach Johnny Sain would work with the pitchers. Again the Yankees were likely the best team in the American League.[26]

Near the end of March, as the regular season approached, Houk, a motivator who was straightforward, quick to smile, but gruff when needed, sat down with Mantle and subtly appealed to his better nature. Mantle had a productive but unspectacular season in 1960, batting .275 (his lowest average since his rookie mark of .267 in 1951), producing 40 home runs and 94 RBI, despite often playing hurt. The slugging switch-hitter finished second in the MVP balloting to Maris, but to Stengel, his best was never quite good enough. Instead of harping on Mantle's shortcomings, Houk praised his performance, saying he needed to be the team's leader and unofficial captain. The most talented player on the league's most talented team, Mantle was also the most respected. "He's one player all the players like," Houk said, adding, "Just think how much they'll like him if he goes out and shows them the way."[27]

Mantle, at once flattered and humbled, reacted positively, as Houk expected. "You can't be a leader in anything by popping off or yelling louder than everybody else," Mickey was quoted as saying to several New York writers, who, as writers usually did, cleaned up his diction. "There are other things mixed up in it." The other things, Mantle explained, were the person's actions. Admitting he would like to be the leader Houk wanted, the long-time All-Star said he hadn't thought about it. A man of action and quick wits, he continued, "They will follow you only if they respect your actions on the field." Even though the two were not close, Mantle pointed to the great Joe DiMaggio as his role model when he came to the Yankees in 1951. "You'd watch Joe do this better than anybody and do that better than anybody. You never heard him make any speeches. He just played ball better than anybody else. That's what made him a leader."[28]

Mantle naturally displayed many of the attitudes of others who came of age during the postwar era. Almost everyone had heard their parents say, "Actions speak louder than words." Mantle's was a generation whose parents lived through the Great Depression and World War II, and most of them grew up being self-reliant. Many weren't well educated, but most were hard-working, careful with money, and unwilling to ask for help. The Yankees and the Tigers expected to follow the lead of peers like Mantle and Kaline, who were outstanding performers, but had different personalities.

As he did with Mantle, Houk instilled confidence in his players. Firm, fair, and empathetic, the manager showed great skill in figuring out his athletes and their roles in New York's expected pennant drive. Indeed, every Yankee was under contract when the camp officially opened on Wednesday, March 1. Hector Lopez arrived on a flight that morning from Panama, and he soon signed a deal for $20,000. During the previous spring, the Yankees had seven holdouts when training began. For fans in New York, the media capital of America, the team announced that 130 games, including three exhibitions, would be televised on WPIX, Channel 11. For the Bronx Bombers, such widespread coverage was hardly new, but it reached a peak in 1961, particularly surrounding the quest to break Babe Ruth's single-season home run record, but that coverage didn't begin in the spring.[29]

At Lang Field, in addition to the usual calisthenics (professional athletes did not yet lift weights, do strength training, or take steroids), the players engaged in familiar drills such as playing "pepper" as well as batting, infield, and outfield practice. The Yankees also featured the return of "old-timers" to rekindle memories of the team's glory years. The greatest of the living stars was Joe DiMaggio. All teams like to publicize former great players, but few had as many Hall of Famers as the Yankees. With Stengel, whom DiMaggio disliked, gone, Joe was all smiles.

DiMaggio, 46, looked almost the same as when he last graced center field at Yankee Stadium. In Florida for two weeks to help publicize spring training, the famed star, also known as Joe D, Joltin' Joe, or the Yankee Clipper, had gained five pounds around the waist and sprouted gray hair around the temples. Handsome, talented, and regal, DiMaggio had led the Yankees to their 18th pennant and 14th World Series championship in 1951. Not even Babe Ruth or Lou Gehrig could boast a greater string of team titles, and writers and photographers loved getting close to the legendary figure. Dan Daniel (born Markowitz) was the dapper, longtime, "gee-whiz" oracle of sports writing who had traveled with and covered the Yankees since Ruth's era. Full of opinions on old-time baseball, Daniel proclaimed that if anyone was capable of breaking into his all-time great outfield of Ruth, Tris Speaker, and Tigers legend Ty Cobb, it was DiMaggio.[30]

The ostensible purpose of DiMaggio's presence was to serve as a batting coach for two weeks, but later Houk called it "good public relations."[31] DiMaggio may have been making himself available for a job within New York's organization, as Daniel hinted, but Wally Moses was the team's hitting coach. DiMaggio supposedly spent some time on fielding techniques with Maris and Lopez as well as youngsters Lee Thomas and Jim Pisoni.[32] In fact, DiMaggio, intensely private and rarely amiable except with writers, would hardly have attempted to convey hitting or fielding tips to Mantle, or Maris, or any other Yankee. "Actually," DiMaggio remarked in 1961 to Tom Meany (who ghosted DiMaggio's 1946 autobiography, *Lucky to be a Yankee*), "I never volunteered any advice to Mickey or any other ballplayer."[33] But stories about the great Hall of Famer offered interesting reading for the folks back in New York.

Outfielder–first baseman Lee Thomas was traded to the expansion Angels on May 8, 1961, along with once-sensational reliever Ryne Duren, who was suffering the ill effects of alcoholism (he later stated so publicly), and right-hander Johnny James. New York received outfielder Bob Cerv, the ex–Yankee slugger who was traded to Kansas City after the 1956 season and taken by LA in the expansion draft, and Tex Clevenger, a cheerful right-hander who pitched five years for Washington before the Angels drafted him.

Houk, like every manager, was forever concerned about his pitching staff. Commenting on the first two exhibition losses to the St. Louis Cardinals by scores of 6–1 and 4–2, Houk, who hated losing, pointed out that New York lost five of six to St. Louis in the spring 1960, but went on to win the pennant. A master of making the best of difficult situations, the Major said the first game was lost on one pitch, a Ryne Duren fastball that Ken Boyer turned into a three-run triple, and in the second game, two errors led to three unearned runs. Still, Houk liked the Yankees' pitching. He praised right-handers Art Ditmar and Jim Coates in the opener and Whitey Ford, Bob Turley, and Ralph Terry the following day. Houk also liked the early arrival of Bill Stafford. After finishing Army training, the big right-hander from upstate New York was stationed at Fort Lee in Virginia, and he would be discharged by April 15. Stafford went 3–1 with a 2.25 ERA in eight starts in 1960, and Houk saw him as a rising star.[34]

Luis Arroyo was projected by Houk to be one of New York's top relievers, but Ryne Duren, once the Yankees' "Flame Thrower," had produced two fine seasons and a third good one. Duren, a flamboyant, hard-drinking, near-sighted showman who wore "Coke bottle" glasses and fired a fastball reaching nearly 100 miles per hour, posted a 6–4 record and led the league with 19 saves in 1958. The burly "Rhino" followed up with a 3–6 mark and 14 saves in 1959, the year the Yankees fell to third behind the pennant-winning White Sox and the improved Indians. Those were big numbers for a reliever in the 1950s. Duren, posting a 3–4 mark and eight saves in 1960, once again fanned more batters than the innings he pitched, striking out 67 in 49 innings.

Arroyo, called "Yo-Yo" by Casey Stengel, a nickname the Puerto Rican lefty received when pitching at Greensboro of the Carolina League in 1949 (fans there had a hard time drawling Luis' last name), first made it to the majors with the St. Louis Cardinals in 1955. The stocky, 5'8½" southpaw had good stuff, starring in the winter league for Puerto Rican teams since the late 1940s. In 1956–1957 he enjoyed a good winter for San Juan, and his manager was Ralph Houk, who liked what he saw. Yankees scouts followed Arroyo, particularly after Cincinnati acquired him in 1959. Adding a screwball in 1960, Arroyo hurled for the Havana Sugar Kings, the Reds' Triple-A club, and the team relocated to New Jersey in July. The Yankees, needing good left-handed talent for the bullpen, bought his contract on July 20.

Arroyo looked more like a professor than a ballplayer, wearing horn-rimmed glasses away from the ballpark. Living with his family in a modest apartment in Brooklyn, Arroyo, a quiet, cigar-smoking, hard-working father of five children, rode the subway to Yankee Stadium. More effective out of the pen than the harder throwing Duren, Arroyo, known as a nice guy, posted a 5–1 mark with a 2.87 ERA in 1960. He saved seven games, impressing Stengel and especially Houk.[35]

Toward the end of March 1961, Arroyo, pitching batting practice before a game with the Milwaukee Braves, suffered the kind of injury that can happen to any pitcher. The batter lined a shot back at his head, and he reacted by flinging up his hand. He was hit on the wrist, suffering a fractured ulna bone. Team doctors said the lefty would be out at least three weeks, causing him to miss the rest of spring camp.[36] Houk had liked Arroyo's performance in 1960, and he kept the reliever on the active roster. He had just ten days of training, but the rubber-armed southpaw suffered no ill effects from the injury in 1961. Arroyo first appeared in the second game of a doubleheader in the Bronx on Thursday, April 20, hurling 1⅓ hitless innings of relief and racking up a save by protecting Bob Turley's second victory, a 4–2 win over the Angels. As the season progressed, Arroyo and his screwball only got tougher.

Mantle and Maris played their way through spring camp, but for Maris, named MVP in 1960 (he outpolled Mantle and Brooks Robinson by a narrow margin, 225–222–211), life was already different. He spent a good part of the winter attending banquets and accepting awards, including the MVP and the Hickok Belt as Athlete of the Year. He was a celebrity, and he would soon approach the status Mantle had known for years. By the time the Marises reached St. Petersburg in late February 1961, his wife Pat was two months pregnant with their fourth child. Their car broke down in Georgia on the trip from their home in Raytown, a suburb of Kansas City, Missouri. After the car was towed and repaired, the Maris family journeyed on to St. Pete, where Pat was hospitalized for more than a week. Roger helped keep house for his kids, Sue, little Roger, and Kevin, the toddler, before his mother arrived one week later. Concerned about his wife and his children, Maris was often distracted from baseball. Houk said in his 1962 book, *Ballplayers Are Human, Too*, about Maris that spring, "He still couldn't hit a lick."[37] In his book following the 1961 season, *Roger Maris at Bat*, the slugging outfielder recalled, "I hit only one home run and very little of anything else in twenty-five exhibition games."[38]

Mantle, who didn't have his family with him, enjoyed a better spring, connecting often enough for home runs and living the good life, but the Yankees lost two-thirds of their exhibitions. Houk, attacked by many of New York's writers, held his own in verbal exchanges, and he remained patient because the core of his team was intact. Tony Kubek later wrote, "In spring training, we didn't take much of anything seriously except getting in shape for the season, and it should have been obvious to anyone that Ralph wasn't playing those games to win."

Mickey Mantle, who won the Triple Crown with his outstanding season in 1956, was easily the most famous star of the 1961 Yankees. Most fans and writers hoped "The Mick" would be the Yankee to break Bath Ruth's single-season home run record of 60 (National Baseball Hall of Fame, Cooperstown, New York).

Kubek indicated what really happened that spring in St. Petersburg had little to do with the stories appearing in the papers. For fun one night, Moose Skowron, a big, friendly guy, became the Yankees' chauffeur, cap and all, and drove for Mickey and Whitey Ford, both famed celebrities who caused a stir at restaurants where they dined.

Perhaps the most fun came on a day when Joe DiMaggio invited the players to stay after practice because his beautiful blonde ex-wife, Marilyn Monroe, wanted to play ball. Joe D had a softball and some bats, and various Yankees took turns pitching to the sexy movie star. "She hit the ball," Kubek recalled, "ran around, and we had a great time." DiMaggio invited Kubek and several others to dine out with them two nights in a row, and Marilyn, the center of attention, wanted to talk baseball, while the ubiquitous photographers took loads of pictures.[39]

The Yankees played their last exhibition contest in St. Pete against the Cardinals, their longtime training partner, on April 7. The Yankees had lost their first eight games at Lang Field before defeating the Tigers on March 29. Against the Cardinals, Maris, following base hits by Clete Boyer and Bill Skowron, became the hero when he singled off tall right-hander Ron Kline, the ex–Pirate, to win the game in the 11th inning, giving reliever Jim Coates the 5–4 win.[40]

Tony Kubek, All-Star shortstop and later author of the 1987 book, *Sixty-One*, was an important part of the Yankees' exceptional infield that led the American League in 1961 with 180 double plays (National Baseball Hall of Fame, Cooperstown, New York).

Overall in Florida, Houk evaluated his players, the Yankees posted a 10–17 record, Mantle was the biggest star, and the players got in condition to open the regular season on April 11.

Spring in Lakeland

Once the advance camp for minor leaguers and prospects ended and the Tigers' rookies and veterans, along with wives and families, arrived in the last week of February, Detroit's spring drills got under way at Henley Field. Bob Scheffing wanted to strengthen the infield, so he was looking at the "Big Five" from Denver, notably third baseman Steve Boros, second sacker Jake Wood, and first baseman Larry "Bo" Osborne. Scheffing also spent time talking with Kaline. The Tigers needed him to rebound from his 1960 season. Hopefully he would return to form as a fine hitter, a great outfielder, and a role model for younger players.

Scheffing and the Tigers, however, faced different expectations than did Houk and the Yankees. Regardless of what writers projected, the Yankees players all expected to win the pennant. With two exceptions, 1954 and 1959, the Bronx Bombers had won every pennant since Casey Stengel began as manager in 1949. Players who arrived from the minors or via trades knew they were coming to a winner. Luis Arroyo was happy when the Yankees purchased his contract from the Reds the previous July, and he proved it by his performance on the field.

The Tigers, on the other hand, aspired mainly to reach the first division. Nobody in Lakeland entertained thoughts of the Tigers winning first place. While the Yankees were winning pennants in the 1950s, the Bengals' best records were second place in 1950 and fourth twice, in 1957, when New York took another flag but fell to the Milwaukee Braves in the World Series, and 1959, when the Yankees finished third. The Tigers lacked the tradition and expectation of winning, not to mention the World Series paychecks that seemed built into New York's organization. Therefore, many of the writers covering the Bengals were cynical even of first-division projections, especially after Detroit's fall to sixth place in 1960.

Instead, sportswriters, who were traveling on expense accounts and needed to send back interesting stories, highlighted whatever was new or different, including new players and a "youth movement." By 1961 the Tigers and most fans believed they would be a winner when they proved it by consistently winning more games. Until then, most observers figured when the pressure mounted, their heroes would flop, as in the past.

Along with featuring Kaline and Colavito, Watson Spoelstra, the Tigers' beat writer for the *Detroit Free Press*, and Joe Falls, writing for the *Free Press* since 1960, highlighted the progress of Billy Bruton and Bubba Morton, two of Detroit's new black stars. The Tigers had a long record of futility in one-run games, fashioning a 19–31 record in 1960, and 11 of those losses came in a row. Detroit's record for the past six seasons in one-run contests was a combined 111–167. Falls, more cynical than most, enjoyed writing about "inside" parts of the game. He pointed out that little plays such as the bunt, the stolen base, and the hit-and-run could win big games.

Fortunately, Bruton had the skills needed for winning close games. In one at-bat during an intrasquad game, the left-handed batter bounced a hit-and-run single to right field, advancing Ozzie Virgil to third base. "It wasn't much of a play," Falls wrote, "but it's something the Tigers haven't had in years." Nobody could remember when Detroit's number two hitter could be counted upon to advance the base runner.

Playing the exhibition opener in Sarasota against the White Sox, Bruton drove a sharp single to right field in his second at-bat, and the hit put the Tigers ahead to stay. With two outs and two runners aboard in the fourth inning, Bruton topped a grounder toward third base, and with his "blinding speed" he beat the throw to first. Bruton's infield hit kept the inning alive, and Kaline followed with a bases-loaded double. Up next, Colavito hit a 400-foot home run (he hit four homers in Florida), so the Bengals scored six runs instead of one in the inning. Detroit won, 14–7, and while wins in the spring don't count in the standings, this game showed the kind of baseball the Tigers could play with more speed, better base running, and good clutch hitting.

The following day in Orlando against the Minnesota Twins, Bruton again displayed his heads-up play. The Tigers had runners on first and second base, with Bruton at first. George Thomas, a versatile outfielder promoted from Denver, looped a ball down the right field line, and the runner at second headed for third. The quick-witted Bruton started for second, but he tagged up when he saw the ball curve foul. If the right fielder made the catch in foul territory, he could advance. If the outfielder dropped the ball, as he did, he couldn't advance anyway. Overall, Bruton rapped

Billy Bruton, acquired from the Milwaukee Braves before the 1961 season, sparked the Tigers' outfield by providing speed, savvy and a good throwing arm in center. Bruton also inspired younger black players and many fans with his first class abilities and his positive demeanor (Detroit Historical Society).

four hits in seven trips in Detroit's first three exhibitions, but more importantly, he reached base in seven out of ten plate appearances. The veteran's on-base percentage was excellent.[41]

Detroit's training season was full of surprises. For example, Dick Brown was hitting .400, and with his peak being .263 as a rookie with Cleveland in 1957, nobody expected this, not even Liisa, his pretty Finnish wife. Jake Wood had hit in 11 straight games, and with Frank Bolling gone to Milwaukee, Wood won the second base job from Chuck Cottier, the former Braves utility infielder. Veteran Don Mossi looked so good in the spring that Bob Scheffing thought about opening the season with the 6'1" southpaw, who had excellent control and usually pitched hitters low and away. The dependable Mossi, who finished the 1960 season with a sore arm and a 9–8 record, was strong again. More importantly, Al Kaline, who usually started slowly, was taking hours of extra batting practice, working hard on conditioning drills, and logging more time in the outfield. Hustling like a wide-eyed rookie, he was hitting well, a hoped-for follow-up to his disappointing 1960 season. He finished the spring in Florida with a team-best .456 average.

Such good news was making Scheffing's first spring with the Tigers satisfying. Along with Jake Wood and Steve Boros, former Denver stars who were winning starting positions at second and third base, respectively, Bubba Morton was a pleasant surprise. Morton was coming off two straight seasons at Detroit's Triple-A club, one at Charleston and one with Denver. "He figured to get a quick, polite look this spring," Falls commented, "and then the inevitable ticket back to his Rocky Mountain home." Instead, the 5'10", 175-pound Morton, who grew up in Washington, D.C., was hitting with power (he batted .357 in Florida), running the bases with daring, and making excellent catches.

Even the doubting denizens of Detroit's press box were comparing Morton to the great Minnie Minoso in his glory years, but Morton apparently had little chance of making the Tigers, who already had Charlie Maxwell pushing for a regular job. Maxwell, who hit 24 homers and drove in 81 runs in 1960, was reduced to throwing out the warm-up ball between innings in Lakeland. Further, Detroit had reserves such as hard-working George Thomas, the multi-talented outfielder who reportedly threw as well as Kaline and batted .283 with 13 home runs and 81 RBI at Birmingham of the Double-A Southern Association, and George Alusik, another 6'3" outfielder who produced an even better season at Denver, batting .329 with 26 circuit clouts and 106 RBI. The bespectacled Alusik, hoping to be Detroit's slugger of the future, had an exaggerated notion of his worth to the ball club, holding out for a better contract in 1961. Instead, Alusik was given a one-way airline ticket to Denver, where he again produced good numbers (.298, 14 homers, 81 RBI). Recalled on August 1, he arrived in Detroit in time to struggle during the pennant race, averaging just .143 in 16 plate appearances.

Morton, bright, friendly, and gentlemanly, gave the Tigers his best shot, playing right field, left field, and third base. He hit one pinch-hit homer against the Philadelphia Phillies, belted another four-bagger and two singles against the St. Louis Cardinals, and added a pinch-hit double that set up the winning run against Kansas City. Hitting .375 with nine runs scored, he was earning the respect of everyone in Lakeland, fans, players, and team officials included. The Tigers had signed the versatile Morton as a third baseman out of Howard University in 1955, after he completed a stint in the Coast Guard. He had played the outfield and displayed good skills for six minor league seasons, the last two in Triple-A ball. He hit .296 with nine homers and 66 RBI at Denver in 1960, and he looked good in 1961.

By the end of March, Scheffing made the first dozen cuts to his team. Afterward, talking to the writers, he expressed an unusual faith in younger players. "There is always a temptation to bolster a club by adding two or three veterans who, you like to think, have one or two good years left in them," the Bengals' manager said. "Sometimes it works, briefly anyway, but the time comes when you have to go to the young ones you have in the minors and who have shown they are ready for a trial up here."[42]

Two of the most important younger players were Wood and Boros. Wood, born on June 22, 1937, grew up in a diverse, working-class neighborhood. His father, Jacob, Senior, came from Virginia, and his mother, Roberta, grew up in North Carolina. Being sensitive to discrimination, they raised their nine children to treat others fairly. Jake, a New Jersey native, didn't experience the effects of segregation until, after signing with Detroit, he traveled to Florida and moved into Tigertown for advanced spring training in 1957. Lanky and fluid at 6'1" and 170 pounds, Wood batted right-handed and played shortstop, but he was switched to second base at Fox Cities of the Three-I League in 1959. Quiet, polite, and friendly, he excelled at the plate and in the field, batting .300 or more for five ball clubs in four minor league seasons, finishing with a .305 mark, 34 stolen bases, 12 home runs, and 76 RBI for Triple-A Denver in 1960.

Having the opportunity in 1961 was crucial. "I went to spring training, and from day one, I had a good spring camp," Wood said later. "You don't know what somebody can do or what they can achieve, if they're given the opportunity. I got the opportunity."[43]

Steve Boros, the highly-touted MVP of

Playing for Bob Scheffing in 1961, Steve Boros took over for the Tigers at third base. In his first season as a regular, Boros hit .270 with five home runs and a career-high 62 RBI (National Baseball Hall of Fame, Cooperstown, New York).

the American Association in 1960, grew up in a close-knit family in Flint, Michigan, and became a bright student, a gentleman, and a standout athlete. Born on September 3, 1936, Steve, one of five children, helped his father Steve, Senior, and his mother Helen operate a small market near the family's home. Playing sandlot ball and varsity sports at Northern High, he received a baseball scholarship to attend the University of Michigan. Excelling in all phases of the game, he made some All-American teams as a third baseman in 1957. After signing a bonus contract with Detroit, Boros spent his first season with the Tigers, hitting just .146 in 42 plate appearances. He learned the professional game in 1958 at Charleston, Birmingham, and Augusta, hitting a combined .252. In 1959 he played at Birmingham, averaging .305 with 16 homers and 85 RBI. A right-handed batter, he enjoyed a fine year in 1960 with Denver, batting .317, belting 30 home runs, producing 119 RBI, and making the All-Star team. Boros twisted his ankle playing in Puerto Rico that winter. When the 6'0" 185-pounder was training with the regulars in Lakeland, he was labeled "solid."[44]

More importantly, Boros received an opportunity similar to Wood's— third base was open. Eddie Yost, the veteran of 16 seasons who was known as the "Walking Man," was taken in the expansion draft. Scheffing needed a regular third baseman. Boros was ready, willing, and able.

Chico Fernandez, who figured to be the Tigers' shortstop, seemed less able than Boros. Fernandez, a Cuban who first made the majors with the Brooklyn Dodgers in 1956, was traded to the Philadelphia Phillies on April 5, 1957. He was the Phillies' regular at shortstop in 1957 and 1958, and a reserve in 1959, when his average slipped to .211. On December 5, 1959, the Tigers acquired Fernandez and right-hander Ray Semproch for veteran Ted Lepcio and two minor leaguers. Fernandez, who was single and lived alone, contributed a solid season in 1960. He averaged .241, two points higher than Detroit's league-worst team average of .239, but he fielded .947, and his 34 errors topped all regular AL shortstops. He was liked by Tigers fans and he liked playing for Detroit, but he needed to step up his game. By the end of spring training in 1961, Scheffing was telling writers that the Cuban had an indifferent attitude.

Worse, Detroit had no ready alternative. Joe Falls, taking his cue from Scheffing, found little to praise about the friendly Fernandez: "He moves about slowly in the field and it looks like too much of an effort for him to run out grounders." As a result, the manager was looking at all of his short-stops. Unfortunately, "[Ozzie] Virgil, a utility man his entire major league life, seems to lack the instincts to play shortstop on a regular basis." Scheff-ing said that Virgil could fill in, but he doubted whether he could handle being the everyday shortstop. The pilot looked at Chuck Cottier, but so far he couldn't hit. Overall, Fernandez showed more flashes of brilliance along with his many pedestrian efforts. Falls noted that Scheffing had one option: to go with Chico, and "hope he feels like playing."[45]

Scheffing thought about giving a chance to Dick McAuliffe, who batted .259 in an eight-game trial with Detroit in 1960 after hitting .301 for Knoxville of the South Atlantic League. Given some Triple-A seasoning, which he received for two months at Denver in 1961, McAuliffe would have to learn on the job. In any event, Scheffing knew that all the minor league experience in the world wasn't the same as handling the job in the major leagues. By the third week of June, McAuliffe was sent a ticket to fly from Denver to Detroit. For the remainder of the season, the aggressive, hard-charging, left-handed batter from Hartford, Connecticut, was platooned with the right-handed batting Fernandez, but shortstop was the Tigers' weakest position.

Dick McAuliffe, a sparkplug infielder, began in the Tigers' system with Jake Wood at Erie in 1957. In 1961 McAuliffe was called up from Denver in mid–June, and he batted .256 in 80 games, playing shortstop as well as third base (Author's collection).

Lineups of the Tigers and the Yankees

Loaded with talent, the Yankees had the best team in the league, a lineup of experienced, established stars. New York's batting order from Game Seven of the 1960 World Series was, from the top, Bobby Richardson, at second base, Tony Kubek at shortstop, Roger Maris in right, Mickey Mantle in center, Yogi Berra in left (backed up by Hector Lopez), Bill Skowron at first, John Blanchard at catcher (only because Elston Howard's little finger on his right hand was broken in Game Five), Clete Boyer at third, and the pitcher. With Howard in good health, the Yankees could hardly open the 1961 season with a better lineup.

Besides longtime lefty ace Whitey Ford, Houk's rotation featured several right-handers. Art Ditmar, a finesse hurler who threw a hard, sinking fastball along with a good curveball and a slider, signed as an amateur free agent with the Philadelphia Athletics in 1948. After three seasons with the A's, part of 1954 in Philly and all of 1955 and 1956 in Kansas City, the 6'2" Ditmar, from Winthrop, Massachusetts, was traded to the Yankees in early 1957. He had given the Yankees four good seasons, the first two starting and relieving, depending on how Stengel needed him. A fierce competitor, he wasn't afraid to keep a hitter off-balance by throwing at his head. His best season in the Bronx came in 1960, when he fashioned a 15–9 record, but he lost twice to the Pirates in the 1960 World Series. Early in 1961, Ditmar's fastball wasn't sinking. He was 2–3 on June 14 when the Yankees traded him along with little-used Deron Johnson to Kansas City for the reliable Bud Daley. A confident left-hander who had led the A's with 16 victories in 1959 and in 1960, Daley previously toiled for mediocre teams.

Besides Ditmar, Houk planned to pitch Ralph Terry and Bill Stafford. Terry, the 6'3" right-hander from Big Cabin, Oklahoma, who served nearly two years with the Yankees' Kansas City "cousins" after being part of the Billy Martin trade on June 15, 1957, saw his career take off with a 10–8 mark and a 3.40 ERA in 1960. Terry, 25, who originally signed with the Yankees in 1953, could win the big game, which Houk liked, but he also gave up home runs, which any manager dislikes. An experimenter, Terry, a sensitive guy who was always thinking, might fire two blazing fastballs for strikes, followed by a slow curve or a slider. Stafford, 22, a 6'1" right-hander who grew up playing ball in Catskill, New York, threw a curve, a change, and a good fastball with a devastating sink. After going 11–7 for the Yankees' Richmond club of the International League in 1960, he was 3–1 in eight starts for New York. An intelligent fellow who might talk to the baseball, Stafford dressed unusually for a big leaguer, often wearing loafers, blue jeans, and a button-up shirt, but on the mound he was all business. He thought carefully about his pitches, often a batter or two ahead.

Houk also relied on Jim Coates, 28, the 6'4" right-handed country boy from the northern neck of Virginia who looked and acted like a hillbilly (recalled Houk).[46] Coates climbed the Yankees' system starting with D-ball in 1952, making two appearances for New York at the end of 1956. The sidearmer was sent to Richmond in 1957, where he was 14–11. He started 1958 with a 2–0 mark before breaking his pitching arm. Coates missed more than a year, but he worked his way back. With his intimidating, often-inside fastball, good control, and scowling appearance, he had a 6–1 record as a rookie in 1959. The "Mummy," nicknamed for his habit of sleeping with both eyes open, pitched well in 1960, going 13–3 as a spot starter and reliever.

Finally, Rollie Sheldon, 24, the 6'4" right-hander, was trying to jump to the Yankees from Class D Auburn of the New York–Penn League, where he had a fine 15–1 ledger in 1960. All of New York's pitchers were proven major league winners, except for the bright, poised, and talented Sheldon. But Sheldon, who came from Putnam, Connecticut, and pitched one good season at the University of Connecticut before signing with New York in 1960, showed great potential, especially with his low fastball and his slider, which was a better pitch than his curve.

The 1961 baseball issue of *Sports Illustrated*, dated April 10, analyzed all 18 major league clubs, including each team's strong points, weak points, "big ifs," rookies and new faces. *SI* pictured Kubek, Maris, Skowron, and pitcher Art Ditmar as four key Yankees. Kubek and Maris had the flat-top haircuts so popular at the time among athletes, and more than half of all the players pictured had that hair style. The Yankees, wrote the editors, "have power hitting, good defense and front-line pitching." In 1960 the Bombers led the league with 193 home runs and 746 runs scored, and the pitchers led the loop with 42 saves and a 3.52 ERA. Mantle with 40 and Maris with 39 home runs swung the biggest bats, but Skowron (26 homers), Berra (15), Boyer (14), and Kubek (14) were also longball threats. *SI* said the infield of Skowron, Richardson, Kubek, and Boyer was one of the best. Howard, a fine catcher with a rifle arm, would play more under Houk. As it looked at the end of spring training, the starting rotation of Ford, Ditmar, Terry, Turley, and Stafford "are talented enough to make any manager smile."

The weaknesses were secondary pitching and the bench. The editors figured Jim Coates' ERA of 4.28 and his ineffectiveness late the previous season might be signs of trouble. Luis Arroyo, who was sharp on occasion, "cannot be regarded as a day-in, day-out stopper," an observation that proved to be quite inaccurate. The big *if* was the manager. If Stengel's genius helped the Yankees win ten of 12 pennants, Houk might have a problem. For rookies, righty Rollie Sheldon could help, and African American catcher Jesse Gonder offered good left-handed hitting. Danny McDevitt, the ex–Dodger, and Bill Short, who had a brief trial in 1960, were left-handers that could boost the rotation. Nobody at *SI* had a clue about Arroyo's imminent success.

The writers said not to bet against the Yankees: "This team is loaded in a league without much competition. The only thing that might hurt them is their unaccustomed lack of depth."

The Tigers, on the other hand, failed to impress the editors of *Sports Illustrated*. Pictured were hurlers Jim Bunning and Frank Lary along with outfielders Al Kaline and Rocky Colavito. The magazine's writers overlooked the talent of Arroyo for the Yankees, and they missed the potential of Norm Cash for the Tigers. Detroit's strong points included the "best out-field in the league—maybe—and good pitching." Kaline had a "miserable" season in 1960, but was back in his favorite position, so his hitting should improve. Bruton, after seven steady seasons at Milwaukee, should be a top-notch center fielder. Colavito, like Kaline, had a subpar year in 1960. The cleanup hitter batted .249 with 35 home runs and 87 RBI, but the Indians' hero, although traded to Detroit, had a clause in his contract supposedly paying a bonus for *fewer* than 40 homers.[47] Frank Lary, Jim Bunning, and Don Mossi were reliable starters. Hank Aguirre was a "solid reliever." In fact, Terry Fox would prove more reliable coming out of the pen.

Detroit's weaknesses were the infield, the catching, and secondary pitching. *SI* called the infield "awful," saying Cash at first base provided the only "flicker of class." Whether Cash could hit as well as his .286 standard of 1960 remained to be seen. Chuck Cottier at second, Chico Fernandez at short, and Steve Boros at third "are not major league hitters, unless Boros surprises." Dick Brown would be the catcher, despite his .231 lifetime mark after four seasons, and Harry Chiti was named as the backup. Instead, 30-year-old rookie Mike Roarke became the backup, and Chiti was traded to the Orioles on July 21, 1961, for former Tiger Frank House, at one time Detroit's slugging catcher of the future. Finally, Paul Foytack, once good for 15 wins a season, was 2–11 in 1960 with a big 6.14 ERA. Foytack suffered torn muscles under his right arm in 1960, and while he won 11 games in 1961, he never pitched 200 innings in a year again.

"Detroit has no *ifs*," stated *SI*. "Everything is obvious, and bad." Face-tiously, the editors figured maybe Charlie Maxwell could be an *if*, that is, if the Tigers could trade the outfielder–first baseman for "an infielder, a catcher or six pitchers." New faces were Bruton and Cottier. Wood, who hit .305 in the American Association, could take the second base job away from Cottier, and Boros, the American Association's MVP, was Detroit's "best-looking rookie."

SI called Detroit's outlook desperate: "Assuming Kaline and Colavito do improve on their last year's performances, which is likely, the first division still appears too far away. A better bet is a collapse to seventh."[48]

At the same time, *Baseball Digest* ran its popular "Scouting Reports" covering rookies. For the Yankees in 1961, *BD* featured brief profiles and assessments of ten recruits. Two players of particular interest were right-handers Johnny James and Rollie Sheldon. James pitched in relief for the Yankees in 1960, enjoying his best season, going 5–1 with a 4.36 ERA in 43⅓ innings. The magazine said about James: "Major league material. Good fast ball, good curve and—most important—can get both over the plate." In fact, James was traded to the Angels on May 8. Starting three games, he worked 71⅓ innings there, but he failed to earn a save while finishing ten games. His mark was 0–2 and his ERA was 5.30. *BD* fared better on Sheldon, calling him one of the "better-looking prospects in the league" and saying he had "poise and know-how beyond his years." In fact, Sheldon produced an 11–5 record with a 3.60 ERA in 21 starts.[49]

For the Tigers, *Baseball Digest* evaluated 16 rookies, and several were notable for what happened in 1961. Boros was termed an excellent prospect who could take over Eddie Yost's slot at third, if he improved his hitting. "Outstanding power and speed but must brush up on defense." Boros held down the "hot corner" most of the season, until he broke his collarbone in late July, but his hitting bounced back after he returned. Mike Roarke was called an excellent defensive prospect. "Weak at bat but [the Tigers are] wise to forget this; value is in receiving." The statement proved correct, because Roarke became one of the league's better receivers. Wood was pegged as having all the "tools" needed, plus he had "exciting" speed. He was a good hitter, but a slow starter. "Must cut down on strikeouts." Indeed, Wood enjoyed his best season of seven in the majors, hitting .258, but he led the league with a record 141 strikeouts. Finally, Terry Fox, a reliever, was deemed a fair prospect. "Because he's such a good competitor and likes to win so much, he may make a solid relief pitcher."[50] As the season progressed, Fox paced the Tigers' bullpen, like Arroyo did in more spectacular fashion for the Yankees.

J. G. Taylor Spink, the editor and publisher of *The Sporting News*, argued that teams winning the pennant and the World Series must improve, or fall back. Thus, Spinks chose the Los Angeles Dodgers to top the National League and the Baltimore Orioles to win the AL.[51]

Actually, the projections of magazines like *Sports Illustrated* and *Baseball Digest* as well as newspapers such as *The Sporting News*, all of which were staffed with knowledgeable observers, show why managers and coaches know more about players and teams than do writers and fans. Games are won and lost by talented, determined, quick-thinking players on the field, not by the managers, and certainly not by self-styled experts in the press boxes of ballparks or the editorial offices of magazines and newspapers.

And so the Tigers and the Yankees, loaded with players looking to make their mark in 1961, were ready to embark on their separate but linked odysseys in what became one of baseball's most glorious seasons.

3

Opening the Expansion Season: Baseball in April

Opening Day in 1961

On April 11, 1961, in the bottom of the seventh inning at Tiger Stadium, with the temperature hovering near 50 degrees, Jake Wood, waiting in the on-deck circle, motioned to Steve Boros as he headed home on Larry "Bo" Osborne's two-out pinch-hit single to center, cutting Cleveland's lead to 7–3. Applause rippled through the stands on Opening Day as the crowd of 41,643, with little excitement, watched in anticipation, hoping their favorites would keep the rally going. Osborne took a lead off first base as Wood stepped into the batter's box. In his first three major league at-bats, Wood grounded to shortstop twice and hit a fly ball to deep center. Now he was looking for a fastball. Cleveland right-hander Jim Perry, who had given up three runs on six hits, checked for the sign, went into his stretch, and delivered a hard one at the top of the high strike zone,[1] the kind of pitch Wood loved.

Wood, a right-handed-batting rookie who stood tall in his stance, stepped easily, took a hard cut, and met Perry's delivery, driving the ball on a high arc toward the green seats in the upper deck in left, and sent the crowd into the loudest round of cheering and clapping of the afternoon. Exhilarated, Wood, who later called the four-bagger the beginning of his "emotional roller coaster" with the Tigers, trotted around the bases feeling like he belonged in the major leagues.[2] His long blast cut the Indians' lead to 7–5, but the visitors prevailed as Perry finished the game by retiring the last seven Tigers in a row. Clinching the outcome, Cleveland's Bubba Phillips, a former Tiger, hit a two-run homer in the top of the eighth, and the Tribe won, 9–5.

The loss gave Bob Scheffing, nervous enough to keep tapping one foot on the top dugout step for much of the game, bad and good news. First, veteran right-hander Jim Bunning, the future U.S. Senator who had endured

48

an 11–14 season in 1960, struggled early and left for a shower in the Indians' six-run second inning. Phil Regan, Jim Donohue, and Bill Fischer followed on the mound, but the damage was done as Cleveland coasted behind the seven-hitter by Perry. Scheffing, looking for a silver lining, praised Wood, who played well at second base. The first African American originally signed by Detroit and debut for the Bengals, Wood hit the ball hard in three of four trips. "That's a great way to break in," Scheffing said. "Both he and Steve Boros [third base] are going to be all right in the infield."

Scheffing liked the performances of several young Tigers. He praised the two hitless innings thrown by 6'4" Jim Donohue, the 22-year-old rookie right-hander from St. Louis who was drafted out of the Dodgers' system following the 1960 season.

Jake Wood is shown in the Tigers' home uniform with the left field stands behind him. On Opening Day, April 11, 1961, Wood hit a home run into the upper deck in left field during the Tigers' 9–5 loss to Cleveland (author's collection).

That summer Donohue had posted a combined 9–7 mark, but 7–2 in relief, for two Triple-A teams. Hard-throwing Phil Regan, a tall right-hander who grew up in Wayland, Michigan, began his major league career with a 0–4 record for the Tigers in 1960 but learned a slider pitching in Puerto Rico in the winter, relieved Bunning. Regan worked 3⅓ innings, allowing Willie Kirkland's RBI triple in the fourth. Donohue, keeping his pitches low, blanked the Indians for two frames, and Bill Fischer, the one-time White Sox right-hander who was traded by Washington to Detroit on July 22, 1960, yielded two runs in the last two innings.[3]

Watson Spoelstra of the *Free Press* called the opener a success, notably for the strong performances of Wood (a home run in four trips, good defensively at second base), Boros (one single in four at-bats, good job at third base), Osborne (an RBI single), and Donohue. Scheffing dismissed Bunning's failure as "just a bad game," adding that the lanky sidearmer wouldn't lose many times when he received five runs from his teammates. Considering that two inches of snow covered the ground in Detroit 48 hours before game time, the weatherman wasn't optimistic the contest could be played on Tuesday. But the sun was shining brightly, and more than 40,000 of Detroit's long-suffering fans came out to see a younger team of Tigers open the 1961 season.

The familiar stadium looked good to the folks who attended. The Bengals had spent more than $100,000 in improvements to brighten the old ballpark, last renovated and expanded in 1938. Mayor Louis Miriani made his ceremonial first pitch from the field box of owner John Fetzer, and a few minutes later, after his late arrival, Governor John B. Swanson duplicated Miriani's toss. Last but not least, Jesse Simmons, 84, from Armada, a small town 45 miles north of the ballpark, was recognized for watching his 54th straight Opening Day game in the Motor City. Surely Simmons set a new record in determination and longevity for Tigers fans.[4]

On the same gray, chilly afternoon at Yankee Stadium, New York fell to the Minnesota Twins, 6–0, as Pedro Ramos, the rubber-armed Cuban right-hander, spun a three-hit shutout. Whitey Ford dueled Ramos on even terms for six innings, but in the top of the seventh, the Twins' Bob Allison led off with a long home run to left field, Earl Battey doubled, and Reno Bertoia, the ex–Tiger "Bonus Baby," walked. Billy Gardner advanced the runners with a bunt, and Ramos singled sharply to center, driving home two more runs. Ralph Terry, who fashioned a 10–8 record for the Yankees in 1960, took over and stopped the rally. One inning later, Bertoia, following a single by Allison, lined a homer into the lower deck, just inside the left field line. Facing sidearming right-hander Jim Coates in the ninth, Minnesota scored the final run on a sacrifice fly by Harmon Killebrew, who played mainly first base in 1961. Ramos retired 14 straight Yankees to end the contest.

The first game of New York's regular season attracted a small crowd of 14,607 in the Bronx, but the only hits most fans enjoyed were singles by Yogi Berra, batting third in the order, Bill Skowron, hitting sixth, and Ford, the pitcher. Ramos, who won 11 games but lost an American League–high 18 in 1960, showed a hopping fastball, a better curve, and effective changes of speed in his pitches. "Ramos is changing up better on his curve," observed shortstop Tony Kubek, who batted in the seventh slot. "That's a pitch he hasn't shown me in previous seasons." Roger Maris, at this point hitting fifth, had a quiet day. He reached second base when left fielder Jim Lemon dropped his fly ball leading off the second inning. One out later, Ramos walked Kubek but pitched out of the jam. Maris, using his favorite Louisville Slugger, struck out and flied out to right. The Twins dominated the Yankees in their own ballpark, an impressive feat.[5]

Ralph Houk, who rented a historic 14-room house with Bette and their children in Saddle River, New Jersey, and drove to the stadium daily, said little about the game. The Bronx Bombers had nothing to prove, and he knew his ball club would bounce back. The Yankees of recent seasons always came back. Houk said again that he probably wouldn't platoon, like Casey Stengel liked to do. Dan Daniel said the main question heard after spring training was, "Will the Yankees miss Casey Stengel so much that this will beat them?" The answer was no, according to Daniel and most other sportswriters. Instead, New York was again favored to win the pennant.[6]

Tigers Win Eight Straight

After Opening Day, the Yankees and the Tigers had identical 0–1 records, but Detroit wasted little time moving into first place by winning eight games in a row. The Tigers were scheduled for an open day on Wednesday, April 12, but Thursday's game with Cleveland was snowed out.

The White Sox arrived on a cold Friday for a three-game series, and Detroit won the first two, but Sunday's game was postponed due to cold, wet weather. Frank Lary, the determined, hard-throwing right-hander who had become one of Detroit's aces by fashioning a 21–13 mark in 1956, his second full season in the Motor City, almost racked up a no-hitter. Jim Landis, a right-handed batter up with two outs in the fifth, smashed a grounder between short and third. Shortstop Chico Fernandez moved over, tried to backhand the ball, but couldn't make the play, and the fleet Landis reached base. Spoelstra, the official scorer and *Free Press* writer (a typical arrangement for baseball teams of the era), ruled it a hit. First, Spoelstra said the play was very difficult, and second, the runner could not have been thrown out even if the ball had been fielded cleanly. Lary walked two but yielded no other blow that came close to being a hit.

The Tigers roughed up stocky southpaw Frank Baumann, the one-time bonus pitcher who began his career with the Red Sox in 1955, for three runs on five hits in two innings. Detroit scored four more runs on five hits in the third, including Rocky Colavito's first home run, a two-run clout to deep left. Turk Lown came on to snuff the rally, but the Tigers led, 7–0, and Lary was on top of his game. Afterward, Lary told Spoelstra, the scorer, that he was just doing his job, giving "Waddy" (the players' nickname for Spoelstra) a friendly tap on the back. Spoelstra wrote that he would never forget Frank's "friendly response" to a tough call.[7]

On Saturday, April 15, another cold afternoon, Don Mossi, the third of Detroit's "big three" starters, pitched well for 5⅔ frames and defeated the Pale Hose, 6–2, thanks to relief help from Terry Fox. The Tigers' big blows were home runs by catcher Dick Brown, who launched a drive into the upper deck in left field just inside the foul line, and Billy Bruton's three-run blast. The left-handed-hitting Bruton, who batted second for most of the season behind Wood, drove one of Bob Shaw's fastballs into the upper deck in right for a 6–1 Bengals lead. Mossi, the 32-year-old southpaw from Daly City, California, tired in the sixth, giving up two singles and two walks to force in one Chicago marker. Fox, the six-foot rookie right-hander from Chicago, ended the rally and pitched one-hit ball for the final three innings, earning the save. Fox didn't have the screwball that made Luis Arroyo into the AL's best reliever, but showed a hard fastball, a good breaking ball, and tight control.

Bob Scheffing liked what he saw, and his team's second victory lifted the Tigers into a tie for first place with Cleveland and Minnesota, also sporting 2–1 records. In addition to Wood and Boros, each of whom made several good plays in the infield, Scheffing praised Brown for his receiving, his first home run, and his throw to second base gunning down the speedy Luis Aparicio, who had led the majors with 51 thefts in 1960. In addition, Bruton's first American League hit was the three-run homer, and Fox saved his first game, preserving Mossi's win. Mossi showed his left arm had recovered from the injury that limited him in 1960 to a 9–8 record in 22 starts, all made before August 29.[8]

The Tigers had two open dates scheduled for the next week, but cold weather moved the team's planned bus ride to Cleveland back from Tuesday to Wednesday. Playing on a windy, cold day in huge Municipal Stadium, where the waters of Lake Erie lapped against docks not far behind the outer wall of right field, Fox won in relief in the opener, 5–2, and Lary triumphed easily in the Thursday game, 11–4. On Wednesday Jim Bunning hurled six innings and allowed two runs on two hits, but the Tribe scored twice in the first, on Tito Francona's RBI double and Brown's wild throw to second on a steal attempt. The Tigers scored on Al Kaline's RBI double in the fourth, and Bunning left for a pinch-hitter in the seventh. Detroit clinched the game with four runs in the eighth, and Fox earned the win with three innings of scoreless relief. On Thursday afternoon Detroit won behind Lary, who gave up four runs on eight hits, while his teammates reached one-time phenom Gary Bell and two relievers for 11 runs on nine hits, with Norm Cash belting his first home run, an opposite-field, three-run blast to left in the fifth that upped the Tigers' lead to 7–3. The Bengals traveled home that evening with a 4–1 record, second to the Twins' 5–1 ledger.

On Friday, April 21, the expansion Los Angeles club took the field for the first time at Tiger Stadium to open a three-game series, but if the Angels had visions of moving out of last place, they were sorely disappointed, because the Tigers swept all three games. Mossi won his second game on Friday by a score of 9–1, boosted by Colavito's second homer, a three-run blast to deep left-center that staked the Tigers to a 3–0 lead they never lost. Cold weather lingered in the Midwest, and Saturday's game was moved to Sunday as the first half of a twin bill.

In Sunday's opener, Bob Bruce, who had posted a 4–7 mark for Detroit in 1960, hurled eight strong innings of four-hit ball. Bruce, however, lost his stuff in the ninth, giving up a home run to veteran slugger Ted Kluszewski, the longtime Reds' hero, and a double to ex–Yankee Bob Cerv. Bruce won his first (and only) 1961 game, 3–1, saved by Jim Donohue, who retired two hitters with the bases loaded in the ninth, after Terry Fox faltered and hit the only two batters he faced.[9] The Tigers' three runs came on seven hits, and Dick Brown started the scoring in the fifth inning with a home run to center, his second of the season. In the fateful sixth, Kaline hit a one-out single, and Colavito bounced a bad-hop grounder past third base for a double. Cerv's throw to second base hit the ankle of umpire Ed Hurley, bounding away and allowing Kaline to score. Cash walked, and Boros singled to center for a 3–0 lead.

Returning from the stadium's warm clubhouses for the cold nightcap, the Tigers and Angels gave the small crowd plenty of anxious moments and excitement. Bunning opposed ex–Pirate Ron Kline, who was traded to the Cardinals in 1960 and sold to Los Angeles on April 10, 1961. Each team scored in the third inning, the Angels on Albie Pearson's RBI single and the Bengals on Bruton's RBI double. In the tenth, with the score still 1–1, Ken Hunt, pinch-hitting for Kline, singled to score Ken Aspromonte. Bouncing back, the Tigers tied the score on a pinch-hit home run, a line drive into the left field seats by longtime Red Sox first sacker Dick Gernert, obtained by the Tigers from the Chicago Cubs on August 31, 1960. After Gernert's blast, Donohue blanked the visitors in the 11th, and Brown's clutch single, following walks to Cash, Boros, and Chuck Cottier, clinched the first (and only) victory of 1961 for Donohue, after three hours and 11 minutes. The two wins kept the Tigers in first place with a 7–1 record, followed by the fast-starting Twins at 7–2.[10]

Facing the Yankees

Late on Sunday evening, April 23, shortly after President Kennedy and his top advisers saw the ill-fated Bay of Pigs invasion fail in Cuba, the third-place Yankees arrived in Detroit to open a three-game set on Monday at 1:30, the usual starting time for Tigers day games in 1961. For the opener,

Houk used right-hander Bob Turley, who had led the AL in wins with his 21–7 season in 1958, but was unable to win ten games in either of the next two seasons. Frank Lary, dubbed the "Yankee Killer" because of his 23 life-time wins against New York, had won his first two starts, but he endured a shaky first inning. The tough right-hander allowed two-out singles to Maris, Mantle, and Yogi Berra, catching instead of playing left field. Berra's hit scored Maris, and Mantle scored when Colavito misplayed the ball.

The Tigers quickly replied, scoring twice in their half of the first. Wood, leading off as he did for most of the season, drew a walk from Turley, who, with bone chips in his elbow, had lost the great fastball that once made him a big winner. Bruton doubled to center, and Kaline plated one run with a grounder to short. Colavito fanned, Cash walked, and Boros hit a double to left that tied it 2–2. Cash led off the fourth with a home run, his second of the season, smashing a Turley fastball deep into the upper deck in right. In the fifth, Boros, who had singled in the fourth after Turley knocked him down with a high, inside fastball, singled again to score Kaline, who had doubled.

The Tigers turned a big double play in the seventh that cut off a rally. With Detroit ahead, 4–2, Skowron, always dangerous with his power to all fields, reached Lary for his second homer of the year, a blast into the left field balcony. Rookie Deron Johnson, playing third base for the injured Clete Boyer, singled to left. Bobby Richardson topped a grounder to Boros at third which he legged out the hit. With runners on first and second, Houk used left-handed-hitting rookie Jesse Gonder to bat for reliever Johnny James. Gonder grounded one just to the right of second base, and Wood raced over, gloved the ball, tagged Richardson, and, in one smooth motion, threw to first for the twin killing. Lary ended the threat on Kubek's fly to right. The hard-throwing Alabama hurler walked Mantle in the eighth, but recorded a 4–3 victory.[11]

The Tigers had plenty of heroes, notably Boros and Wood, the team's two young infielders. Boros went 3-for-4, lifting his average to .333 and knocking in the eventual winning run with a single in the fifth inning, but he even drew a round of applause after striking out in the eighth. Wood, who singled in three trips to raise his mark to .286, also drew a walk, scored once, and showed his skill with the glove by turning the key double play. Colavito, not yet winning in the applause department, was booed when he fumbled Berra's single in the first. In the third he was booed again when he foolishly tried to stretch his single to center into a double. Colavito, averaging just .226 after going 1-for-4, was big and strong at 6'3" and 190 pounds, but no speedster. Many fans were riding the former Indians slugger because their longtime hero, Charlie Maxwell, the slugger from Paw Paw,

Michigan, became a reserve when Bruton arrived in 1961, leaving Kaline in right field and Colavito installed in left.[12]

On Monday evening the Tigers and the Yankees were guests at a civic event typical of the era, a charity dinner held at Cobo Hall downtown. Two thousand people paid for seats at the tables set up in the arena where the NBA Pistons played home games. Comedian Joe E. Brown emceed the event, and Mickey Cochrane shared his memories from the 1934 World Series–winning Tigers. Yankees broadcaster Phil Rizzuto introduced the visiting New Yorkers, and Tigers announcer Ernie Harwell presented the Bengals. The 20th annual Capuchin Charity Dinner raised $10,000 to feed hungry Detroiters. "Whenever you see Tigers and Yankees breaking bread together," remarked Tigers owner John Fetzer, "that's always good enough to bring out 2,000 people."[13]

On Tuesday a steady rain and cold weather forced postponement of the second game, but Detroit's writers wrote about the Tigers' "kids," Boros and Wood. Kaline, 26, a veteran starting his eighth full season, was asked if Detroit could make a run for the pennant with a young infield. Perhaps a prophet, he said the young Orioles had played well in 1960 before finishing second, eight games behind the Yankees. Detroit's oldest player in the infield was Chico Fernandez, 29. The others, Norm Cash, 26, Boros, 24, and Wood, 23, were in their first full seasons. Kaline, dubbed "the rocking-chair kid" due to his seniority, liked Detroit's chances with the young guys.[14]

On Wednesday afternoon the two teams defied the cold, the kind of weather that makes a player's hands sting when he hits the ball, and the Yankees won a slugfest in ten innings, 13–11. Whitey Ford, not yet in top form, lasted 6⅓ innings, but "Slick," as the Yankees liked to call him, gave up an uncharacteristic ten runs on 11 hits. Bill Stafford bailed out Ford and Ryne Duren hurled a hitless eighth, while Luis Arroyo collected his first win by pitching two scoreless innings. Don Mossi, the Tigers' stellar southpaw, didn't pitch as well as Ford, departing after four innings in which he yielded seven runs on seven hits. Veteran Paul Foytack and rookies Joe Grzenda and Jim Donohue followed, but nobody could stop the Yankees. Lefty Hank Aguirre pitched the ninth and tenth frames, giving up Mantle's seventh home run, a long drive to left-center with Hector Lopez aboard via a single, to make the final score 13–11.

The hard-swinging Colavito socked his third home run, a solo blow off Ford, but the awesome Mantle, now averaging .342, was the big story. Batting left-handed, he smashed his sixth homer, a two-run blast into the fifth row of the upper deck in right-center field, in the eighth inning. Batting right-handed, he socked his seventh homer to win the game. Tony Kubek hit a bases-empty homer, his first, off Mossi in the second inning, and Roger

Maris, batting .200, belted his first round-tripper, a two-run drive off Foy-tack in the fifth. Richardson, Kubek, and Lopez, playing left field, each rapped three hits for New York. Chico Fernandez, who lifted his average to .294, enjoyed one of his best days ever, going 4-for-5, scoring once, and knocking in three runs. Kaline, batting .349, singled twice in six trips, and Colavito, now averaging .265, added a single to his home run.[15]

The day's action left the surprising Tigers in first place with an 8–2 record, the Twins half a game back at 8–3, and the Yankees third at 6–4. Bob Scheffing, talking to writers after the series, credited Detroit's fast start to several factors, notably the torrid pace set by Al Kaline, whom he called the "fighting leader" of the inspired Bengals. Scheffing cited Sunday's game against the Angels when Kaline, standing on the top step of the dugout with his cap off, was clapping for Charlie Maxwell to come through for Detroit (Maxwell singled). Dick Brown won that game with an 11th-inning single, and Scheffing called Brown one of the Tigers' biggest surprises. He figured Brown to average .250 or more (his lifetime average before 1961 was .231): "That fellow is strong and hits the ball hard." A newcomer, Brown was already well liked in Detroit. Jake Wood called Brown a "model team-mate," one who treated everyone with respect.[16]

Scheffing praised the steady infield play of Steve Boros and Wood. Wood, the fastest runner on the ball club, had scored easily from first base when Bruton doubled. "I don't know anybody else who could have done that except Mickey Mantle," Scheffing remarked. Further, the pitching was strong. Frank Lary and Don Mossi were 5–0 in the first two weeks, Jim Bunning was pitching effectively, though without winning, and Terry Fox and Jim Donohue looked good in relief. Scheffing wasn't elated because the season was young. "Detroit is quite restrained at this stage," commented Watson Spoelstra, "but the town is sure to go wild if the Tigers keep it up."[17]

Yankees fans were disappointed with the slow start of their favorite team, except for Mantle, who was lighting up American League pitching. Dan Daniel compared the current ball club to the 1960 Yankees, as both teams were just above .500 in late April. In 1960, however, New York continued to play .500 ball (13–13) in May, but in the month of June, the Bombers caught fire and fashioned a ledger of 21–8. By the end of June, Casey Stengel said they would win the pennant, and he was right. The difference was that Maris hit well early in 1960, and he carried the Yankees in June. Now the opposite was true: Mantle was hitting well early. He hit five home runs in the first ten games of 1961, and against Detroit, he hit numbers six and seven.

What was wrong with Maris? For one thing, his timing was off, and opposing pitchers, realizing that, were throwing pitches by him that Maris would have ripped at this point in 1960. He was barely hitting .160 before the Yankees traveled to Detroit, where he finally produced his first home run. Houk believed that Pat Maris' problems in carrying her fourth child caused "a serious reaction on Roger." After looking briefly for a place for his family to live in New York, Maris decided instead to send them back to their home in Raytown, Missouri. Despite his struggles at bat, Maris was "the same spectacular man on defense he was when he was slugging the ball last year." Daniel called him a fighter.[18]

Mickey Mantle

Two of the fastest-starting stars of the 1961 season were longtime heroes Mickey Mantle and Al Kaline. Mantle, muscular, bull-necked, and exceptionally well coordinated at 5'11" and 195 pounds,[19] was starting his 11th big league season. He was hitting .342, with seven home runs and 15 RBI, after the Yankees split two games with the Tigers. "The Mick," who averaged .298 in his 18 major league seasons, was enjoying the prime year of his career, despite living with damaged right knee ligaments, osteomyelitis in his left leg, and various other injuries that slowed him and, occasionally, caused him to miss a few games. Still, Mantle was responsible for more stories being turned out by baseball writers than any other athlete of his time. The most famous Yankee since Joe DiMaggio, he was the leader by his presence and his actions on the diamond, in the dugout, in the locker room, and even away from the ballpark.

Greatness was thrust on Mantle from the time he arrived and blasted 400-foot home runs in exhibitions during the spring of 1951, explained New York scribe Dick Schaap, sports editor of *Newsweek*. Mantle, young and inexperienced in that rookie season when the great DiMaggio was closing out his Hall of Fame career, "stepped into a world he never made and found that it is, at times, a hard and terrible thing to be afflicted with greatness." Schaap was writing about Mantle, but every star, indeed every major leaguer, experienced a version of the same burden. Writers said that Mantle hit harder than Ted Williams, slugged farther than Babe Ruth, ran faster than Ty Cobb, fielded better than DiMaggio, and more. When folks repeatedly read such accolades, most of them believe the glowing words. But when the uplifted hero falls short of perfection, he is not ignored but rather criticized, booed, or worse, and most Yankees fans, used to winning, were poor losers. Life-styles and salaries of major league stars look great and glorious to readers, especially to boys dreaming of wearing big league uniforms, but the price of fame is invisible to all except the most informed observers, and the cost to players can be high.

Called the successor to DiMaggio, who was surely the most talented and graceful player of his generation, Mantle, with his smiling image shown on the covers of magazines, alongside newspaper articles, and on television, came out of small-town Oklahoma as an inarticulate young man who had a tough time making sensible comments to the self-anointed lords of the press. He was shy and bashful, and shyness isn't easy to overcome, especially in the glare of New York's publicity machine. But fans, looking for the greatness promised by his potential, saw his shyness as arrogance, or worse. Mantle didn't tip his hat or acknowledge the fans, because he didn't know how. When running out a home run, he kept his head down and circled the bases, as did most of his peers in the 1950s. Yankees fans wanted the slugger to love them, but Mantle shied away, and often this resulted in a chorus of boos when he struck out, hit a mere single, or made a mistake on the bases or in the field. Thus, Mantle stumbled, he swore, he slumped, he suffered, and nobody was there to help him. The ethic of the majors in those years was that each player made it on his own, or he went back to the minors, as Mantle did in 1951.[20]

If fans were upset, Mantle was upset, and he usually blamed himself, which is hardly an unusual reaction of the professional athlete who doesn't live up to his own perceived potential. It wasn't until his Triple Crown exploits of 1956, batting .353, hitting 52 home runs, and driving in 130 runs, that he became famous in America, a stature he never escaped.

Greatness on the diamond doesn't translate to greatness away from the ballpark. Mantle was no intellectual. After Mantle appeared on the "Perry Como Show" during the 1956 season, one writer said, "Saw you on TV last night, Mickey. Did you use a script or was that ad lib?" Mantle, not knowing what "ad lib" meant, finally said, in his Oklahoma drawl, "Gee, I dunno." The hero was flawed. Nobody accused Babe Ruth of being a scholar, but somehow Mantle was different.

Mantle, who didn't like the press getting involved in his private life, was often moody. Yankees fan and author Peter Golenbock, who interviewed Mantle before publishing his 1975 book, *Dynasty: The New York Yankees, 1949–1964*, pointed out that Mantle, a lover of night life along with buddies like Whitey Ford, might answer writers' questions with yes or no replies, or if he didn't want to answer, he could say, "How do I know?" Often he avoided answers, or he replied with terse comments that were unquotable, maybe unprintable. He was a master of locker-room humor and practical jokes, and he could be funny and light-hearted, or crude and profane. Among teammates, he could be effusive and fun. Around outsiders, he was often difficult.[21]

The rugged, blond, pale-eyed slugger followed up his 1956 plateau of greatness by declining, at least statistically, for the next four seasons. In

1957 he improved his average to .365, but he homered "only" 34 times and racked up 94 RBI, a great season for most players. The Yankees won the pennant, but lost the World Series to the Braves in seven games, and Mantle suffered a shoulder injury at second base that made it hurt to bat left-handed for years. In 1958 he saw his average slip to .304, but he led the league with 42 home runs while contributing 97 RBI. The Yankees played the Braves in another World Series, this time winning the championship in seven games. In 1959 The Mick's average dropped to .285, but he contributed 31 home runs and 75 RBI, all mortal statistics. The Yankees placed third, missing just their second pennant since 1948, and the booing by fans was probably the worst of the decade. In 1960 his average again declined, this time to .275, the lowest mark since he hit .267 as a rookie. But he led the league with 40 home runs, one more four-bagger than teammate, rising star, and league MVP Roger Maris. Mantle produced 94 RBI, but he was 18 below the league-best 112 generated by Maris.

The turning point for Mantle and the fans came in a game at Yankee Stadium against Baltimore on August 15, 1960. One day earlier the Yankees had lost a doubleheader to fifth-place Washington, and Maris was injured. In the sixth inning of the nightcap, Clete Boyer singled, and Maris singled him to third. Hector Lopez hit a bouncer to the shortstop, and Maris barreled into second base, breaking up the double play but taking a knee in the ribs from Billy Gardner. Mantle, with Lopez at first, grounded to third, but, frustrated with his failure to get a clutch hit and feeling the pain of ligament damage in his right knee, he trotted to first base as the Orioles completed a double play that running hard might have prevented. Worse, the hustling Maris had been injured one play earlier. With the inning over, New York fans booed loudly as Mantle waited by first base for someone to bring his glove from the dugout. Instead, Stengel replaced Mantle, and the booing increased.[22] Mantle was humiliated, Stengel was upset, and fans were angry.

The following day, when his name was announced as number three in the order against visiting Baltimore, Mantle was greeted with one of the worst cascades of boos, catcalls, and name-calling ever witnessed in the Bronx. In the second inning, Baltimore's Ron Hansen hit a solo home run, and in the third, the Orioles scored again on ex–Yankee Gene Woodling's RBI single. In the last of the fourth, with the Yankees trailing, 2–0, Mantle, following a single by Lopez, stepped to the plate against right-hander Jerry Walker, and again the slugger endured the crowd's abuse. Pretending not to hear, he slammed a two-run homer into the Yankees' bullpen in right center. After his usual head-down trot around the bases, he surprised the crowd of 24,233 by tipping his cap, a happy gesture that brought forth cheers along with more boos.

In the eighth, with the Orioles leading, 3–2, on a Jackie Brandt home run, Mantle faced reliever Hoyt Wilhelm, the knuckleballer. Lopez, who drew a walk, led off at first. Mantle popped up to the catcher, but Clint Courtney, wearing an oversized mitt, dropped it. Given new life, Mantle, who had the extraordinary ability to hit a home run when one was most needed, lined a two-strike knuckler into the right field seats, winning the game, lifting the Yankees ahead of the Orioles into first place by half a game, and causing the fans to roar in approval.[23] After the game, he said, "I wanted to be good tonight more than I ever wanted to be good in my life."

The following day, Peter Golenbock concluded, the writers ignored Mantle's faults and gave him kudos, explaining his injuries, praising his courage, lauding his perfectionism, and admiring his human qualities. The writers and fans were finally shifting to Mantle's side.[24]

The Yankees played well through September, posting a 20–7 record that month. New York, winning the pennant by an eight-game margin over Baltimore, faced the Pittsburgh Pirates in the World Series. In dramatic fashion the Pirates, playing at home at Forbes Field, won the championship in the final inning, 10–9. All Mantle did was bat .400 (10-for-25), walk eight times, score eight runs, hit one double and three home runs, compile a slugging percentage of .800, and produce 11 RBI, one fewer than the 12 of Bobby Richardson, the Yankees' second baseman and the World Series MVP.

In the decisive seventh game, with the Pirates leading in the ninth, 9–7, Richardson, a good contact hitter, and Dale Long, pinch-hitting, both singled off veteran Bob Friend, the third of four Pittsburgh pitchers. Danny Murtaugh sent in lefty Harvey Haddix, and Roger Maris fouled out. Mantle, embracing the pressure, singled to right, bringing home Richardson, sending pinch-runner Gil McDougald to third, and making the score 9–8. Yogi Berra drove a hard grounder just inside the first base line, and Rocky Nelson made the play, stepping on first to retire Berra, and trying to tag Mantle for the game-ending double play. Mantle, reacting instantly, hook-slid back to first, avoiding the tag for the third out, allowing McDougald to score and tie the game at 9–9. In the Pirates' ninth, Bill Mazeroski, who liked high pitches, led off against Ralph Terry. On a 1–0 count, Terry, recalled catcher Johnny Blanchard, threw a high slider that didn't break, and Mazeroski hit the game-winning home run over the wall in left field,[25] crushing the Yankees.

Afterward, Mantle cried in the locker room, not for himself but for his team, and most of the Yankees were in an emotional state, though few had done as much as "The Mick" to win. On the plane home to Dallas that night, Mantle was still having fits of tears. When Merlyn said it was just a game, she didn't understand that her husband felt like he let everyone down.[26] "They were the tears of a man who had tried his hardest," wrote Dick Schaap, "pained and tired, and had done his best."

Mantle heard cheers for his inspired play over and over again after his two-homer game against Baltimore on August 15, even more so during the 1960 World Series. Asked about it, the ultimate jock grinned and replied, "It seemed good. It felt good. I liked it." But he knew the cheers could change. Smiling, he said Yankees fans would let him know when he made mistakes.

Mantle's comments to writers throughout the World Series, usually made in a relaxed mood, suggested he had changed. The most famous Yankee was more at ease with himself. He answered most questions with brief remarks, often accompanied by a grin. Sometimes a smile or a joking comment can turn opponents into friends, and Mantle, however slowly, was learning the art of ballpark public relations. The game's once-fastest center fielder was still the greatest hero, the best of his Yankees generation. He was no baseball god, but he was Mickey Mantle.[27]

More charming than ever, he was off to a great start in 1961. Maybe this was the year the superhero in pinstripes would challenge the Babe's hallowed home run record.

Mantle loved baseball, and he said he loved his wife, but he frequently didn't behave as a loving husband. All baseball players lead split lives, spending half a season (81 games, starting in 1961) on the road. Mantle married his high school sweetheart, Merlyn Johnson, a pretty brunette who was once a drum majorette, on December 23, 1951, in Commerce, Oklahoma.[28] The couple had four sons: Mickey Junior (born in 1953), David (1955), Billy (1957), and Danny (1960). Most biographers concede that Mantle was an alcoholic for most of his adult years, and his wife and three sons became problem drinkers too. Once Mickey was wearing the Yankees uniform, he began having trysts with an older woman, Holly Brooke. Later, Mickey's late-night escapades with women were a concern for Casey Stengel. "Mantle's dalliance with Brooke," wrote biographer Jane Leavy, "set a precedent for a double life that persisted long after the relationship ended and would continue throughout his married life."

The Mantles' first marital address was the Concourse Plaza Hotel at the corner of 161st Street and Grand Concourse, and dozens of other Yankees rookies and their wives sooner or later lived in the building's affordable residential apartments, partly because they were within walking distance of Yankee Stadium. Mickey and Merlyn had a small efficiency apartment with no air conditioning, but in mid–1953 they moved across the Hudson River, like most Yankees families, and rented in the New Jersey suburbs.

By 1961 Merlyn was taking care of four boys, and her life was difficult and lonely. "When we all moved over to New Jersey," recalled Lucille McDougald, a good friend, "Merlyn just stayed with the kids. She more or less faded into the background."[29] Since 1957 the Mantle family had lived the "extravagant life" in Dallas in a $65,000 home.[30]

For much of the summer of 1961, Mantle lived with Roger Maris, at Roger's invitation, and Bob Cerv in an apartment in the Queens, located on the Van Wyck Expressway several blocks from the Stadium. Supposedly Mantle and Maris were "feuding" over issues tied to the home run race, but it was nonsense produced by a handful of overzealous writers. Mantle and Cerv had twin beds in the bedroom, and Maris slept on a studio couch in the living room. They rented for $251 a month, killed time by watching TV programs like *The Andy Griffith Show*, played gin rummy and hearts for no money, listened to music, mostly records from Maris' collection, drank a few beers, and ate cold cuts, pizza, and, once in a while, steaks. A few hours before a game, the three sluggers rode in Maris' new Oldsmobile convertible to the Stadium and moved into their pregame routine, which, for many big leaguers, included signing autographs for half an hour.[31]

Al Kaline

Al Kaline was no glamorous superstar, but he was Detroit's greatest player since Hank Greenberg, maybe even since Ty Cobb. Like Mantle, Kaline seemed destined for baseball's Hall of Fame, but that kind of recognition remained in the distant future. Like Mantle, it took Kaline years to be comfortable with writers, because he also began as an inarticulate rookie from whom great things were expected. The Baltimore native was reserved, reticent, even naïve, but sincere. The expectations of the writers and the fans can be hard for even the greatest individuals to meet, and in that sense, Kaline and Mantle shouldered a similar burden.

Kaline played sparingly as a "Bonus Baby" in 1953, his rookie season (he was 7-for-28 in 30 games), but he took over right field in 1954 when his glove was better than his bat. Also like Mantle, he achieved superstar status too soon, in his case by leading the league in hitting with a .340 mark in 1955. In addition, Kaline belted 27 home runs and contributed 102 RBI, figures that he surpassed only a handful of times. Crew-cut with blue-eyes and a sly grin, the youthful Kaline, who turned 21 on December 19, 1955, was tall, fast, and agile at 6'2" and 175 pounds. He batted right-handed, whereas Mantle was the most famous switch-hitter in the game. Kaline would never produce a 30-homer season, but his excellent play in the outfield would endear him to thousands of fans. Countless kids grew up in Michigan dreaming they could "be" Al Kaline, the same way that kids who loved the Yankees wanted to be like Mickey Mantle.

Kaline followed his batting championship of 1955 with an equally good if not better year in 1956, when he hit .314, after a very slow start (he didn't reach .300 until he went 3-for-6 in a win over the Yankees on August 3). The All-Star right fielder hit the same number of home runs in 1956, 27, but he drove in a career-best 128 runs, just two behind Mantle, who enjoyed his only Triple Crown season. However, Kaline, like Mantle, tailed off statistically in the following four seasons. In 1957 he batted .295 with 23 home runs and 90 RBI, the top average for the Tigers, second in homers, one less than Charlie Maxwell, and eight more RBI than Maxwell. Detroit, led by new manager Jack Tighe, placed fourth in the league with a 78–76 record, but the Tigers finished 20 games behind the pennant-winning Yankees.

In 1958 Kaline enjoyed another good season, but his .313 average ranked third for Detroit behind reserve outfielder Gus Zernial's .323 mark and the .319 season of Harvey Kuenn, the Tigers' other big star ever since Kuenn's rookie season of 1953, when he batted .308 and led the AL with 209 hits. In 1958, Kaline showed less power, hitting 16 home runs, and first baseman Gail Harris led the Bengals with 20 homers. Kaline led the ball club in RBI with 85, and Harris was second at 83. Detroit, with Tighe replaced by Bill Norman on June 10, slipped to fifth place with a 77–77 record. Despite the efforts of heroes like Kaline and Kuenn, the Tigers were mediocre again.

Kaline and Kuenn came through with fine individual performances in 1959, but the Tigers remained in the middle of the league, producing a losing record of 76–78 and finishing fourth, 18 games behind the first-place White Sox, while the Yankees skidded to third. After the Tigers lost 15 of their first 17 games, Bill Norman was fired and replaced by Jimmy Dykes on May 2. In a Sunday doubleheader against the Yankees on May 3, Charlie Maxwell, soon dubbed the "Sunday Slugger," cracked four home runs, each longer than the previous one, to jump-start Detroit with two victories over New York. The Bengals gradually rose as high as second place on June 20, but two days earlier Kaline was struck on the side of the face with a thrown ball, suffering a fractured cheekbone when he was leading the team at .351. The All-Star right fielder sat out a week, but for the rest of the summer, when Kaline surged, so did the Tigers, and when he slumped, so did his team. Kuenn won the AL batting title with a .353 average and Kaline ranked second at .327. Maxwell led the Tigers with personal bests of 31 home runs and 95 RBI, and Kaline was second with 27 homers and 94 RBI.

Kaline came back in 1960 prepared for another good season, hoping trades by general manager Bill DeWitt, serving his second year with the Bengals, would help the Tigers rise above the middle of the league. One important trade, though largely unnoticed at the time, came when Detroit swapped third baseman Steve Demeter, who hit .111 for the Bengals in 1959, to Cleveland for first baseman Norm Cash, who batted .240 with four home runs and 16 RBI in a reserve role for Chicago when the White Sox won the pennant. Cash went on to play 15 good seasons for the Tigers, but Demeter went hitless in five plate appearances for the Indians in 1960 before disappearing into Triple-A ball for ten seasons.

Detroit made a blockbuster trade on April 17, 1960, when Cleveland's popular slugger, Rocky Colavito, who tied for the AL home run crown with 42 in 1959, came to Detroit, and the Tigers sent Kuenn, the 1959 batting champion, to the Indians. Colavito became a powerful cog in the Bengals' machine that challenged the Yankees for the pennant in 1961, while Kuenn hit .308 for the Indians in 1960 before going to the San Francisco Giants and enjoying four more good seasons. DeWitt got the better end of both deals, but his impulsive trading cost him the position as Detroit's GM after the 1960 season.

Kaline endured a rough season in 1960 as the Tigers fashioned the league's worst batting average, .239, while Cash led his new team with a .286 mark. Colavito, as expected, was Detroit's big gun, averaging .249 (he batted .266 lifetime in 14 seasons) and leading his new team with 35 home runs and 87 RBI. Kaline, an All-Star since 1955 and a Gold Glover since 1957, batted .278, his lowest average since 1954, with 15 homers and 68 RBI.

Kaline, like Mantle, received a lot of flak from the fans in 1960, but in his case, the furor came mainly over his investment in a stable of race horses with two other Detroiters, the Red Wings' famed Gordie Howe and businessman Frank Carlin, a friend of both athletes. Kaline dropped out of the HKC Stables when Commissioner Ford Frick raised the question of gambling. Kaline, surprised by the controversy and not personally involved with gambling, was also beset by an injured left knee that slowed him most of the season. He started slowly, hitting .238 by June 1, and he didn't handle the uproar over the race horses well. In August team physician Dr. Russell Wright discovered that Kaline had low blood pressure, which was sapping his energy. After starting on medication, Kaline boosted his mark from a low point of .224 on August 14.

Ten days earlier, the impulsive Bill DeWitt and Cleveland's frenetic Frank Lane capped their love of trading with a major league first: Detroit sent manager Jimmy Dykes to Cleveland, and the Indians sent manager Joe Gordon, a Tigers coach in 1956, to the Motor City. It didn't matter. The

Indians finished fourth with a 76–78 record, and the Tigers were sixth at 71–83, their worst mark since finishing last with a lousy 50–104 ledger in 1952. To wipe the slate clean, John Fetzer bought the controlling interest in the Tigers after the 1960 season, and shortly afterward he renamed the classic ballpark Tiger Stadium.

Kaline never received the booing that Mantle endured for years, but he faced high expectations that he himself shared. He masked his disappointment with his team's annual performances by saying as little as possible to writers, partly because he didn't feel comfortable talking about himself and his achievements, and partly because he wasn't good at it. Still, Kaline had a presence in Detroit that set him above other players, although that wasn't his intention. Mantle had a similar presence in New York, but he was more comfortable around teammates, many of whom were buddies, notably Whitey Ford and Yogi Berra, two longtime Yankees greats.

Kaline, like Mantle, started his professional career right after high school, but he signed a bonus contract in 1953 and never spent a day in the minor leagues. New York GM George Weiss reportedly tried to trade for Kaline after the 1958 World Series, but John McHale, then Detroit's GM, nixed the deal. Still, as Kaline and every other major leaguer knew, a ballplayer can never be sure whether, or when, he might be traded. Baseball is a business, and star athletes put fans in the seats—and nowadays they sell team gear too. The ball club wants to know what the player achieved today, not last year. As long as Kaline kept up his All-Star level of performance, despite the Tigers' middle-of-the-pack finishes, he had job security, but not certainty. One day in 1959, after Detroit started with a 2–15 record and ticket sales were off, Mantle and Ford pulled Kaline aside after a game and said they heard the Yankees wanted to deal Bill Skowron and a pair of minor leaguers for him. When Skowron broke his wrist in July, the trade rumors faded.

Al Kaline (left) talks with Mickey Mantle before a game at Yankee Stadium. Kaline and Mantle, the respective superstars of their teams, were often pictured together (National Baseball Hall of Fame, Cooperstown, New York).

Still, every year the Bengals finished out of the first division, talk arose over trading Kaline.[32]

Kaline, like Mantle, married his high school sweetheart, but the similarity ends there. Al and Louise Hamilton took their wedding vows on October 16, 1954, after his first full season as Detroit's right fielder. He met Louise, whose family moved from West Virginia, at Baltimore's Southern High. She played softball, understood baseball, and was willing to talk baseball. That was important to Al, whose life was dedicated to baseball. Returning to Baltimore and talking about his high school years in 2004, the year Al and Louise celebrated their 50th wedding anniversary as well as the year Southern High was converted to a condo, he said, "I was always a shy guy. Girls didn't exactly fall over me. It's not like I was a great quarterback or something."[33]

Kaline liked his privacy, despite dealing with his growing celebrity status. The Kalines had two sons, Mark (born in 1956) and Mike (1963). Kaline returned home to Baltimore after the first two seasons, but the couple moved to an upscale suburb northwest of Detroit, Birmingham, after he won the 1955 batting title, and it seemed like a good idea to live near Detroit (a few years after 1961, the Kalines moved to elite Bloomfield Hills, 20 miles northwest of downtown Detroit). Kaline was, for all practical purposes, a ballplayer in a gray flannel suit. Characteristic of most people's values in the 1950s, he never rocked the boat. A clean-living gentleman off the diamond, Kaline was a family man. His wife and sons were very important to him, and he lived a secluded life without hint of scandal. The worst you could say about the Tigers' biggest star was that he hired a company to promote his 1955 batting title, and, later, he bought into a racing stable as an investment. A superstar athlete and a contented husband and father, he represented the ideal major leaguer to dozens of writers as well as to legions of Tigers fans.

Wives are part of ballplayers' lives, and Louise Kaline, a bright, attractive brunette, socialized with other Tigers' wives, and most of them attended Detroit's home games. Traditionally, the women sat together behind the Bengals' dugout in the first two rows of reserved seats, just behind the sections of field box seats that ran from first to third base in the lower deck. Merry Sue Roarke, the wife of Mike Roarke, Detroit's backup catcher in 1961, remembered that all of the wives were friendly, but each one had to learn how to live in the public eye. The wives got along, accepted each other, and rooted for their husbands to play well.

"It's like you have to get used to being in the spotlight," explained Merry Sue, "because that's not how anyone grows up." They were living a public adventure together as well as living similar lives. "One girl said one day, 'I don't care if you're the 25th player on the club, you're a major league player. Don't take anything from anybody.' That's kind of how they all felt, 'You're one of us.' That was nice."[34]

In any event, star athletes live complicated lives, as Mickey Mantle discovered early, and so did Detroit's favorite son. When he interviewed Kaline at the Oakland Hills Country Club for his 1997 book, *The Tigers of '68*, George Cantor, an intellectual sort who was one of the best writers for the *Free Press* in the 1960s, offered insights into Kaline and his life. Kaline lived on a level above other players, inherently so because of his superior talent. By 1961 he was long since the face and heart of the franchise. Later, when the conservative Jim Campbell became general manager, nobody was allowed to earn more than Kaline, no matter what. "He truly was," Cantor observed, "in Rocky Colavito's words 'a little tin god' in the Detroit organization."

Perhaps because of his upbringing in a working class neighborhood, Kaline

One of the Tigers' new baseball families in 1961, Mike Roarke talks with his wife Merry Sue, who is dressed fashionably, before a game at Fenway Park in Boston (author's collection).

was careful, conservative, and correct in his life. But Cantor found that a few of the younger players resented Detroit's superstar. Some thought that Kaline set himself apart on purpose. Others believed that he couldn't play through injuries, the opposite of what Mantle did for the Yankees. People's evaluations of others depend on their own values and perceptions, and lesser players sensed more favorable treatment of Kaline, including in salary. Still, the Baltimore native was a great baseball player. Explained pitcher Johnny Podres, who came to the Tigers later from the Dodgers, you had to see Kaline in action to appreciate him. "He never makes a mistake."[35]

Wrapping Up April

After leaving Detroit on Wednesday evening, April 26, the Yankees finished the month by beating the Indians twice and splitting a Sunday doubleheader at expansion Washington, finishing April with a record of 9–5.

In the two-game home stand at Yankee Stadium, the Bombers defeated the visiting Tribe, 4–3, behind a steady performance by right-hander Art Ditmar, a finesse pitcher. Left-handed batting Tony Kubek, the quiet, rangy, 6'3" shortstop from Milwaukee who lived with a teammate in the Stadium Motor Lodge eight blocks from the ballpark, hit three singles in four trips off former Giants southpaw Johnny Antonelli, who gave up all 11 hits in 6⅔ innings. The Indians opened the scoring with two runs in the third inning, and clutch-hitting Hector Lopez, batting third, knocked in one run with a sacrifice fly in the Yankees' third. Deron Johnson tied the game at 2–2 with an RBI single in the fourth, and Mantle, in the cleanup slot, knocked in the go-ahead run with a sacrifice fly in the fifth. In Cleveland's sixth, Jimmy Piersall, a right-handed batter with a volatile temperament and a history of wacky antics on and off the diamond, tied the score with a sacrifice fly, but Mantle, smashing a triple to deep right-center in the seventh, drove in the eventual winning run. Ditmar blanked the Indians the rest of the way, boosting his mark to 2–0.

Friday's cold weather caused a postponement, but on Saturday the Yankees beat the Indians again, this time 4–2. Ralph Terry won his first game, aided by Luis Arroyo, who pitched the eighth and ninth frames to record his second save. The Yankees opened with three runs in the first inning off Jim Perry, thanks to a sacrifice fly by Roger Maris, a single by Mantle, and Yogi Berra's two-run homer to deep right. Woodie Held, a one-time Yankee prospect, got one run back for the Tribe on his solo clout in the fourth, but Maris singled home a run in the fifth, boosting New York's lead to 4–1. Cleveland's final marker came on Vic Power's run-scoring single in the sixth, but when Terry tired in the eighth, Arroyo stifled the Indians.

Traveling to Washington (the first 162-game season featured many two-game series), the Yankees split Sunday's twin bill with the Senators. Whitey Ford upped his record to 3–1 in the opener before a typically small DC crowd of 21,904. The southpaw hurled six innings, Bill Stafford yielded a run, and Arroyo got his third save with two hitless innings. Against right-hander Dick Donovan, the ex–White Sox star who kept his pitches low, Berra singled home Mantle in the fourth. In the seventh, pinch-hitter Jesse Gonder, a catcher from Oakland, California, who soon had a reputation for being outspoken about racism when most African American athletes were reluctant to say much, knocked in a run with a grounder, and Kubek's RBI double made the lead 3–2. Clete Boyer hit an RBI single in the eighth, and Arroyo saved New York's 4–3 victory, after yielding Harry Bright's sacrifice fly in the eighth.

In the nightcap, former Tigers southpaw Hal Woodeshick pitched eight effective innings, squaring his record at 1–1, saved by ex–Tigers lefty Pete Burnside, who retired the final two Yankees to preserve the Senators' 2–1 victory. Rollie Sheldon, dubbed the "Rookie from Class D" by Joe Trimble of the *New York Daily News*, worked seven innings, but didn't get enough run support. The visitors collected ten hits, but they scored only in the ninth, when Lopez led off with a single off Woodeshick. Facing 6'4" reliever Dave Sisler, a star basketball and baseball player who attended Princeton on an academic scholarship, Mantle singled, and Skowron singled for one run. After Elston Howard popped out, Burnside came in to retire Maris and Boyer on grounders. The Senators scored on Gene Woodling's RBI single in the fourth and catcher Dutch Dotterer's RBI double in the fifth. When the day ended, the Yankees were second at 9–5, one game behind the league-leading Tigers at 10–4. The surprising Twins were third with a mark of 9–6, the White Sox were fourth at 7–6, and the Indians, Orioles, and Red Sox were tied for fifth with .500 marks, three games back.

Ralph Houk claimed he wasn't worried. "I believe our pitching depth to be as good as any opponent," the manager told feisty Joe King, "and that's why I am not apprehensive over doubleheaders, so long as we do not have to play more of them than any other club." Houk named Art Ditmar, Bob Turley, and Whitey Ford as starters for the next series against the Twins in Minnesota. Houk liked the performance of Sheldon, who gave up five hits, walked two, and fanned eight. The rookie, more mature than most, refused to buckle with runners on base, instead getting the ball low without letting up. "He kept firing real fast and got the ball over in the jams," said Elston Howard. Sheldon, who pitched with a stiff overhand delivery, was surprising everyone with his effective hurling. Houk said the Bombers' one weak position was third base, hence the opportunity received by Deron Johnson, who, along with an ineffective Art Ditmar, was traded to Kansas City on June 14, 1961, for 6'1" southpaw Bud Daley, who survived on wits and breaking balls like the knuckler, slider, and curve. Houk showed he was going with a largely set lineup by starting Mantle, Kubek, Skowron, Richardson, Lopez, and Maris in the first 14 games.

To date Mantle had been spectacular. When he didn't hit a home run, he helped the Bombers with his other skills. In New York's 4–3 win at Washington on April 30, Mantle, batting in the top of the fourth with Maris at first base and one out, grounded into a force play at second, but he beat shortstop Coot Veal's throw to avoid the double play. Dick Donovan was pitching to Berra when Mantle stole second. On the next pitch, Berra laced a single to left and Mantle raced around to score for a 1–0 lead. Batting with two outs in the sixth, Mantle singled and again stole second. This time

Berra bounced back to the pitcher, so Mantle was stranded as the inning ended. Clete Boyer singled home the eventual winning run in the eighth, Arroyo recorded his third save to preserve Ford's third victory, but Mantle's play was instrumental in the win. Afterward, Houk, when asked about Mantle as the team leader, remarked, "The way he is hitting and the way he is fielding, I don't think he has to do any more to lead."[36] The Mantle of Triple Crown fame was back for the Bombers.

New York played .556 ball for the first ten games (5–4, and one tie), and Maris was hitting just .161 (5-for-31). Tony Kubek recalled, "That is what a lot of writers forget about sixty-one. It was Roger who started slowly while Mickey carried the team. Houk was getting booed by the fans, and the writers were skeptical, but Mickey kept it from being a lot worse."[37]

While New York finished April with a twin bill split in Washington, Detroit followed the loss to New York on April 26 by splitting two games at home with Boston and dividing a two-game set with visiting Baltimore, before starting on a seven-game road trip to Washington and Chicago.

Hosting the Red Sox at Tiger Stadium on Thursday, April 27, the Bengals totaled only five safeties off two Boston hurlers in a 5–2 defeat. Boston right-hander Ike DeLock lost his control in the third inning, surrendering a single to Jake Wood and four straight walks, and the last two passes to Rocky Colavito and Norm Cash forced in two runs. Manager Pinky Higgins called right-hander Dave Hillman out of the pen, and the former Cub blanked the Tigers on three hits the rest of the way. Jim Bunning, on the other hand, gave up four runs on six hits and two costly errors in seven innings, and southpaw Joe Grzenda, once a prized fastballing prospect from Scranton, Pennsylvania, who overcame an arm injury in 1959 and managed to make the Tigers in 1961, gave up the final run on three singles in the eighth.

Friday's night game was postponed due to the chilly weather, but on Saturday afternoon the Tigers bounced back, led by three long home runs. Colavito victimized right-hander Tom Brewer, leading off the second inning with his fourth home run, a solo clout to left that gave the Bengals a 1–0 lead. Detroit scored four runs in the fourth, topped by Wood's second homer of the season, a drive into the seats in right-center field for a 5–0 lead. After two errors and a walk in the fifth, Dick Brown connected for his third home run, a grand slam that upped the lead to 9–0 and sent Brewer to the showers. The Bosox got to Frank Lary for two runs in the seventh, capped by Vic Wertz's RBI double. Hank "High Henry" Aguirre, or "Mex," the 6'4" southpaw who was one of seven children of Mexican-born Joseph Aguirre and Californian Jenny Alva, took over and blanked Boston, recording his first save and boosting Lary's mark to 4–0. Every starter except

Boros collected one hit, and Boros walked and scored on Brown's four-bagger.

The Tigers finished the home stand by splitting a Sunday doubleheader with Baltimore, winning the opener, 8–2, with Phil Regan getting his first victory and Hank Aguirre his second save, and losing the nightcap, 4–2, as Paul Foytack pitched into the seventh inning, when he surrendered three straight home runs. Boros swung the big bat in the first game with two singles and a double in three at-bats. Towering Walt Dropo gave the Orioles a 1–0 lead with his first homer of the season in the second inning, and Jerry Adair's run-scoring single in the fourth made the lead 2–0. The Bengals moved ahead in the seventh with three runs, thanks to Chico Fernandez's RBI single, a pinch-hit RBI single by Bubba Morton, batting for Regan, and Wood's sacrifice fly. The Tigers put the game away in the eighth with five runs, the last one scoring

Hank Aguirre, the Tigers' tall southpaw from California, came out of the bullpen 45 times for Detroit in 1961. Aguirre posted a 4–4 mark and saved eight games (National Baseball Hall of Fame, Cooperstown, New York).

on a wild pitch to Wood by right-hander Jack Fisher, allowing Mike Roarke, who had replaced Brown, to trot home. In the nightcap, righty Hal "Skinny" Brown won his first game, outdueling Foytack, who defeated himself by throwing three gopher balls in a row in the top of the seventh. Big-hitting Jim Gentile started the assault, connecting for his fourth home run, Gus Triandos belted his second, and Ron Hansen got his first. Foytack, who had injured his arm in 1960, had not yet worked himself into shape. Cash rapped two of Detroit's four hits, including his third home run, a solo four-bagger.

As April ended and the season moved into the warmer month of May, the Tigers were looking good. Bob Scheffing, growing bolder about his team as the wins piled up, observed, "If the pitching stays as good as it was in the first three weeks, we ought to be in the [pennant] race." Scheffing cited the maturity of his pitching rotation, praising Frank Lary, Jim Bunning, Don Mossi, and Paul Foytack. The manager also pointed to the improvement of Chico Fernandez, now hitting .271. He indicated that Fernandez didn't get himself into good shape in the spring, but since the season opened, his performance had picked up sharply. Jake Wood, fielding well, showed good power when he belted an upper deck home run to left in the opening game and a long homer to right-center on April 29.

The Tigers had plenty of highlights. Cash and Kaline were the team's biggest hitters, with Cash averaging .333, hitting three home runs and driving in 14 runs in the first 14 games. Kaline was also batting .333, and he led the team with 19 hits, including six doubles and a triple, but no home runs. The relief pitching shifted when Terry Fox developed a sore arm (a recurring condition for Fox). After posting one win and one save, he hadn't pitched in a week. Hank Aguirre made three appearances, taking the loss when the Tigers fell in extra innings to the Yankees on April 26, but saving one game against the Red Sox and another against the Orioles. Also, Dick Brown's receiving met the high standards the manager wanted, and Brown beat the Red Sox on April 29 with his first major league grand slam.

In addition, the Tigers, as usual, were active in the community. On Saturday, April 29, before the Bengals took the field in the afternoon against the Red Sox, 4,000 high school athletes attended a special clinic at Tiger Stadium. Scheffing and his coaches provided most of the instruction, and Charlie Maxwell won the most cheers by slugging several balls into the right field stands in a hitting exhibition. One fun feature from the Bill DeWitt days remained, as the Dixieland Band strolled through the stands and played between innings of home games.[38]

Baseball in the spring during the first expansion season looked good in New York as well as in Detroit, and longtime fans of the Yankees and the Tigers were looking forward to more excitement from their heroes. Regardless, few writers or spectators had any idea that the 1961 season would develop into an exciting pennant race featuring a display of home run power never before seen in the major leagues.

Charlie Maxwell, Detroit's stellar left-handed hitting slugger since 1956, when he enjoyed a .326 season with 28 home runs and 87 RBI, was very popular in Detroit. On Saturday, April 29, "Ol' Paw Paw" headlined the clinic at Tiger Stadium for 4,000 high school ballplayers (author's collection).

4

The Tigers Lead the League in May

Maris Finds His Timing

A strong hitter with a compact left-handed swing, Roger Maris, whenever he was in a groove, stroked home runs with regularity. On Wednesday, May 17, with the first five weeks of the 1961 season gone and the Yankees in second place, five games behind the surprising Tigers, Maris, the American League's 1960 MVP, finally found that groove, even though New York fell, 8–7, to the visiting Washington Senators. Two days later the Bronx Bombers took a two-day trip to face the Cleveland Indians, the team that originally signed Maris. Against the Tribe, Maris belted two more home runs, both in a losing cause. On Sunday, back at Yankee Stadium to open a three-game set against Baltimore with a doubleheader, Maris went 3-for-4, homering in the opener to lift New York to a 4–2 victory. The Yankees fell in the nightcap, and Maris went hitless in two trips, but he walked once and drove in one run with a sacrifice fly. A week later the Fargo slugger launched another streak, homering four times in four games, cracking two of those four-baggers in the Yankees' 12–3 rout of the Red Sox at Fenway Park on May 30.

In his 1962 book *Roger Maris at Bat*, co-authored by Jim Ogle of the *Newark Star-Ledger*,[1] Maris recounted his first home run streak starting against Washington on May 17. New York was losing, 8–2, when he batted against 6'2" left-hander Pete Burnside, the former Tiger, in the eighth inning. Facing Burnside in the sixth, Maris, hitless in two trips, had bunted for a base hit. Rejecting another bunt in the eighth and looking for a pitch he could pull, got a fastball that he lined into the right field seats, cutting New York's deficit to 8–4. Maris recalled a "great feeling of relief" when he hit homer number four: "It had come off a left-handed pitcher and it was my first of the year at the Stadium." The Bombers lost, 8–7, but they were starting to hit.

The Yankees traveled to Cleveland for two games, and lost both, but Maris found his "long-lost timing" in the defeat on Friday, May 19. In the first inning at cavernous Municipal Stadium, Maris socked home run number five off 6'4" Jim Perry, son of a tobacco sharecropper from Williamston, North Carolina, who won a league-high 18 games for the Tribe in 1960. In the sixth frame Maris started a three-run rally with a single, but Indians rookie southpaw Bob Allen pitched a scoreless ninth to preserve Cleveland's 9–7 victory. In Saturday's 4–3 loss, Maris, facing righty Gary Bell in the third inning, hit homer number six, a solo blast to deep right that gave the Yankees a 1–0 lead. Maris had no other official at-bats, but he was hit by a pitch in the first, walked in the sixth, and lifted a sacrifice fly in the eighth as New York scored twice for a 3–3 tie. The Indians won on John Romano's RBI double in the eighth, and the Yankees couldn't score off ace reliever Frank Funk in the ninth.

Back at Yankee Stadium, New York split a twin bill with Baltimore on Sunday, May 21. Before a noisy crowd of 47,980, the Yankees won the opener, 4–2, as Maris enjoyed a 3-for-4 day, hitting his seventh home run, a solo shot off right-hander Chuck Estrada in the first inning. Lopez and Whitey Ford contributed RBI singles, and Maris singled home the winning run in the seventh. Baltimore's Dick Williams hit a solo homer in the eighth off Ford, who hurled a scoreless ninth to boost his ledger to 5–1. The Bombers lost the nightcap, 3–2, but Maris hit a sacrifice fly in the sixth to drive in Bobby Richardson, who had tripled, for a 1–1 tie. In the seventh, Orioles lefty Steve Barber singled home two runs for a 3–1 lead. But in the ninth, after Barber walked the first two Yankees, Hoyt Wilhelm came out of the bullpen. Clete Boyer beat out a bunt to load the bases, but Wilhelm, whose knuckleball carried him into the Baseball Hall of Fame in 1985, got Yogi Berra to bounce into a double play, allowing a run to score. The Birds' six-foot right-hander closed the game by inducing Richardson's pop fly to second base. Rollie Sheldon, who gave up Baltimore's three runs, lost, dropping his mark to 0–2.

Clete Boyer, the Yankees' rifled-armed, slick-fielding third baseman, averaged .224 in 1961, but he connected for 11 home runs and contributed 55 RBI (author's collection).

The Yankees thumped the Orioles

on Monday, 8–2, with Clete Boyer socking a timely three-run home run, his second, to clinch matters. Veteran Art Ditmar (2–2) lasted only 3⅓ innings, and Jim Coates, the hard-throwing Virginian who won 13 games in 1960 and another 11 games in 1961, held the O's until the seventh inning. In the Yankees' seventh, John Blanchard, the left-handed batting catcher who pinch-hit in the first inning when Maris' eyes blurred after taking eye drops, and Mantle drew walks. Berra hit an RBI single, and Elston Howard, at first base with Berra catching, hit into a fielder's choice at second, scoring Mantle. Bobby Richardson walked, Coates fanned, and Tony Kubek singled for a 5–1 lead. After the O's scored once in the eighth, Ralph Houk yanked Coates for Luis Arroyo. The screwball ace, who also threw a passable fastball and a dinky curve, retired the side on a double play and a fly ball. Boyer homered in the eighth, and Arroyo added a scoreless ninth.

Despite questions about his eyes (Houk "blew his top," telling writers that he wished Maris had taken the eye exam before hitting four straight homers),[2] Maris was feeling good. In fact, co-owner Dan Topping suggested he get the eye exam due to his slow start. Regardless, Maris later revealed the kind of self-doubts that most players experience when they're slumping. "My doubts about hitting twenty-five homers for the year began to disappear," he concluded. "During the long stretch without homers I despaired of getting that many, but now I felt I was in the groove and moving."[3] At that point Maris was batting .248 with seven home runs, including four in four games. He had contributed 19 RBI, driving in 15 runs so far in May. Mantle, off to a faster start, was hitting .302, but after slugging seven homers in April, hit only three more before May 29. Also, he had knocked in just two runs since May 4.

Partly as a result, the American League standings after the games of Monday, May 22, showed New York in third place with an 18–15 record, 5.5 games behind league-leading Detroit (25–11) and two behind Cleveland (21–14). Writing in *The Sporting News*, Joe King of the *World-Telegram & Sun* concluded, "these Yankees under Ralph Houk are the same old inconsistent Yankees they were under Casey Stengel."[4] King and Arthur Daley of the *New York Times* were two influential writers who criticized Houk as the Yankees' losses mounted.[5] Regardless, Maris was hitting the ball hard, Mantle was already enjoying a big season, Ford was off to a 5–1 start, and Arroyo was the best Yankees stopper out of the pen since Joe Page posted league highs with 60 appearances, 48 games finished, and 27 games saved in 1949.

Maris' slow start hindered the Yankees in April and the first half of May, and Detroit's Rocky Colavito hurt the Bombers when he enjoyed his first two-homer game of the year to sink New York at the Stadium in the

Bronx, 8–3, on Saturday, May 13. One day earlier, Colavito, reacting to a few fans who were heckling his father, Rocco, leaped into the box seats behind third base and bulled his way toward the senior Colavito, until several fans and ushers managed to restrain his 6'3" and 190 pounds of "outraged energy" before any blows were struck.[6]

Colavito had a short fuse at the ballpark. According to one Tiger, Colavito once confronted Joe Falls, the acerbic *Free Press* scribe, in the clubhouse after a game at Tiger Stadium. When Falls walked into the room full of ballplayers, with soggy towels, spiked shoes, and other equipment lying on the floor and a couple of other writers walking around looking for interviews, the powerful Colavito grabbed Falls, lifted him up, pinned him against the wall, and declared, *"Don't you ever write a story about me again!"* Similar to the day at Yankee Stadium, Colavito, usually a genial, friendly fellow, was ready to defend a perceived threat to his honor.

Roger Maris (left) shares a laugh with right-hander Jim Coates after another Yankees victory. Coates gave the Yankees an important boost in 1961, fashioning an 11–5 record, making 32 appearances in relief, and saving five games (National Baseball Hall of Fame, Cooperstown, New York).

Tigers' Stars Shine

Detroit played consistently good baseball in the warmer weather, and every man used by Bob Scheffing, seemingly blessed with a magic touch, helped the team. On Tuesday, May 2, the Tigers began the month at expansion Washington by winning two out of three games, all played in the evening, when fans in the DC metropolitan area (who resented the old Senators, now the Twins, for leaving) were more likely to come out to Griffith Stadium, the venerable ballpark that featured a 31-foot fence in right field. Jim Bunning, boosted by a two-run homer by Norm Cash, won the opener, 6–3, hurling a complete game, scattering 11 hits, and lifting his record to 1–2. But on Wednesday night, Frank Lary dropped his first game in five decisions, 5–4, as the Senators scored all five runs on six hits in six innings. The Tigers outhit the home team with nine safeties, but after scoring three runs in the second on Dick Brown's homer and Billy Bruton's two-run single, they managed only one more tally. Larry Osborne, batting for Lary, hit an RBI double in the seventh, but Joe McClain (7⅔ IP) and Dave Sisler combined for the win.

In the finale on Thursday, crafty Don Mossi won a two-hit shutout, 6–0, with Bruton, Kaline and Boros rapping two hits each and Cash going 3-for-4 and driving home a run. Mossi, using his three-finger grip (instead of the traditional two fingers), mixed his pitches well, displayed sharp control and, as usual, spotted the ball without losing velocity or ball movement. In addition, the California southpaw was a master at changing speeds and location, two requisites for pitchers to be effective. Ahead 1–0, the Tigers took a 3–0 lead in the seventh on Mossi's bases-loaded walk and Wood's sacrifice fly. Cash singled home one run in the eighth, and Bruton clinched matters with a two-run single in the ninth. In the Senators' ninth, Mossi gave up a two-out single to Willie Tasby, the first everyday black player for the Red Sox in 1960, but the lefty closed the game on a fly to right.

Traveling to Comiskey Park to open a four-game set on the evening of Friday, May 5, the Tigers battered White Sox pitching to win all four contests, capped by a doubleheader sweep on Sunday. Paul Foytack, enjoying his first good outing, evened his mark at 1–1 with 7⅔ innings of solid pitching in the first contest. Detroit won, 8–4, as Jim Donohue finished the eighth, and Hank Aguirre, the tall, fun-loving left-hander who saw baseball in terms of living a romantic dream, worked a scoreless ninth for his third save. Wood, Kaline, Colavito, Cash, and Boros each contributed two hits, and Chico Fernandez went 3-for-5 and scored a run. On Saturday the teams staged a slugfest, and the hard-throwing Bunning, who didn't have his usual command, allowed six runs on seven hits in four innings. Aguirre gave up Sherman Lollar's RBI double, tying the game at 8–8 in the eighth. Unfazed, the Tigers won by scoring three times in the ninth, Jake Wood's run-scoring single broke the tie. Aguirre claimed his first victory, after Terry Fox earned the save.

Both teams hit the opponent's pitchers hard in the Sunday twin bill, but the Tigers had the biggest belters and won each tilt by a two-run margin. In the opener, Lary, with his control not sharp, failed in the sixth when slugger Roy Sievers clubbed his sixth homer, and his second of the day off Lary, a grand slam that gave the Chisox a 6–2 lead. Detroit's Joe Grzenda, the 6'2" lefty, retired three hitters to end the inning, and when the Bengals scored five runs in the seventh, Grzenda won his only game of 1961. Wood slugged a two-run triple, and, after walks to Kaline and Colavito, Cash singled in a run, and Colavito scored on Bob Shaw's wild pitch. Wood gave

Detroit its final 8–6 margin with a solo homer in the eighth, his third of the year.

In the nightcap, Phil Regan, off to a surprisingly good start after posting an 0–4 record in 1960, turned in a sterling effort, scattering eight hits to improve to 2–0 as the Tigers won, 5–3. Chicago right-hander Cal McLish, who was 4–14 for Cincinnati in 1960, allowed all five runs on eight hits in five innings. Cash's grounder with the bases loaded in the first inning opened the scoring. The White Sox replied with two runs in the second, but the Tigers took a 4–2 lead in the third, aided by Fernandez's two-run single. Colavito scored the last run in the fifth with a homer to left. Minnie Minoso, the slick-fielding, Cuban-born outfielder, led off Chicago's eighth with his second homer of the year, cutting the lead to 5–3, but Regan prevailed.

Following Detroit's sweep, the Tigers led the AL with a 16–5 record, the Yankees were second at 13–7, two and a half games back, and the Twins, Orioles, and Indians were all tied for third with 11–10 ledgers, five games behind.

Scheffing's good news was that many of the Tigers were playing at a high level. Billy Bruton, who went 2-for-5 in the nightcap, was starting to hit, averaging .237 after the day's action (up from .190 when May began). Chico Fernandez, whom Jake Wood called "a big league shortstop,"[7] rapped one single in the nightcap, but his 1-for-7 day actually lowered his average to .297. The Cuban glove whiz, not known for hitting, had contributed ten RBI to date. Norm Cash, Al Kaline, and Rocky Colavito, as they would all season long, were swinging the biggest bats. Kaline, who collected two singles and a double, was hitting a nifty .326 with seven two-baggers, although he had not yet connected for a home run. Colavito, who picked up three hits on Sunday, was averaging just .229, but he had five home runs and 14 RBI. Cash was the league's biggest surprise, hitting .342. Cash had four homers, one behind Colavito, but was driving in runs at a furious pace, leading the Tigers with 23 RBI in 21 games. Scheffing was happy, and Detroit's fans anxiously awaited their team's return to Tiger Stadium.

Roger Maris

Roger Eugene Maris, who made an indelible mark on the Yankees and baseball in New York, never really left his roots in the small-town Midwest. He was born on September 10, 1934, the second son of Rudy and Connie Maras. Roger changed his name legally to Maris in 1954, as did his father, mother, and brother, largely because of his mother's longstanding feud with members of the Maras family and her resentment of their roots in Hibbing, Minnesota.[8]

Rudy and Connie Maras, married in mid–1932, had their first son, Rudy, Junior, on June 18, 1933. Rudy, Senior, the son of immigrants, had been employed at a variety of jobs, and by the time Roger was born in 1934, he was working as a repairman for the Great Northern Railroad. The second Maras son, who always admired his older sibling, remained close to Rudy all their lives, and later, when Roger operated a Busch beer distributorship in the Tampa Bay area, Rudy was his partner. Their parents, however, often bickered, partly because Connie, by all accounts a dark-haired, hot-tempered beauty, saw other men while her husband was away. By 1941, when work was picking up on the Great Northern, Rudy's foreman, moving to Grand Forks, North Dakota, offered him a promotion. Despite his wife's objections, Rudy made the move. After World War II ended, Rudy got a transfer to Fargo, a town of 30,000 that Roger forever called his home. There the Maras brothers excelled at football, basketball, track, and baseball.

Like most athletically inclined boys during those times, the Maras siblings grew up loving sports. Ironically, Rudy, or "Buddy" to his friends, loved baseball, but at first Roger didn't. As teenagers they played American Legion ball, but Rudy almost literally twisted Roger's arm to get him to the ball field, until their high school years, when Roger liked baseball. Both were exceptional athletes. In communities like Fargo during the postwar decades, baseball was the favorite pastime for boys, but many also played the other popular team sports, football and basketball. Indeed, most young men who made it to the major leagues once had been all-around athletes in high school. Rudy, one year older, stronger, and bigger, was considered the better athlete, and Roger always believed it. Later they transferred to Bishop Shanley, the Catholic high school, because of the school's coach, Sid Cichy. Unlike high school baseball, often limited by chilly weather in the Midwest, football was almost a religion, the biggest sport at any school that fielded a gridiron 11. Roger earned All-State recognition in football as a junior, but Rudy, a senior, wasn't recognized, an omission that rankled Roger.

In American Legion ball in 1949, Roger and Rudy both made it with the Gilbert C. Grafton Post, but in 1950, both played outfield on the post's first nine, coached by Chuck Bentsen. Roger, who batted .367 in 1950, won the team's MVP award, edging out Rudy. Roger, who loved and admired his talented older brother, never bragged about winning the award. A Cleveland scout, Frank Fahey, saw Roger play that August in the American Legion tournament at Dickinson, North Dakota. The 15-year-old star stood 5'8" and weighed 155 pounds, and if he grew, Fahey believed he would make a good major league prospect, because he "could run and throw and had lots of power."[9] In 1951 Roger enjoyed a better baseball season, although a late-summer slump (foreshadowing his pro career) dropped his average to .350, and he was edged out for MVP honors by outfielder-pitcher Don Gronland. Roger, who played hard, believed people should be fairly compensated for their efforts, and he figured it was unfair for him to be bypassed for the team's highest honor.

As a senior at Bishop Shanley in the fall of 1951, with Rudy gone to Santa Clara College in California on a baseball scholarship, Roger, the fleet, rugged, and elusive halfback, scored five touchdowns in one game, four on kick returns and one on a 32-yard run from scrimmage. Fargo's greatest all-around athlete, he enjoyed good seasons on the gridiron, the hardcourt, and the track, but the school missed Rudy's strong athletic contributions. After graduating from Shanley High in June 1952, Roger played city league baseball and accepted a football scholarship from the University of Oklahoma. For more than a year the quiet, modest young man had dated pretty Pat Carvell, also a Catholic, another Shanley student, and his future wife. As a senior, Roger dated Pat exclusively, much to his mother's dismay. Also, his brother Rudy contracted a mild case of polio at college, and even though he later recovered, his dream of playing major league baseball was shattered.

Late in the summer of 1952, Roger traveled to Oklahoma, saw the campus, and took an entrance exam, but he decided college life wasn't for him. Returning home, he contacted Hank Greenberg, general manager of the Indians. Greenberg sent scout Cy Slapnicka to Fargo to offer a contract with a bonus of $5,000 and the promise of $10,000 more, if he reached the majors. The 18-year-old signed.

Maris (to use the name most readers know) climbed through the Indians' farm system steadily, if not in spectacular fashion, hitting well at every stop and, later, with power. In 1953 he trained at Indianville, the Tribe's minor league camp at Daytona Beach that had been a navy air base during World War II. The large majority of players who made the minors in those days weren't major league prospects, but rather they filled minor league roster spots to keep the majors' feeder leagues going. Cleveland's system had two outstanding prospects, fireballing southpaw Herb Score and slugging outfielder Rocky Colavito. Slated for Class D ball, Maris demanded that he be sent to Fargo-Moorhead in the Class C Northern League, and the Tribe's front office acquiesced. There he roomed with returning slugger Frank Gravino, who enjoyed his greatest season, hitting .353 with 52 home runs and 174 RBI. Maris, a line-drive hitter, averaged .325 and belted 18 doubles, 13 triples, and nine homers, one of which landed on a porch across the street from the center field fence. Following the season, Gravino was picked the league's MVP, and Maris was named Rookie of the Year. His conflicted parents were proud indeed of Roger, but their reticent son, although now a star, left the bragging to them.

After spending the winter in Fargo working for a beverage distributor, living in the basement of a friend who worked for the business, and dating Pat, Maris returned to spring camp at Indianville, determined to play Class B ball. Rather than return to Fargo-Moorhead, as asked, Roger, rocking the Indians' boat, threatened to quit baseball. Hank Greenberg, renowned as a Tigers slugger before he became the Indians' GM, realized Maris was just obstinate enough to leave the game. Greenberg authorized Maris' assignment to Keokuk, Iowa, of the Class B Three-I League. Jo Jo White, the center fielder for Detroit's World Series champions of 1935, managed Keokuk. White, impressed by Maris' talent, desire, and all-out style of play, liked him. Not only a good hitter, Maris would steal bases, break up double plays, and make all of the moves a less hard-nosed player might be reluctant to try. White also taught his protégé to pull the ball. Maris made the league's All-Star team, batted .315 with 32 home runs and 111 RBI, helped Keokuk finish in second place, and legally changed his name to Maris.

Cleveland had a very talented team at all positions in 1954, winning the American League pennant with an all-time high American League record of 111–43 and an eight-game margin over the Yankees, although the New York Giants swept the World Series from the Tribe in four games. By that time, Maris had the skills, the mindset, and the work ethic that it took to be a major leaguer. However, he split the 1955 season between Tulsa of the Double-A Texas League and Reading of the Class A Eastern League, after he had a conflict over playing time with Tulsa's manager, "Little Dutch" Meyer. Maris demanded to play regularly. He walked off the diamond after a session when Meyer made him field flies and keep throwing the ball to third base, and Greenberg again intervened, switching the outfielder to Reading. Maris liked Jo Jo White, now Reading's manager. He also became friends with Carroll Hardy, the NFL San Francisco 49ers' halfback, a right-handed batter who enjoyed an eight-year career as a major league outfielder. Recalled Hardy, "Roger had a football mentality too—we both played hard."[10]

According to his teammates, Maris was a "regular guy." He played only 25 games at Tulsa, but playing for White in the Eastern League, he regained his slugging form, hitting .289 with 19 homers and 78 RBI in Memorial Stadium, a pitcher's ballpark, and helping Reading finish in first place. Perhaps equally important, biographers Tom Clavin and Danny Peary pointed out that good reports about Maris' improved play in the East reached George Weiss, the Yankees' GM. Before Maris reached the majors, the Yankees were watching his career.

Training with the Indians at the major league camp in Tucson in 1956, Maris figured he deserved a shot with Cleveland, but Hank Greenberg had other ideas. In addition to having two seasoned outfielders acquired by trade, Jim Busby and Gene Woodling, the Indians had hard-hitting rookie Rocky Colavito, who was ready for the majors after a .268 mark with 30 homers and 104 RBI at Triple-A Indianapolis in 1955. Maris, who hated not playing regularly, was again ready to leave for home when he was sent to Indianapolis. Under manager Kerby Farrell, Maris started slowly, gradually hit his groove, and helped Indianapolis challenge the Yankees' Denver affiliate for the American Association title. Maris displayed his strong, short swing, good speed, aggressiveness on the bases, and skill in the outfield, averaging .293 with 17 homers and 75 RBI. The bat of Fargo's favorite son

helped Indianapolis win the Junior World Series over Rochester, champions of the International League. Back home with his $300 winners' check, Maris married Pat Carvell on October 13, 1956. Content with marriage and family life, Roger and Pat eventually had six children. A few days later, when a player was injured in the Dominican Republic, Rudy Regalado, a friend, called Roger, who brought Pat to the DR for a honeymoon and winter of baseball—until he injured his heel and they went home.[11]

Maris was talented, determined, and quietly efficient. Not a charming person, he was down-to-earth, friendly, and likeable. Virtually every player who pulled on a uniform as his team-

Roger Maris, renowned as a slugger, showed his defensive prowess in this leaping grab of a ball just in front of the low right-field wall in Yankee Stadium (National Baseball Hall of Fame, Cooperstown, New York).

mate, regardless of the level or the sport, liked the no-nonsense, straight-forward Maris. On April 16, 1957, earning the $10,000 in his original contract for reaching the majors, Maris made his debut, lining three singles in five trips and scoring once, but the Indians lost, 3–2. Two days later at Briggs Stadium in Detroit, showing the pop in his bat, he walked once and hammered an 11th-inning grand slam to lift the Indians over the Tigers, 8–3. Maris, appearing in 116 games in 1957, played mainly center field, thanks to his speed, arm, and good glove. He helped the Tribe with 14 homers and 51 RBI, good figures for a rookie, but he was slowed by broken ribs suffered in Kansas City on May 10 when he tried to break up a double play at second base. Hitting .315 at the time, Maris missed two weeks, but the nagging injury led to a final average of .235. New manager Kerby Farrell must have felt snake-bitten: three days earlier, fastballing southpaw Herb Score had been hit in the eye with a drive off the bat of New York's Gil McDougald, and following surgery, Score was out for 1957. Score pitched five more seasons, but was never effective again.

The Indians' lineup featured the popular Rocky Colavito in right field. Colavito, the right-handed batter who hit 21 homers as a Cleveland rookie in 1956, averaged .252 and belted 25 more home runs while contributing 84 RBI in 1957. Left-handed batting Gene Woodling, the former Yankees star, played left field and hit a team-high .321 with 19 home runs and 78 RBI. The Indians' top longball star was veteran Vic Wertz, who always kept his cap on because he was self-conscious about his baldness. The first baseman had debuted with the Tigers in 1947, set a Detroit record for left-handed hitters with 27 homers in 1950, came to Cleveland in a trade with the Baltimore Orioles on June 1, 1954, and contributed 14 circuit clouts and 48 RBI to help Cleveland win the pennant. In 1957 Wertz led the Tribe in homers with 28 and RBI with 105. Featuring aging mound stars like Bob Lemon, Early Wynn, and Mike Garcia, the Indians fell to sixth place, but Roger Maris, then a youthful 22, had a bright baseball future.

Yankees Warm Up

While Maris was working on his timing in 1961, Ralph Houk was searching for the best Yankees lineup. In April and May, New York, despite the best lineup and best bench in the American League, trailed the Tigers. Tony Kubek later acknowledged the pressure from criticism by writers about Houk's skill versus Casey Stengel's, Maris' eye exam, and Mantle finishing May in a week-long slump. "But then there was Whitey [Ford]," Kubek recalled, "telling us everything was going to be all right, and making life interesting to the bullpen."

The issue about Ford was whether the pain he had suffered in his left arm in 1960 meant his career was going downhill. Some doctors thought Ford had neuritis, but in fact, said Kubek, Ford had a pulled tendon in his shoulder compounded by a case of the gout. But in 1961, Houk, talking about Ford with pitching coach Johnny Sain, decided his best left-hander needed more work on a regular basis. In May, Houk began pitching the 5'9" 160-pound Ford every fourth day, whereas Stengel had used his ace every fifth day, partly to save him for occasional big games. When they had run into each other during the previous winter at a basketball game in Madison Square Garden, Houk had asked Ford about pitching every fourth day. Ford agreed. In St. Petersburg, Sain had Ford strengthen his arm by throwing five minutes on the sideline and five minutes of batting practice. They stepped the regimen up to ten minutes on the side and ten minutes to batters, and other pitchers followed Ford's example. Ford, indeed, was a hero and role model to the pitchers.

In addition, Sain taught Ford a new pitch—a controlled, faster curve, or slider. Sain liked Ford's good fastball, his overhand curve, and his usual sharp control. Ford, however, was 32, and his big curve was breaking slower. "It seemed like it took me about five minutes to learn that slider," Ford remarked, "and I'm convinced that it kept me in baseball another five years."

Writing about May 21, when the Yankees split a Sunday doubleheader with the Orioles at the "House that Ruth Built," Kubek noted that New York had totaled 34 home runs, with Maris hitting just five. Art Ditmar and Bob Turley hadn't won in their last seven starts combined, and reserve catcher John Blanchard, who ended up hitting 21 home runs, was 0-for-9 as a pinch-hitter. In the next 17 games New York hit 32 home runs, including seven against the Red Sox at Fenway on Memorial Day, a game that featured two circuit clouts each by Maris, Mantle, and Bill Skowron in a 12–3 romp over Boston.

"Then came the month of June," Kubek wrote, and the pennant race heated up.[12]

After defeating the Orioles two out of three at Yankee Stadium and a day off on Tuesday, May 23, the Yankees hosted the Red Sox twice and won both games. Against Boston on Wednesday, Ralph Terry pitched a three-hitter to win his second game, 3–2, and Maris provided the first two runs with a home run off 6'8" Gene Conley, the versatile right-hander and NBA star. On Thursday Ford boosted his record to 6–1 by pitching seven-plus innings, yielding a three-run homer in the seventh to Jackie Jensen, the former California football great. Arroyo took over in the eighth, allowed one more run on a groundout and held the 6–4 lead, based on early two-run homers by Blanchard, his third, and Kubek, his third.

After two days off due to rain, the Bombers split a Sunday twin bill with the White Sox, losing the opener, 14–9, as Turley failed again (five runs, four earned), but five more Yankees hurlers, including Arroyo, who took the loss, also couldn't hold Chicago. Reliever Turk Lown, the former Cubs right-hander who had served as an Army infantryman during World War II, fighting at the Battle of the Bulge, evened his mark at 2–2, and Billy Pierce, the star southpaw from Detroit whom the Tigers swapped to the White Sox in 1948 in perhaps the Bengals' worst-ever trade, saved the win with two scoreless frames. Bob Cerv, reacquired in a 1960 trade with Kansas City, Yogi Berra, and Bill Skowron homered in a losing cause. Jim Coates, in relief of Art Ditmar won the nightcap, 5–3, helped by Maris' ninth homer, a bases-empty shot. The games of May 28 left New York, with a 21–16 mark, 4.5 games behind first-place Detroit (28–14) and a game behind Cleveland (24–17).

On the road again, the Yankees finished May and opened June by splitting four games with Boston at Fenway Park. On Monday, May 29, Boston's Ike DeLock, the Highland Park, Michigan, three-sport star who had served with the Marines from 1946–1948, outdueled Whitey Ford, who saw his ledger fall to 6–2. New York managed five hits and lost, 2–1, with the only damage coming on Mantle's bases-empty homer, his 11th, in the seventh. Jackie Jensen, the rugged ex–Yankee who had signed with the PCL's Oakland Oaks for a $75,000 bonus in 1949, gave Boston an early 1–0 lead with his fourth home run, and Vic Wertz's RBI single in the seventh won it.

On Memorial Day, Tuesday, May 30, the Yankees won a 12–3 slugfest,

featuring two homers each by Mantle, his 12th and 13th, two by Maris, his tenth and 11th, and two by Skowron, his seventh and eighth, plus one by Berra, his sixth. Ralph Terry, who went 1–2 as a rookie for New York in 1956 before being dealt with volatile Billy Martin to Kansas City in mid–1957, and returned along with versatile Hector Lopez in a trade on May

Ralph Terry, the Yankees' right-hander from Big Cabin, Oklahoma, came through with an impressive 16–3 record in 1961. Terry's 16 victories were second only to Whitey Ford's 25 wins for the Yankees (National Baseball Hall of Fame, Cooperstown, New York).

26, 1959, allowed three runs on five hits in two-plus innings. Terry left with his team leading, 4–2, and Bill Stafford pitched out of the jam, hurled four hitless innings, and recorded his first victory. Jim Coates earned his second save with three scoreless innings. Home runs highlighted the contest, featuring Mantle's three-run clout off Gene Conley in the first. In the eighth, Maris and Mantle sealed the victory with back-to-back blasts, Maris' three-run homer to deep right and Mantle's belt to deep right-center, off right-hander Mike Fornieles.

The rival clubs also split the last two contests. On Wednesday the Bombers won a close one, 7–6, as Rollie Sheldon won his first game, improving his mark to 1–2. Arroyo held the Red Sox for nearly two innings, and Danny McDevitt, the 5'10" lefty known for hard fastballs and control problems before being sold by the Dodgers after the 1960 season, earned his first Yankees' save by retiring the last two outs in the ninth. The visitors built a 7–1 lead, featuring Maris' 12th home run, a solo blast in the third inning. New York scored five runs in the fourth, highlighted by Mantle's 14th homer, a two-run shot.

On June 1, New York lost, 7–5, with Bill Monbouquette winning his fourth game, thanks to a save by rookie right-hander Tracy Stallard, who would later be best known as the pitcher who gave up Maris' 61st home run. Turley, the erratic 6'2" fastballer who pitched with virtually no wind-up, coughed up four runs in two-plus innings, and his record fell to 3–3. Skowron homered twice, numbers nine and ten, but the Yankees fell short.

Rocky Colavito

The hard-hitting outfielder that Cleveland fans adored in 1957 was Rocco Domenico Colavito. Tall, strong, and slow-footed at 6'3" and nearly 190 pounds, the Italian-American had the dark good looks of a rock star. Before long he was idolized by thousands of Cleveland fans, especially teenage girls. Born on August 10, 1933, in the Bronx, Rocco was raised in a close-knit family with two older brothers and two sisters. The Colavitos lived in a poor section surrounded by Italian, Irish, and Jewish neighbors. Rocco, Senior, drove a truck for a local iron and steel corporation for more than 30 years, and Angelina, his mother, was a housewife who died when Rocco was nine. Domenic, then 16, became responsible for raising his youngest brother. Crotona Park was across from the tenement where the Colavitos lived, and the park surrounded the ball field where Hank Greenberg played as a kid. Rocky, as he was later known, played baseball with his brothers on their sandlot team. The youngest Colavito had a strong arm, and his throwing exploits were well known. When he was 16, Rocky heaved a baseball over the roof of the Claremont Park elevated station, a city block away from where he stood. With Yankee Stadium a few blocks away, the aspiring ballplayer, who threw and batted right-handed, idolized Joe DiMaggio, and he copied the Yankee Clipper's mannerisms, his habits, and his stance. Indeed, like thousands of other boys, Colavito dreamed of wearing Yankees pinstripes and taking the field at the nearby stadium where the legendary Babe Ruth hit so many home runs.

During the summer of 1949 Colavito played for the Bronx Mohawks, and the ox-strong teenager was first spotted by major league scouts, including Mike McNally, general manager of Cleveland's affiliate in the Eastern League, Wilkes-Barre. In a tryout at Yankee Stadium, McNally saw enough of Colavito's attitude, arm, and skills to sign him, but major league rules prevented signing anyone until his high school class graduated. Rocky, who quit school after the tenth grade to work and help his family, appealed the ruling. Commissioner Happy Chandler ruled that Colavito could be signed after January 1, 1951. Rocky attended a tryout hosted by the Yankees at their triple-decked stadium in September. Afterward, the front office, seeing him as a strong-armed pitcher, offered a contract worth $3,000. However, Colavito was loyal to McNally, who had approached him several weeks earlier, and agreed to a deal with Cleveland after Christmas. Advised by Domenic, Rocky signed a contingent contract, including a "down payment" of $1,250, that totaled $3,000, not counting the salary of $1,500. The new prospect's career began in 1951 when the Indians assigned him to Daytona Beach in the Class D Florida State League.

Unlike Maris, who refused to play Class D ball, Colavito climbed through the Indians' farm system smoothly, shining at every stop. However, after arriving at Indianville, the Bronx native discovered that he was listed as a pitcher. Determined to play every day, he confronted McNally, who wanted him trained as a pitcher due to his good arm and slow running speed. Greenberg, himself big and slow, had fought the same battle as a young player. Greenberg later starred as a slugging outfielder and first baseman, and he decided in Colavito's favor. Following training camp, Colavito moved into a local rooming house, donned his uniform with number 5 (DiMaggio's and Greenberg's number), and hit the Florida State League. Playing 140 games, tops in the circuit, Colavito showed his durability, his work ethic, his positive attitude, and his bat. Averaging .275, he hit 23 home runs, racked up 111 RBI, and got a promotion to Class B. The Bronx native proved to be a down-to-earth fellow who was liked and respected by teammates and friends.

In 1952 Colavito, the dark-haired New Yorker with polite manners and a bright smile, split the season between two Class B clubs, Cedar Rapids of the Three-I League and Spartanburg of the Tri-State League. After starting in Cedar Rapids, Colavito had to return to New York to face his draft board due to call-ups during the Korean War. Instead, he was designated 4-F by the Army due to his flat feet, a situation not unlike Mickey Mantle being designated 4-F due to osteomyelitis in his leg. Colavito, however, never took the flack and abuse over "draft-dodging" that often rained down on Mantle. He rode the train back to Cedar Rapids and hit two home runs in his first game, but collected only 16 hits in his first 32 games. Hospitalized with a virus, he was finally cured, but his weight fell from 185 to 168 pounds. The Indians sent him to warmer South Carolina, partly to get a fresh start. Thriving at Spartanburg, Colavito averaged .252 with 11 homers and 55 RBI. In the league's new playoff system, he helped his team beat Gastonia in five games to win the semifinals, blasting a pair of home runs in the fifth game.

The following season the Indians sent Colavito to Class A Reading in the Eastern League, and the 20-year-old gained two important life experiences. After the first month, he was hitting just above .200 with no home runs. Kerby Farrell asked him to drop the DiMaggio style, move his feet closer together, and try a crouch, and it worked. Colavito blossomed, leading the league in home runs with 28 and RBI with 121, and he averaged .271. Reading finished in first place but didn't win the championship, although Colavito clubbed six home runs in 12 post-season games. Colavito, who loved his family, also met his future wife, Carmen Perrotti, 17, who was working in a sandwich shop, the Piccadilly, not far from Reading's ballpark. A pretty brunette, Carmen and her family lived in nearby Temple. Before long Rocky was in love, and throughout the winter and the 1954 season, he would take a pile of quarters into a phone booth and call his sweetheart from the hotel of the town where his team was playing ball.

Colavito took another big stride on his road to major league stardom in 1954 with a strong season at Indianapolis, Cleveland's top farm club. Whether or not he was motivated by love, he enjoyed his best season yet, playing 149 games, again hitting .271, leading the league with 38 home runs, and driving home 116 runs. In a precursor of the attitudes developed by folks in Cleveland, the fans in Indianapolis voted him the team's most popular player, and, as it developed, he won the honor again in 1955. Following the season, overcoming objections from his father and her parents that they were too young (he was 21, she was 19), he married Carmen in a big wedding in Reading on October 30, 1954. On their way to honeymoon in Miami, the Colavitos stopped in Lake Worth, Florida, to visit Rocky's roommate and friend, Herb Score, voted the American Association's MVP after winning 22 games.

Colavito figured to make the Indians in 1955. Exceptionally strong (his handshake was enough to crack knuckles), he dressed impeccably in conservative attire and kept himself well groomed, as a successful businessman might. He realized that young people looked up to ballplayers as role models, so he conversed in grammatically correct, even elegant terms, but he behaved like a regular guy, not like a self-indulgent celebrity.

Before traveling to Tucson, Colavito spent the winter pounding his fist into his glove, swinging his bat, and squeezing a rubber ball to strengthen his big hands, all before breakfast. He performed well in Tucson. When camp ended, Score made the big league roster, and it looked like Colavito would too. But Hank Greenberg, with several outfielders returning from the pennant-winning Indians, sent the proud prospect back to Indianapolis. While the fireballing Score cruised through the American League with a 16–10 mark and a 2.85 ERA, Colavito kept the faith and produced another impressive season, batting .268 with 30 home runs and 104 RBI. Called up in September, he batted nine times in five games, connecting for two singles and a pair of doubles. Instantly liked, even loved, by the fans, he knew he was ready for the majors.

At spring training in 1956, manager Al Lopez believed Colavito needed more seasoning. He stuck with the Indians until June 14, one day before the trade deadline. Prodded by Lopez, Greenberg convinced Colavito to go to San Diego of the Pacific Coast League. Colavito, upset, agreed to go on condition that his PCL stint last only a month. He proved himself again, averaging .368 with 12 home runs and 32 RBI in 35 games. After miscommunications lasting a couple of weeks, Cleveland recalled the young slugger on July 23. He lived at the Auditorium Hotel near the ballpark and played right field. On August 1, Carmen gave birth to their son, Rocco III.

During the Tribe's remaining games, Colavito, excited to be a father as well as a big leaguer, became a big hero. On Tuesday, July 24, he collected three hits in his first game back as Cleveland dumped visiting Washington, 11–0, and his bases-loaded triple in the bottom of the eighth upped the lead to 9–0. Living up to his longball promise, he belted 16 homers to add to the five he hit before being sent to San Diego. The Rocky Colavito Fan Club (fan clubs for players were common in the 1950s and 1960s), started by teenager Barbara O'Connor, who at first hoped to be the Tribe's batgirl, cemented the new star's fame. By the end of the season, Colavito, famous for his movie star good looks and smile, was the most popular player in Cleveland.[13]

Colavito, Maris, and 1961

Ironically, two of the American League's top six sluggers in the 1961 season were scouted and signed by the Indians. Rocky Colavito and Roger

Maris both worked their way up through the Tribe's farm system, and both played together for the Indians in 1957 and for part of 1958, until Maris, deemed a problem by general manager Frank "Trader" Lane, was swapped to Kansas City on June 15. They were markedly different individuals, but both would rank high in baseball lore and in career home runs, Colavito with 374 in 14 seasons and Maris with 275 in 12 seasons. Maris enjoyed four of his top five seasons after joining the Yankees in 1960, until he was slowed by injuries in 1965. Colavito hit 25 home runs in 1957, belted 41 in 1958, and banged a league-high 42 four-baggers in 1959. Traded to the Tigers on April 17, 1960, despite being shocked by the trade and uprooted from his home and friends in Cleveland, he launched 35 home runs for Detroit. Pulling the ball less, he peaked with 45 homers in 1961, the year Maris excelled with his 61 homers. Colavito followed his remarkable 1961 season with 37 homers in 1962, the year Maris followed his sensational 1961 season with 33 circuit clouts.

Both sluggers, Colavito, by now a sharp dresser, and Maris, who dressed like a country boy from Fargo, made it tough on AL pitchers for years, both knew the pressure of being a threat to go deep, both originally disliked being traded away from Cleveland, and both found a home with another team following a final trade, Colavito to the Indians in 1966 and Maris to the St. Louis Cardinals in 1967. Maris withstood a huge amount of media scrutiny while he chased Ruth's home run mark in 1961, an extremely harassing circumstance that Colavito never had to face.

In 1957 Colavito played right field and Maris center for Cleveland, but Colavito reaped the accolades of fans and sportswriters. Maris, quiet and reserved, played in Colavito's shadow. Colavito, enjoying his second strong season, belted 25 home runs and contributed 84 RBI. Maris, a hard-hitting rookie who had the defensive skill and good speed to play center field, a position the slower Colavito couldn't handle, tailed off in the second half of the season, finishing with 14 home runs and 51 RBI. In 1958, when the Indians traded to regain aging hero Larry Doby, the Tribe's longtime star center fielder, and Minnie Minoso, once the White Sox's fleet center fielder, Colavito, 24, was moved to right. Maris, one of the Tribe's youngest players at 23, became the fourth outfielder. Every other position player except Colavito and catcher Russ Nixon, 23, was at least 30. Minoso was 32, Doby was 34, and Mickey Vernon was 40.

At the trading deadline, June 15, Maris was swapped to Kansas City along with Dick Tomanek, a left-handed pitcher, and Preston Ward, a left-handed batting first baseman and outfielder, in return for Vic Power, the flashy-fielding Puerto Rican first baseman who could also play third base, and versatile Woodie Held, who could play shortstop, second base, or the outfield. The Indians gave up Maris' potential left-handed power, but considering Cleveland's sixth-place finish and declining attendance in 1957, Maris seemed expendable. Also, Colavito came into his own in 1958, hitting .303 and leading the Indians with 41 home runs and 113 RBI. His future seemed assured, but Maris was dealt to a team that needed a potent bat. Maris, who hit just .225 with nine home runs and 27 RBI in 51 games for Cleveland in early 1958, improved 22 points while hitting 19 homers and driving home 53 runs for the Athletics. Aware of the possibility he could be traded to the Yankees, the Fargo star liked Kansas City, a big city with the feel of a small town. Roger and Pat bought a house for their growing family in the suburb of Raytown. So well did the Marises like their home and the Midwestern environment that Roger kept the house during his seven seasons in New York.

In 1959 Maris enjoyed a solid year with Kansas City and made the All-Star team, despite suffering the removal of his appendix in the first half of the season. Playing for a seventh-place team that fashioned a 66–88 record, he batted .273 with 16 homers and 72 RBI. It was clear to baseball observers that Maris, despite his supposed problems with the Indians, had plenty of talent, skill, and power. The upshot was his trade to the Yankees after the 1959 season. Colavito, helping Cleveland to a second-place finish with his potent bat, was stunned when Frank Lane swapped the home run leader to Detroit on April 17, 1960, for the 1959 batting champion, Harvey Kuenn, who hit .353. Calling Colavito a "hamburger" that he gave up to get a "steak," Lane couldn't see the fans' emotional attachment to Colavito.

Still, Maris and Colavito, handling the adjustments needed to a new team and a new city, both enjoyed good years in 1960. Maris helped the Yankees win the pennant with his 39-homer, 112-RBI season, while Colavito whetted the appetite of Tigers fans with his 35-homer, 87-RBI year.

The Yankees had a proven left-handed, pull-hitting slugger in Maris to go with the switch-hitting Mantle, and the Tigers had a proven right-handed slugger in Colavito to go with Al Kaline, even before Norm Cash blossomed as a longball threat. In many ways, thanks to trades by Cleveland's Frank Lane, the stage was set for the Tigers and Yankees to battle for the 1961 pennant.

Tigers Win on the Road

While the Bronx Bombers were flying high by early June, the Tigers continued playing well in May and June, getting good hitting, if not as many home runs, and good pitching, if not as many clutch performances out of the bullpen. Still, every game highlighted the role of two or more hitters, including youngsters (in baseball terms) like Jake Wood and Steve Boros, veterans like Billy Bruton and Chico Fernandez, and key reserves, notably Charlie Maxwell, Bo Osborne, and Bubba Morton. The Tigers' stellar mound trio continued to be Frank Lary, Don Mossi, and Jim Bunning, while Phil Regan, yet to lose a game, became a reliable fourth starter. Dick Brown was still hitting the ball better than expected, and Norm Cash was averaging .336 with 11 homers after the Tigers tied the A's, 4–4, on June 1. Most baseball writers as well as legions of fans expected the Yankees to win consistently and roll toward another pennant, but many Detroit writers and Tigers fans were becoming believers in the Motor City's most famous pro team.

Starting on Tuesday, May 9, the Tigers hosted Washington for three days and four games, and the teams split the series. Afterward, Detroit flew out to start a long road trip that lasted until the final Sunday in May, playing four times against the Yankees, three games against the Orioles in Memorial Stadium, two against the Red Sox at Fenway Park, two against Kansas City at Municipal Stadium, three against expansion Minnesota at Metropolitan Stadium, and, finally, three games against expansion Los Angeles in the 22,000-seat bandbox called Wrigley Field, home to the Pacific Coast League's LA Angels before 1961. Altogether, the Tigers would play 17 games in 17 days, representing a considerable amount of air travel, living out of suitcases, eating at hotels, killing time, and riding to and from ballparks in buses and taxis.

Against the Senators, the Tigers won the first and third games, lost the second and fourth tilts, and held onto first place with an 18–7 record. In the first game of the doubleheader at Tiger Stadium on May 9, Mossi improved to 4–0 with a four-hitter, winning, 7–2, despite giving up back-to-back solo home runs to Willie Tasby and catcher-outfielder Gene Green in the fourth inning. Seven players each drove in a run for the Tigers, led by Wood and Brown with two hits. In the nightcap, Paul Foytack (1–2) hurled five innings but lost, 5–4, and sidearming left-hander Joe Grzenda gave up the last two runs. Tasby, a right-handed batter with pop in his bat who hit a career-best 17 homers in 1961, and southpaw swinger Gene Woodling, one of five Senators to hit ten or more homers in 1961, connected for solo four-baggers off Grzenda, with Woodling's blast giving Washington a 5–2 lead.

The last two games weren't close. On Wednesday, Jim Bunning (2–2) nearly duplicated Mossi's feat, hurling a five-hitter to win, 7–1. Boros knocked in two runs, while Wood, Morton, subbing for Kaline (who had pulled a leg muscle), Colavito, and Bunning each drove home one runner. On Thursday, the Senators ripped Bill Fischer and three relievers for nine runs on 12 hits. Marty Kutyna, a 6'0" right-hander traded from Kansas City to the Senators on December 29, 1960, hurled the last five innings and lifted his ledger to 2–0. The Tigers collected 11 hits, but only Bruton, Brown, and right-handed pinch batter Ozzie Virgil, with his first homer, drove in runs.

Just before the road trip, Kaline, who was hitting .333, praised Bob Scheffing and Detroit's team effort. Players could talk to this manager, Kaline explained. If you saw something from the dugout, you knew he would take care of it. Scheffing was getting 100 percent from his men. "He's a master of handling guys on the bench, fellows like Charlie Maxwell and Larry Osborne." Kaline added, "You get down in the dumps when you're not playing. Scheffing treats them perfectly."

Why had the Tigers come alive in 1961? Kaline said, "Last year, it was up to two or three players to do the job at bat. Now everybody's doing it. Determination and hustle are the big things when you're winning." The team's leader and new spokesman liked the jobs done by the newcomers from Milwaukee, notably Dick Brown, Billy Bruton, and Terry Fox. Last but not least, the Tigers had come from behind to win seven of their first 16 victories. Kaline was happy about that statistic, and so were his teammates that were shouldering the load.[14]

The Bengals launched their East-West odyssey on May 12 with four games at Yankee Stadium. The visitors won single games on Friday and Saturday, thanks to stellar pitching, but the Yankees swept Sunday's twin bill. On Friday evening before a loud Bronx crowd of 23,556 paid, Frank Lary, proud of his "Yankee Killer" fame, scattered 11 hits for a nail-biting 4–3 victory. Art Ditmar dueled Lary on even terms until the fourth inning, when Colavito lined a one-out triple to right center and scored on Steve Boros' sacrifice fly. In the bottom of the frame, Hector Lopez, liking outside fastballs, gave the Yankees a 2–1 lead by lining

Yankee Killers: Rocky Colavito, holding his potent bat, and Frank Lary, nicknamed "Yankee Killer" by the writers, were pictured in the Tigers' clubhouse after providing the power in a 4–3 victory at Yankee Stadium on May 12, 1961. Colavito tripled to deep center in the fourth, and he scored the game's first run on Steve Boros' sacrifice fly. Lary hurled a complete-game victory, and he homered in the ninth to provide Detroit's winning margin (National Baseball Hall of Fame, Cooperstown, New York).

a home run into the right field seats after Bill Skowron doubled. Yogi Berra made it 3–1 in the fifth with an RBI double. Ditmar got in trouble in the sixth, giving up singles to Bruton and Kaline, and, after one out, Osborne walked to load the bases. Ralph Houk brought in Arroyo, and Boros knocked in one run with a sacrifice fly, leaving the Tigers behind 3–2. In the seventh, Lary, a timely hitter, doubled, and Wood singled for a 3–3 tie. In the ninth, Lary launched his sixth career home run to left field off reliever Jim Coates, giving Detroit the final 4–3 margin. In the Yankees' ninth, Lary gave up a two-out single to Blanchard and a walk to Mantle, pinch-hitting for Lopez, but Detroit's ace ended it on Clete Boyer's grounder.

After the game, Lary talked and joked with writers, telling them he hit a shoulder-high fastball for his home run. Enjoying a 2-for-4 night at the plate, his first hit was a double, and he slid head-first into second to beat the throw. Bob Scheffing had used Lary more than once as a pinch-runner, saying he knew how to slide and the risk to his best pitcher wasn't great. The bulldog right-hander was peaking at age 31, earlier pitching a one-hitter against the White Sox and now beating the Yankees with their own weapon, the home run. "Besides," wrote Watson Spoelstra, "Lary has turned the Tigers into the reasonable facsimile of a legitimate contender."[15]

On Saturday afternoon Phil Regan, with sharp control and a good slider, improved to 3–0 by winning a five-hitter, 8–3. Regan did yield bases-empty home runs to Blanchard, his second, and Berra, his third, and the game was tied at 3–3 when the Bengals batted in the eighth inning. Cash drew a leadoff walk, Boros flied out, but Brown lofted his fifth home run, a high drive into the left field stands for a 5–3 Tigers lead. Regan set down the Bombers in their eighth inning, and in the ninth, Bob Turley gave

Dick Brown, playing his first season as the Tigers' regular catcher, was a standout until suffering a split finger in mid–July. On May 13, Brown belted homer number five to help Detroit beat the Yankees, 8–3, in New York (National Baseball Hall of Fame, Cooperstown, New York).

up a leadoff double to Wood. Houk called for reliever Danny McDevitt, and the sidearming southpaw fanned Bruton but walked Kaline. Up stepped Colavito, who had thrilled his Bronx backers with a solo homer in the fifth, his sixth round-tripper. Finishing his customary bat-behind-the-back warmup and related gyrations, the colorful slugger hit number seven, boosting the Tigers' lead to 8–3. After the win, Detroit led the league with a 20–7 record, and New York was second at 14–10, but the Yankees fell 4.5 games off the pace.

Sunday's twin bill had plenty of thrills, and the Yankees won twice. In the opener, the teams went back and forth for 11 innings before Yogi Berra sealed a 5–4 victory with a run-scoring pinch-hit single. Mossi worked the first seven innings and allowed four runs on seven hits, notably two-run homers by Bob Cerv and Bill Skowron. After Detroit scored once in the ninth to cut the deficit to 4–2, big Bo Osborne, batting for Chico Fernandez, hit a two-run double into the right field corner for a 4–4 tie. In the Yankees' ninth, Hank Aguirre, usually effective on the mound but clueless as a batter (he hit. 085 lifetime), came in for Bill Fischer. Aguirre hurled scoreless ball in the ninth and tenth. In the fateful 11th, Mantle singled, Skowron fanned, and Blanchard flied out. Yankees fans, used to victories, grew restless. Lo and behold, Maris drew a walk, Kubek hustled out an infield hit, and Berra, batting for Jim Coates, singled home the game-winner.

In the nightcap, Bunning, hardly showing his dominating form, coughed up seven runs on eight singles, three walks, and a wild pitch in two innings. Hurling three frames each, Fischer and Jim Donohue together allowed the Yankees one run and three hits, but the Tigers' comeback fell short. Colavito, bashing his eighth, and Brown, socking number six, homered in the second inning for a 5–2 deficit. Wood tripled leading off the fifth, and Bruton singled for one run. Charlie Maxwell, playing left field in place of Kaline (Colavito moved to right when Maxwell played left), lived up to his Sunday reputation with his first home run of the season, cutting the lead to 7–5. Each team scored once more, but Coates, the tall, intimidating right-hander, took over for Ralph Terry in the fifth and finished the tilt, earning both wins on Sunday. Houk was relieved, because the Yankees needed both wins to keep the race close.[16]

For league-leading Detroit, the continuing journey saw the Bengals beat the Orioles in Baltimore three straight times, with Foytack, Lary, and Regan picking up the victories. Detroit fell twice in Boston, with Bunning hurling a five-hitter, but losing, 1–0, on Don Buddin's RBI double, and Aguirre losing in relief, 4–3, on Jackie Jensen's RBI single in the tenth inning. In Kansas City for games on Sunday and Monday, May 21–22, the Tigers won both, as Lary spun a six-hitter for his seventh victory, Boros connected for his first home run, and Colavito cracked his tenth homer. On Monday the surprising Regan improved to 5–0 and won in a breeze, 10–2, with a 12-hit attack that featured Cash's sixth circuit clout.

The traveling Tigers moved to Bloomington, Minnesota, the town where the friendly, popular, big-hitting Harmon Killebrew hosted a pre-game TV interview show, and a Dodge dealer had welcomed each of the Twins to town with the gift of a new car. But the Bengals won two of three games, and Kaline, not Killebrew, swung the biggest bat, going 6-for-14, belting his first three home runs, and driving in seven of Detroit's 16 runs.

At Metropolitan Stadium, built on a cornfield for the minor league Minneapolis Millers in 1956 and later reputed to be the most poorly maintained ballpark in the majors, Bunning pitched well in the night opener on Tuesday, May 23. The intense right-hander worked seven-plus innings, and Aguirre (2–3) won in relief. Kaline blasted his first homer in the sixth inning for a 2–0 Tigers lead, and the Twins scored in the eighth. In the ninth, matching a major league record of three consecutive home runs for the 46th time, Cash slugged his seventh, Boros connected for his second, and Dick Brown belted his seventh homer for the 5–2 victory.[17]

On Wednesday night, Mossi (5–0) needed three innings of relief by Bill Fischer, who protected a 5–2 Tigers lead, although he gave up two runs on Killebrew's 11th homer in the ninth. Facing Camilo Pascual in the third inning, Kaline homered for a 1–0 lead. In the fifth, Kaline singled, Colavito clubbed his 11th homer, a two-run shot, and Cash singled, stole second, and scored when Killebrew misplayed Boros' grounder to first. In the last of the fifth, Zoilo Versalles, who went 4-for-5, homered to cut the Twins' deficit to 5–2. Fischer came out of the pen in the seventh, and, pitching steadily, he earned his first save.

On Thursday night the Tigers fell, 7–6, in 11 innings when slugger Jim Lemon, following Lenny Green's double and ex–Tiger Reno Bertoia's sacrifice, singled off

Don Mossi, Detroit's stellar left-hander who compiled a 15–7 record in 1961, had a 14–3 mark before the Tigers arrived in New York for the crucial three-game series with the Yankees on September 1 (National Baseball Hall of Fame, Cooperstown, New York).

rookie Jim Donohue (1–1), the fourth Tigers reliever. Foytack was charged with four runs in seven-plus innings, and Fox, Aguirre, Fischer, and Donohue couldn't hold Foytack's 5–2 lead. Kaline hit his third home run and Cash slugged his eighth, giving Detroit a 5–0 first-inning lead. But Lemon got his chance in the 11th, and Donohue couldn't preserve the 6–6 tie.

The Bengals' 17-game journey came to a disappointing end after Los Angeles beat first-place Detroit two out of three. The visitors won the Sunday finale, 9–4, when Bunning (3–4), working six good innings, and Fox, with sharp control, recorded his third save by holding the Angels to Ken Hunt's homer in the ninth. Charlie Maxwell, playing left field with Colavito in right (Kaline's back was sore), knocked in two runs with a single in the third inning and a homer in the sixth. Bruton hit a two-run double in the seventh. In the eighth, Cash, who knew actor Dan Blocker and had taken teammates to the set of "Bonanza," slugged his ninth homer off Ryne Duren, who then walked Boros and gave up Brown's eighth homer for a 7–3 Tigers lead.

In Friday's opener, Lary hurled a complete game but lost, 5–4, dropping his mark to 7–2. Colavito hit the game's only homer, a two-run blast in the seventh inning that tied the game at 4–4, but Earl Averill, Junior, the former Cubs catcher-outfielder taken by the Angels in the expansion draft, hit an RBI double in the eighth for the winning score. On Saturday, Regan, lasting 4⅓ innings, lost his first game after five wins, 10–1, and was ejected for cursing umpire Ed Hurley after being fined the usual $50 for throwing at a batter. Only Bruton's third homer avoided a shutout. Slugger Ted Kluszewski, who had started his career with the Cincinnati Reds in 1947, and Ken Hunt, who had two trials with the Yankees before belting 25 homers in 1961 for the Angels, swung the big bats. Big Klu, a left-handed belter who stood 6'2" and weighed 225 pounds, went 2-for-3 with his eighth homer, a three-run clout in the fifth that gave LA a 7–0 lead. Regan then decked Hunt. Hunt, a right-handed hitter who was tough at 6'1" and 205 pounds, got up and went 4-for-5, banging his seventh homer off Bob Bruce, who replaced Regan, for an 8–0 LA edge.[18]

Chasing the Pennant

Calling them "Victorious Vagabonds," Joe Falls observed that after fashioning a 10–7 record on the transcontinental trip, the Tigers were still in first place, 3.5 games ahead of the second-place Indians, with the Yankees not far behind. Falls saw two main reasons for Detroit's early success. First, he credited Kaline's .307 average, 46 hits, and 24 RBI, whereas in 1960 at this time, he was averaging .232 with 21 hits and 14 RBI—a huge difference. Falls observed that Detroit had a better bench than in previous seasons. For example, Kaline had missed five games so far due to assorted injuries, most recently the finale with the Angels when he wrenched his back ducking out of the way of a ball headed for the dugout. Still, the Tigers filled in with Charlie Maxwell and Bubba Morton. Maxwell played two games, rapping four hits, including two home runs. Morton also filled in for Kaline, and in Baltimore the rookie unloaded a two-run triple.[19]

Back at Tiger Stadium, Detroit finished May and opened June inauspiciously by dropping two of three games and tying another with sixth-place Kansas City. After a day off on Monday, May 29, the Bengals split a Memorial Day doubleheader before a record crowd of 51,791, winning the first game, 5–3, when Norm Cash slammed a grand slam off the facing of the third deck in right center in the eighth inning. Cash's upper-deck blast, his tenth of the season, sent the packed stadium into a state of hysteria, and even the grounds crew was cheering as Cash, grinning, jogged around the bases. In the fateful eighth, Wood popped to short, Bruton walked, and Kaline singled. Rookie right-hander Bill Kunkel replaced tiring southpaw Jim Archer, another rookie, but Colavito walked. Ex-Indian Bud Daley came from the pen to replace Kunkel. Cash, who proved again that he could hit lefties as well as right-handers, launched his four-run bomb, and Bill Fischer (1–1) earned his first victory with two innings of work!

The remaining three games left the Tigers with two losses plus a tie. In the holiday nightcap, the A's roughed up Paul Foytack for six runs in 2⅔ innings, topped by Norm Siebern's three-run homer in the third. Bob Bruce replaced Foytack with two outs and two runners aboard, walking Andy Carey and permitting a two-run single to pitcher Jerry Walker. When the fourth frame was over, KC had an 8–0 lead the Tigers couldn't overcome, despite a three-run seventh that made the final score 9–3. On Wednesday, Kansas City won again, 6–4, victimizing Frank Lary, who gave up all six runs in 6⅓ innings. Leo Posada, a second-year outfielder, rapped two hits, and Joe Pignatano, the former Dodgers catcher, went 4-for-4 with three RBI. On Thursday, June 1, the two clubs were tied when a violent hailstorm hit Detroit in the bottom of the eighth with the Tigers facing right-handed reliever Dave Wickersham. Earlier, Cash had connected for his 11th homer, Kaline rapped two singles, Bruton and Fernandez each batted in a run, and Boros' grounder in the seventh tied the game at 4–4. The statistics counted, and the game would be replayed later.

After the games of June 1, the AL standings showed Detroit in first place with a 29–16 record, followed by Cleveland (26–17), two games behind, and New York (23–18) was third, percentage points ahead of Baltimore (25–20), both four games back. The Detroiters believed they were ready to race with the Yankees for the pennant. On the other hand, the seasoned New Yorkers believed the pennant was theirs to win, regardless of the roaring Bengals.

5

Detroit and New York
Win Big in June

Tigers Keep Winning

Detroit, after closing out May by losing two out of three games to the Kansas City Athletics at Tiger Stadium, opened June by tying one game with the Athletics before hosting a four-game series against the Minnesota Twins. New York, after splitting four games at Boston, flew to Chicago to take on the White Sox for three games at Comiskey Park starting June 2. The Tigers, fashioning records of 10–4 and 19–12 in April and May, respectively, continued to play well with a 19–10 mark in June. But the Yankees, following ledgers of 9–5 in April and 14–12 in May, caught fire with a league-best 22–10 record in June, making Ralph Houk's ball club look like the nearly invincible Yankee teams of the 1950s. On June 23, Detroit traveled to Cleveland for a four-game set at Municipal Stadium, and the Bengals won the first three, dropping the deflated Tribe to third place with a 41–30 mark. Afterward, the Indians lost more games than they won, finishing 1961 in fifth place with a losing record of 78–83.

Only four of ten AL ball clubs—the Yankees, Tigers, Orioles, and White Sox—compiled winning records for the 1961 season, and fourth-place Chicago, at 86–76, finished 23 games out of first place. By late June, the pennant race was all about the Yankees and the Tigers.

When the Tigers tied the Athletics in the rain-shortened clash on Thursday, June 1, Cash, who went 1-for-2 and cracked his 11th home run, was batting .336. Already people were bringing signs to the ballpark with phrases like "Stormin' Norman" or "Crash Cash" to wave when the increasingly popular first baseman made a good play or came up to bat. Detroit's radio-TV duo—George Kell, the former Tigers All-Star third baseman who was elected to the Baseball Hall of Fame in 1983 and was in his third season as the team's broadcaster, and Ernie Harwell, a longtime play-by-play man now in his second year as Kell's partner—started using the nickname

"Stormin' Norman," and it stuck. When the Texan enjoyed another good day at the plate, which was happening frequently, writers wanted to know why Cash was a big-time slugger after averaging .286 in 1960. He heard the same questions over and over, and his usual reply was, "I don't know why I'm hitting like this. I'm using the same bat and the same swing." Detroit's newest star added, "The bat weighs thirty-one ounces and is probably the lightest bat in the league. Maybe it's swinging quick. If you're fast enough, you have more of a look at the ball."[1]

Cash did have an idea why his bat was quick, but he wasn't telling anyone, not as long as he could pull on a big league uniform. He was "corking" his bats by drilling a half-inch hole about eight inches long into each bat's heavy end and plugging the top two inches with cork, sawdust, and glue. Twenty years later, Cash told *Sports Illustrated* that his tactic gave him the weight of a heavier bat while making it swing like a lighter bat. Earl Weaver, who began his stellar career as Baltimore's manager in 1968, also explained to *SI*'s Steve Wolf how to cork a bat, indicating the drilled hole could be plugged with Plastic Wood. Said Weaver, "You can't spot a good job with a magnifying glass."[2] Although what Cash and others did was illegal, there is little indication that umpires check bats as much as they do pitchers for illegally applying a substance to the baseball, thus making the ball drop or otherwise move in an unusual fashion.

Actually, Cash's personalized bats mainly gave him a psychological edge. He was well-coordinated, strong, and quick, and he saw the ball well. Bob Scheffing, who got the same questions repeatedly about Cash, said, "For pure unadulterated brute strength at the plate, Cash must be bracketed with Mickey Mantle and Eddie Mathews." The Tigers' skipper concluded, "He swings a light bat, as he told you, and I mean he swings it." Scheffing didn't exaggerate. Cash swung the bat quickly and hard, putting his uncanny strength into his compact, slightly uppercut swing. The good news was that the Tigers gave Cash a chance to be a regular in 1961, and he responded in remarkable fashion. Indeed, he was living his baseball dream.

Cash was king in Detroit, a role that belonged to Al Kaline before 1961, but being the top Tiger carried obligations. Everyone wanted Cash's autograph, or more. Kids in the neighborhood walked, bicycled, or arrived in a car with their parents to ring the doorbell whenever Cash was at home, and, being the friendly, easygoing fellow that he was, the new Tigers hero would sign his name on just about any item. Cash's image appeared on billboards around Detroit, and he was asked to endorse products ranging from pizza to autos. A variety of clubs and organizations wanted him for a speaker, and, of course, they paid for his services, usually $50 or $100, sometimes more. In 1961 he probably earned $5,000 in extracurricular income, although often he appeared without charge. He couldn't seem to say no. Whenever he left Tiger Stadium, a line of autograph seekers was waiting, and he obliged. Celebrity has advantages and disadvantages, and the Tigers' star was learning that day by day.[3]

Joe Williams, the respected columnist and sports editor of the *New York World Telegram & Sun*, the writer who came to Cash's house to speak to him after the Washington twin bill on June 11, pointed out that the Tigers' slugging hero was earning a "coolie wage." Cash, said Williams, hit home runs for Detroit, and Sunday he became an "Olympian," hitting one clear out of the park, a feat never before accomplished by a Tiger, although Ted Williams and Mickey Mantle had hit such Olympian blasts. Going into the game with Boston on Monday, June 12, Cash, with 17 homers, was trailing Roger Maris by three and Mickey Mantle by one, and he was tied with Rocky Colavito at 17, one less than Cash hit for the entire 1960 season. Also, Cash's .370 average was one point below Jimmy Piersall's league-leading .371. Saying Cash (who earned an estimated $13,000 in salary in 1961)[4] was well below Mantle's pay, Williams, an astute observer, called Cash "the lowest salaried .370 long ball hitter the majors have known in decades."[5]

Nine days earlier, on June 2, the Twins arrived in the Motor City for single games on Friday and Saturday and a twin bill on Sunday. The Tigers, showing their versatility, won the first two, closely contested pitchers' battles, but on Sunday the Bengals unloaded the heavy lumber and won twice with home runs. On Friday night Jim Bunning, showing good control, squared his record at 4–4, winning a four-hit shutout, 2–0, and Rocky Colavito and Al Kaline slugged home runs for the margin of victory. A crowd of 22,141 waited during a rain delay of one hour before the game started, but Colavito, hitting cleanup, slammed his 13th four-bagger off the facing of the upper deck in left field, narrowly missing becoming the first major leaguer to clear Detroit's left field roof. On Saturday the smooth Don Mossi nearly matched Bunning's shutout, but the Twins, totaling seven hits, scored on Bob Allison's RBI single in the ninth. Charlie Maxwell, pinch-hitting for Dick Brown in the sixth, drew a bases-loaded walk off Pedro Ramos for a 1–0 lead, and Colavito hit number 14 in the eighth for the final edge of 2–1, lifting Mossi's mark to 6–0.

On Sunday the Tigers whipped the Twins twice by six-run bulges, 10–4 and 9–3, for a sweep of the series. Frank Lary won the opener, giving up four runs on nine hits and boosting his record to 8–3. Typically tougher with runners on base, Lary was backed by five home runs. Cash smashed a bases-empty homer, number 12, in the second inning. With the Tigers ahead, 4–1, in the last of the eighth, Dick Brown cracked his ninth four-bagger after Steve Boros walked. Chico Fernandez, playing better than ever, connected for his second round-tripper, and after a single by Lary, Wood blasted his fifth home run for a 10–1 lead. In the nightcap, right-hander Bob Bruce, a native of Highland Park, Michigan, and a one-time Alma College hurler, looked good at first, but he left after loading the bases two outs in the third inning. Paul Foytack, struggling all summer with soreness in his pitching arm, came in from the pen and got Jim Lemon on a fly ball. Mixing his pitches well, the veteran right-hander contributed 6⅓ strong innings for the victory, evening his mark at 3–3. This time the power came from Colavito, who smashed a three-run home run to deep left in the first, his 15th, and Bubba Morton, playing right field with Kaline in center, who connected for his first homer, a three-run blast that gave the Tigers a 6–1 lead in the second. In the eighth, Cash, who went 2-for-3, singled, Boros sacrificed, Fernandez singled him home, and Mike Roarke belted his first circuit clout, a two-run drive to left for the 9–3 final margin.

When Sunday's games were over, Detroit led the league with a 33–16 record, and speculation centered on whether the Tigers were in the pennant race for the long haul. Following a two-game sojourn to Chicago, red-hot Cleveland, having won six in a row and 18 out of 22 since May 14, would arrive in Detroit on Thursday for a four-game showdown. The Yankees, meanwhile, ranked third with a 25–19 mark, 5.5 games behind Detroit, and the Orioles were fourth at 26–22, 6.5 games off the pace. Lyall Smith, one of several *Free Press* scribes covering the Bengals, summarized the season, notably Bob Scheffing's decision to trade Frank Bolling to Milwaukee and start Jake Wood at second base. Also, Eddie Yost was placed in the expansion draft after Scheffing decided Steve Boros could handle third. The Tigers kept young outfielders Bubba Morton and George Thomas as reserves, along with popular veteran Charlie Maxwell.

Regardless of personnel, nobody figured the Tigers for more than a first-division finish, and fourth place was considered realistic. Thus, the question: Did Detroit need more pitching, more power, and more experience to stay in the pennant race with so many younger players on the roster? If so, the trading deadline was June 15. "It won't be easy," Lyall Smith concluded, "But I'd trade."[6]

Regardless, the Tigers traveled to Chicago, lodged at their usual digs, the Sheraton Towers, and dropped a pair of night games to the White Sox. On Monday, June 5, at Comiskey Park, located within smelling distance of Chicago's South Side stockyards, Phil Regan, who took the mound with a 5–1 record, lost after being roughed up for five runs on nine hits in six innings, including three-fourths of a 4-for-4 outing by Jim Landis. Chicago lefty Frank Baumann boosted his ledger to 4–4 by spacing seven hits to win, 8–0. Jake Wood went 3-for-4, but Baumann, tough in the clutch, allowed no extra-base hits. On Tuesday evening Jim Bunning, the sidearmer who was not yet his stellar self, lost, 7–1, hurling 6⅔ innings and allowing all seven runs on 11 hits. Veteran right-hander Early Wynn, the ex–Indian, worked 3⅓ innings, and late-inning specialist Turk Lown, the Brooklyn native who loved eating turkey, earned his third win with 5⅔ innings of relief. Detroit's run scored on Brown's bases-loaded grounder in the fourth for a 1–0 lead. The Chisox replied with three in the fourth and one more in the sixth, and Landis upped the lead to 7–1 with a two-run single in the seventh. Cleveland, with a 32–17 record, now led Detroit, now 33–18, by .006 percentage points, and New York was third at 28–19, three games behind. The Tigers flew home for a day off to prepare for the first-place Indians' arrival on Thursday.

Bengals Battle for First

Joe Falls hyped the Indians on Thursday, June 8, the opening day of the crucial four-game series, pointing out that Cleveland was the hottest team in the league. Before dumping the expansion Senators, 11–0, the previous day, Cleveland was hitting a "slightly sensational" .286 as a team (the Indians and Tigers finished the 1961 season tied for the AL lead with .266 marks). The Tribe featured three of the league's top hitters, center fielder Jimmy Piersall (currently at .368), catcher John Romano (.357), and ex–Reds second baseman Johnny Temple (.328). Manager Jimmy Dykes was high on his team. In addition to Piersall, Romano and Temple, Dykes praised first baseman Vic Power (.296). The pilot was pleased with his bullpen, featuring Frank Funk, the right-hander from Washington, D.C., who posted a 4–2 record as a rookie in 1960, Barry Latman, the tall right-hander from Los Angeles who came to the Indians in a 1960 trade after three seasons with the White Sox, and Bob Allen, the 6'2" rookie lefty from Tatum, Texas, who was 3–2 with a 3.75 ERA and three saves in 1961. At that point in 1961, Funk, Latman, and Allen together had won 13 games in relief and saved several more.

Bob Scheffing and the front office figured Detroit needed to bolster the pitching staff, notably the bullpen. The Tigers dealt infielder Chuck Cottier to Washington to get Hal Woodeshick, the former Tiger who was 3–2 with one save and a 4.02 ERA in 40.1 innings for the Senators. Woodeshick, once a hot prospect from Wilkes-Barre, Pennsylvania, who debuted for Detroit in 1956 with a 0–2 record, was traded to Cleveland and produced a 6–6 ledger for the Indians in 1958. The 6'3", 200-pound lefty enjoyed his best seasons later with the National League's expansion Houston Colt .45s.

Detroit also sent Jim Donohue to Los Angeles for Jerry Casale, a once promising right-hander from Brooklyn who had spent nearly two years in the Army before debuting with the Red Sox in 1958. Now 27, Casale enjoyed a career-best 13–8 record for Boston in 1959, but he started 1961 at 1–5 for the Angels. Casale, who battled a sore arm in 1960, could start and relieve with his good fastball and good size, 6'2" and 200 pounds (he had no decisions and a 5.25 ERA in three games for Detroit in 1961). Donohue was seen as a "disappointment," having a 1–1 mark and just one save after finishing the game in eight of 14 appearances before the trade on June 7.[7]

When the first-place Indians, riding their nine-game win streak, arrived for a doubleheader on Thursday, June 8, they found the Motor City awash in "pennant fever," a type of hysteria peculiar to baseball fans that had not gripped Detroit since the Tigers and the Yankees battled for first place in 1950. The old, gray-walled stadium seemed to enclose an "epidemic disaster area," symptoms of which, wrote *Free Press* staffer Neal Shine, include "uncontrollable clapping and stomping, periods of deep depression and high elation, and radical behavioral changes."[8]

For the first game Scheffing picked the 6'1" Mossi, the ex–Indian famed for his big ears, slightly crooked nose, and clutch pitching, and he scattered five hits over seven innings but lost, 1–0. The southpaw gave up the game's

Many Tigers fans liked to enjoy a beautiful baseball day by sitting in the center field bleachers at Tiger stadium. Those tickets cost 75 cents in 1961. On a clear summer day in Detroit, bleacherites could talk baseball and see the Tigers forever (photograph by Irwin Cohen).

only run in the first inning on doubles by Johnny Temple and Vic Power. Terry Fox threw two bad pitches to open the eighth, giving up a double to Temple and a bunt single to Piersall. Aguirre took over, retired Chuck Essegian on a foul fly ball, and induced Power to ground into a double play. Aguirre also pitched a hitless ninth, but too late. Jim Perry, supposedly "too nice" to win in the majors, allowed nine singles in seven-plus innings. The tall right-hander escaped a bases-loaded jam in the fifth when Wood lined to the pitcher, and Perry's quick throw doubled Mossi off first. Frank Funk earned his fifth save with two scoreless innings, Mossi's record fell to 6–1, and the crowd of 48,550 was disappointed, restless, and chattering.

Fortunately for Tigers fans, Lary, with his pitches catching the corners, won another tight game on Thursday, 2–1, hurling a six-hitter, striking out eight, and walking none. Big right-hander Wynn Hawkins, who went 4–4 as a rookie for Cleveland in 1960, took the loss, giving up both Tigers runs in his five innings. Cash, swinging the hot bat, slugged his 13th home run to deep right in the second. Maxwell, giving Bruton a rest (Kaline played center), went 1-for-4, but Paw Paw knocked in the decisive run with a bases-loaded forceout in the fifth, scoring Lary, who started the rally with a one-out single. Hawkins escaped further damage when Colavito lined into an unassisted double play. Bearing down, Lary yielded only an RBI double to pinch-hitter Don Dillard, and the split left the Tigers, at 34–19, half a game behind the 34–18 Tribe.

The twin bill featured a variety of exciting moments and, considering the missiles thrown at Jimmy Piersall in center field, a few lowlights. The sometimes zany, always outspoken Piersall was the target of a golf ball, a firecracker, and bottles, and the police did catch a 15-year-old who tossed a metal can opener. Piersall had no kind words for Detroit's fans or for the four ushers, eight plain-clothes cops, and several uniformed police patrolling the outfield stands. Jimmy Dykes threatened to pull his team off the field if Piersall was hit, but it didn't happen. The most excitement came when stocky Bob Hale, who averaged .302 as a pinch-hitter in 1960, batted for the pitcher and grounded to Wood for an apparent double play. Wood flipped to Fernandez, who fired to Cash for what looked like the third out, but Larry Napp called Hale safe. The Tigers, led by Cash, rushed to protest, and Scheffing trotted out to join the rhubarb. Hale took a chance and broke for second. Cash spotted him, turned to make a play, and Hale retreated, but Cash's throw to catcher Mike Roarke, covering first, arrived in time, and Napp called Hale out. This time the Indians went wild, claiming there could be no play with the other team's manager on the field. Regardless, the umpire prevailed, and Lary improved to 9–3.[9]

The two teams split the next two games. On Friday night before a large crowd of 43,427, the Indians won a thriller, 5–4. Regan, whose ability to earn wins in late-inning relief stints later earned him the nickname "Vulture," gave up four of the Tribe's runs on four hits in his five frames, but he departed with the score tied at 4–4. Foytack (3–4) gave up the winning run when ex–Tiger Bubba Phillips homered to deep left in the ninth. Right-hander Bobby Locke pitched into the fifth, when Barry Latman took over, yielding Colavito's RBI double, tying the game. Latman permitted no more hits, and the former University of Southern California star lifted his record to 5–0. On Saturday the Tigers roared back, winning a tight contest, 2–0, behind the five-hit effort of Bunning (5–5), aided by Bill Fischer, who recorded his second save. In the ninth, when Tito Francona followed Piersall's single with a two-out base hit, Scheffing called on Fischer, and he closed the game on Vic Power's bouncer. After Saturday's games, first-place Cleveland (35–19) still led Detroit (35–20) by half a game, and the Yankees, at 32–20, were two games back.

Following the Indians, the fifth-place Senators came to town on June 11 for a Sunday doubleheader, and the Tigers settled for another split. They lost the opener, 7–4, despite Cash hitting two home runs, one over the roof in right field. The Bengals, rooted on by a noisy audience of 21,723 on Sunday, won the nightcap when Stormin' Norman went 4-for-5, including homer number 17. Phil Regan, who retired the final Senators hitter, Coot Veal, in the top of the 11th, improved his mark to 6–2 when Steve Boros' RBI single won the game.

Enjoying a break from the schedule on Monday, the day Joe Williams filed his column on Cash's home-run heroics and low salary, the Tigers played golf at the Hillcrest Country Club in Mount Clemens where sponsors, the local purveyors of beer, gas, and cigarettes, picked up the tab for the food, beverages, and amenities. According to the *Free Press*, the Tigers had been a "sponsors' jackpot" since their eight-game win streak following the Opening Day loss.[10] The Yankees commonly enjoyed such perks based on fame, but 1961 was a new experience for the Bengals.

The Tigers battled the Red Sox for the next three days, winning the first two of three contests, and again Cash, swinging his explosive bat, was the hero, making front-page headlines by blasting homers number 18 and 19 in Tuesday night's 7–1 cakewalk. Enjoying cooler weather after a rain delay, Cash, batting in his usual fifth slot, went 2-for-3 and connected for his fifth and sixth home runs in the last four games. He opened the scoring in the third inning by hitting a savage liner to center for an inside-the-park, three-run homer, aided when Carroll Hardy slipped on the wet turf. Following Kaline's two-run double and Colavito's RBI double, Cash provided the final score of 7–1 with his 19th circuit clout in the seventh, a tape-measure job to the third deck in right center. For Boston, Gene Conley, originally signed by the old Boston Braves in 1950, took the loss, while Mossi scattered 12 hits and improved to 7–1. Maxwell, starting in left (sending Colavito to right), singled twice in four trips. The home runs by the hot-hitting Cash left him two behind Roger Maris, who hit number 21 as the Yankees fell to the Indians, 7–2.[11]

The Bengals, however, divided two day games with the Bosox. On Wednesday afternoon in a "Ladies Day" contest, while the Tigers gave away flowers, trading stamps, and gift certificates, Lary became the league's first ten-game winner by a score of 4–2, thanks to two runs on errant throws by third baseman Frank Malzone. Cash was hitless, but Wood laced an RBI single in the second, Bruton slugged a two-run triple in the fourth, and Malzone's error allowed Bruton to trot home for a 4–0 lead. Lary surrendered two runs in the eighth on four singles and a sacrifice fly, but the Tigers' ace cruised to victory. Maxwell played for Kaline, who had torn tissue between the thumb and finger on his right hand, and Osborne played third base for Boros, who had a pulled muscle in his leg.[12]

In the finale on Thursday, Bunning pitched well until he threw one bad pitch, a changeup, to Vic Wertz, and the long-time slugger hit a grand slam to deep right field to cap a five-run fifth inning. Following two singles, Osborne had booted the pitcher's bunt near the third-base line. One run scored on a forceout, Bunning issued a walk, and Wertz made the Tigers pay. Bill Monbouquette stifled the home team on a four-hitter, 10–1, with the lone Bengals run scoring on Osborne's RBI double in the ninth. New York won at Cleveland, 3–2, and the Yankees, now 37–21, climbed into first place by percentage points, leaving the Indians and the Tigers tied for second with 38–22 records. Worse, Cash had to leave the lineup because of an acute sprain in his

Jim Bunning, Detroit's dominating right-hander, compiled a 17–11 record in 1961, but he didn't move above .500 until June 25, when he defeated the Cleveland Indians, 6–3, and boosted his mark to 7–6 (National Baseball Hall of Fame, Cooperstown, New York).

left instep, and he was doubtful for the upcoming Yankees game in Detroit on Friday night.[13]

Tigers and Yankees Square Off

When the Yankees stepped onto the manicured diamond at Tiger Stadium for a first-place showdown on the evening of Friday, June 16, they looked around at a packed house of 51,744. Spectators filled every nook and cranny of the stadium with the green seats, and most rooted against the "Damnyankees." Outside the storied ballpark at "The Corner" of Michigan and Trumbull, scalpers were offering $2 seats for $4 and getting plenty of takers. By game time there were a few empty seats in the lower deck in right field, but bleacherites in center (75 cents per seat) were jammed into the aisles as well as filling the benches. When the PA announcer read off the Tigers' starting lineup, the crowd gave approval for every starter, but, wrote Judd Arnett in the *Free Press*, they gave a "solid, deep-throated roar for Norman Cash, the new Tiger hero."

Jake Wood ripped a single to center on Bill Stafford's first pitch, and a burst of noise arose around the ballpark. When Bruton laced a single past second, the crowd responded with a surging, protracted roar, followed by more screaming when right fielder Roger Maris booted the ball, and then threw wildly past third base, allowing the speedy Wood to score. Kaline topped one to third, Clete Boyer booted it, Bruton scored, and the bedlam increased. The noise subsided temporarily as Colavito grounded into a double play. Cash, after twirling two bats, stepped up to the plate. A large banner rolled down from the upper deck in right, reading "Stormin' Norman," and another appeared behind home plate: "Cash." Cash promptly singled to center, bringing forth yet another cascade of cheers, and so the night went for the Tigers faithful. Boros ended the inning with a pop fly, and Detroit led, 2–0. In the third, the crowd was delirious again when Bruton led off with a single and Kaline doubled off the screen in left for a 3–0 lead.

The Tigers won, 4–2, and cool Phil Regan, with his fastball and slider hitting the spots and the fans roaring on every strike, spaced six hits. In the fifth inning, Bill Skowron, who waved his 36-inch bat like a ping-pong paddle (despite wearing a corset after a back injury at home in 1959), hit an opposite-field homer, his forte, a two-run shot to right. In the Tigers' fifth, Wood and Bruton singled, and Tony Kubek, the cutoff man, threw to first trying to trap Bruton, but the relay hit Bruton. Scrambling up at third, Wood scooted home for the 4–2 edge. Regan's stuff blanked Mantle and Maris. Both went 0-for-4, and the crowd loved it. Mantle, typically for an away game, drew screams of disapproval when he walked up to the plate. Mantle fanned in the second, and he flung his bat high in disgust. "'Boooooooo,' they yelled half in anger and half in delight," wrote Judd Arnett, "and Mr. Mantle dog-trotted to the dugout, his legs stiff, his head down, as the noise surged and washed throughout the old ball yard." New York featured sluggers like Maris, Mantle, Skowron, Berra, and Howard, but the unflappable Regan, except for one pitch, stifled them, as cheers, "ooohs," and "aaahs" continued unabated on a happy evening.

All such tense contests feature moments of irritation or anger, and Cash, irate, came up screaming after New York's Jim Coates, using his favorite tactic, knocked him down with a high, tight fastball in the eighth inning. The benches cleared, but the uproar soon faded. Chico Fernandez was booed by many Tigers fans when he flipped an obscene gesture seemingly toward the crowd, but it turned out that his finger was intended for Clete Boyer, who fielded his grounder in the fourth and waited to throw until the Bengals' shortstop, with a pulled leg muscle, had to run it out.[14]

Friday's game set the tone for the series. The fans kept lining up to see the Bronx Bombers, with 51,509 paying their way into Tiger Stadium on Saturday night and another 44,459 on Sunday afternoon. On Saturday each team's hitters tried to wear out the opponent's pitchers, and the Tigers hung on for a 12–10 win amid an impressive display of power hitting. With Detroit leading, 8–0, Maris led off a five-run Yankees fourth inning with his 23rd home run, this one off Don Mossi. Eight hitters later, Tony Kubek, the witty, spray-hitting shortstop, drove in the fifth run with a single, knocking Mossi out of the box. Paul Foytack earned his fourth victory by working out of the jam and pitching shutout ball until two were out in the ninth. In what seemed like a heartbeat to fans, most of whom were on the edge of their seats, Boyer homered, his third, Kubek singled, Maris doubled, and Mantle launched a three-run bomb, his 20th. Bill Fischer relieved Foytack, hot-hitting Elston Howard smashed a drive into the left field seats, and Terry Fox finally ended the suspense by getting Skowron to line out to short. The Tigers victimized newly-acquired lefty Bud Daley for four runs in the first, Kaline and Cash each knocked in a run in the second, and Fernandez led off the third with a home run, his third. After the Yankees replied with their first five-run burst, Colavito tripled to right in the Tigers' fourth, scoring on a wild pitch. Kaline, not to be outdone by Yankees sluggers, hit a solo homer in the sixth, and, in the eighth singled home Wood, who had doubled, for a 12–5 lead.[15]

The three-game set climaxed on Sunday on a beautiful, sunny June afternoon before another big audience with a matchup of the two teams' aces. This time the Tigers managed just three singles, and Motor City fans spent a mostly silent afternoon when Whitey Ford, backed by another display of Yankees power as well as by Luis Arroyo's scoreless ninth, struck out 12 and won easily, 9–0. Ford's fifth straight win gave him a majors-best record of 11–2 and a good shot at 20 victories. Ford, who always seemed to get banged up in Detroit, tripped coming up the concrete dugout steps before the game, scraping his knee on the edge of the top step. Joking with writers afterward, he denied that Arroyo, who said he wasn't getting enough work, offered to pitch batting practice. "In a pig's eye you are!" exclaimed Ford, who wanted relievers to be fresh and ready to go. Still, he pointed out that Arroyo, usually efficient, proved his value again in the ninth by disposing of three Bengals on four pitches.[16]

The Closer: Luis Arroyo, the Yankees' bullpen stalwart in 1961, posted a 15–5 record but also saved 29 games, 13 of them for Whitey Ford. Little Luis' good control and tricky screwball helped him dominate hitters (author's collection).

Against Ford that Sunday, Lary, famed as the Yankee Killer, paled in comparison. He was routed in the third inning after yielding five runs on nine hits, a sluggish performance that dropped his record to 10–4. "Lary didn't have a thing today," lamented Bob Scheffing, but in what may have been a prophetic comment, he said, "but if we can take two out of three from those guys for the rest of the season, I'll be more than happy." After the loss, Lary's record against the Yankees was still 25–9, but on this day the bulldog right-hander didn't seem ready to compete.

In the Yankees' first, Bobby Richardson, the classy second baseman who averaged .305 in seven World Series, led off with a single. Hitting second, Clete Boyer, the cannon-armed third baseman who was first signed by Kansas City in 1955 and was traded to New York in 1957, grounded into a double play. Up stepped Maris. Lary, pitching carefully, walked the slugger. Mantle, hitting left-handed, sliced a single to left, but Berra popped up to Cash, ending the inning. Taking the mound, Ford set down Wood, Bruton, and Kaline in order.

Moose Skowron, the number-six hitter, led off the second with a home run into the left field seats, his 13th, and strong-armed John Blanchard, the reserve catcher who would have started on any other AL team, hit the first of his two home runs, a drive to deep right, his fifth of the season. Ex-Athletic Joe DeMaestri, a right-handed batting, good-fielding shortstop subbing for the injured Kubek, topped one down the first-base line. Lary got off the mound slowly, and his low throw was too late. Ford, a left-handed hitter, surprised the pulled-in infield by chopping one over Ozzie Virgil's head at third. Richardson bunted, and Cash, trying for a force at third, threw too late, and everyone was safe. Boyer brought home DeMaestri with a sacrifice fly to Kaline. Maris grounded one to Wood at second and legged out a single when Lary, unaccountably, was late covering first. Mantle lifted a long fly to center that Bruton ran down, but another run scored for a 4–0 lead. Lary escaped the inning when Berra flied out to center.

"The Yanks, who at times looked like Little Leaguers in the first two games," observed Joe Falls, "couldn't do anything wrong and methodically added to their total." In Detroit's second, Dick Brown singled, but that was it. In the visitors' third, Skowron lined a double to left, and Blanchard's grounder advanced the runner. DeMaestri singled for a 5–0 lead, and Scheffing had seen enough. Newly acquired Jerry Casale was summoned in relief, but the tall right-hander couldn't stop the damage. Two singles and an error let in a run in the fifth, Blanchard belted his sixth homer, a solo shot to deep right in the seventh, and Maris connected for number 24 in the eighth, a two-run blast accounting for the final score of 9–0.

After the dispirited crowd filed out, Detroit, with a 40–23 record, was leading Cleveland (40–24) by half a game and New York (38–23) by one game. The pennant race had a long way to go. Indeed, Sunday's main consolation for the Tigers was that the three-game attendance of

The Moose: Bill Skowron, the Yankees' power-hitting first baseman, slugged 28 homers, ranking him third on the team in 1961 behind Roger Maris with 61 and Mickey Mantle with 54 (author's collection).

147,712 topped the previous three-game mark of 142,683 set against the Indians in 1950.[17]

Whitey Ford and Frank Lary

Every team has an ace pitcher as well as maybe two or three more first-line pitchers, and the Yankees' Whitey Ford and the Tigers' Frank Lary were two of the league's best.

Ford, 32, pitching his tenth season for the Yankees, enjoyed a career year in 1961. He recorded his best month ever in June, starting eight games and winning them all. Typical of his season was his performance at historic Yankee Stadium on June 30, when the Bronx Bombers beat the Senators, 5–1. Washington scored in the first inning when Billy Klaus, the ex–Red Sox infielder, tripled to left, and he scored when Tony Kubek threw badly to first on Chuck Hinton's grounder. Ford allowed just four more singles in his complete game, and he got plenty of support from his friends. Roger Maris went 2-for-3, including his eighth double in the sixth inning, a run-scoring liner that bounced over the waist-high fence into the right field stands. Mickey Mantle connected for his 25th homer, a two-run, inside-the-park four-bagger to deep center field. Maris knocked in the last two runs with a single in the eighth. Ford's 14th victory improved the Bombers to 45–27, leaving them in second place, two games behind the league-leading Tigers (48–26).

Edward Charles Ford, an only child, was born in Manhattan, one of the five boroughs of New York City, on October 21, 1928. Four years later, Jim Ford moved his family across the East River, and his son grew up in an apartment on 34th Avenue in the Astoria section of Queens, not far from the Triborough Bridge. The working-class neighborhood was composed of Irish, Italian, and Polish families. Eddie played stickball, football, and roller hockey on the streets as a youth during the Great Depression. His father was a good ballplayer who was always interested in Eddie's athletic endeavors. Later, his parents would take a one-week vacation where they could watch their major league son pitch. Ford came of age during World War II under circumstances similar to many of his baseball contemporaries. A good athlete, the blond-haired city slicker loved playing baseball, and he liked playing first base. He also followed the Yankees and his favorite player, Joe DiMaggio. Like other youths, Eddie would read about his heroes in the sports section of the *New York Daily News*, then a two-cent daily.[18]

Asked by Peter Golenbock why he didn't start out as a pitcher, Ford figured he was "a pretty good hitter. I was a good fielder. I just didn't grow.

I was 5 foot 9, 150 pounds in high school." Ford attended Aviation High, but he was more interested in playing baseball every chance he got. His sandlot team was the Thirty-fourth Avenue Boys of the Queens-Nassau League. As a senior, Ford was told by the school's coach, Johnny Martin, to try pitching. At a tryout at Yankee Stadium in April 1946, the lefty didn't look particularly good in five swings of the bat, and Yankees scout Paul Krichell also suggested pitching. That summer he worked during the week in the mailroom of Equitable Life, and he played on the company's baseball team. Ford played for the Thirty-fourth Avenue team in Sunday double-headers, when he switched between first base and pitcher with his friend Don Derle. Their team won all 36 games as well as the *New York Journal-American* sandlot championship, capped by the exciting title game held at the Polo Grounds. Ford's performance, notably his 18–0 record, impressed several teams. He had a good fastball, but the curve was his best pitch, and he threw both with good control.

In addition to the Red Sox, all three New York ball clubs—the Yankees, Giants, and Dodgers—made offers, but the Yankees offered Ford $7,000. None of the other teams were willing to match that figure, including $3,500 to sign the left-hander, who was considered small by major league standards. Like Mantle, Ford would be a Yankee forever. He signed his contract in October 1946, after the Yankees finished in third place, 17 games behind the pennant-winning Red Sox and five games behind the second-place Tigers.

Ford, witty, bright, and fun-loving, almost to an extreme, valued performing on the diamond. Like Mantle, he loved living the high life away from the ballpark, but mainly among friends. Around strangers or those he didn't know well, Ford was a gentleman, humble and gracious.

Ford was assigned to Binghamton of the Class A Eastern League for spring training in 1947. After a month, manager

Chairman of the Board: Whitey Ford, enjoying his career season, fashioned a remarkable 25–4 record with a 3.21 ERA. Ford's accomplishments in 1961 included winning baseball's Cy Young Award and being named World Series MVP (National Baseball Hall of Fame, Cooperstown, New York).

Lefty Gomez, the Yankees southpaw who made it to the Baseball Hall of Fame in 1972 by fashioning four 20-win seasons in the 1930s and going 6–0 in World Series play, shipped the recruit to Butler, Pennsylvania, of the Class C Middle Atlantic League. As he did at four stops in the minors, "Whitey" (Gomez gave him the nickname) posted a winning record, going 13–4 in 24 games and 157 innings for Butler. Serious, durable, and tenacious on the mound, Ford produced ledgers of 16–8 at Norfolk of the Class B Piedmont League in 1948 and 16–5 at Binghamton in 1949. The Yankees brought him to spring training in St. Petersburg in 1950. Cocky to the point of arrogance, Ford was disliked by many big names on the Bronx Bombers, for example Eddie Lopat. Lopat, the durable lefty who had a 15–10 mark in 1949 and beat the Dodgers once in the World Series, was asked by pitching coach Jim Turner to show Ford the ropes, but Ford resisted advice. Lopat told Turner to forget it, and Ford was soon back in Kansas City, the Yankees' top affiliate in the Triple-A American Association.

Ford pitched well at Kansas City, compiling a mark of 6–3, and he was recalled to New York on June 29, 1950. By that time he understood what it took to stay in the major leagues, and he listened to Turner, Lopat, and other Yankees, becoming a serious student of the game. Ford became close friends with Yogi Berra, who was in his fourth full season en route to a 19-year career that carried him to the Hall of Fame in 1972. Berra, the top catcher in baseball in the 1950s, had a knack for outguessing hitters on the best pitch to call, and Ford seldom shook him off. Berra, an oddball character who kept up a line of chatter from behind the mask, made his pitchers better. "He knew what the hitters were looking for," observed Ford. "He made you bear down." Ford and Berra, managed by Casey Stengel, were two of the biggest stars on the talented Yankees championship teams of the decade, ball clubs missing out on pennants only in 1954 to the Indians and 1959 to the White Sox. Their most famous teammate was Mickey Mantle, whom Ford first saw in late 1950 when he was going 9–1 and Mantle was called up from Class C Joplin of the Western Association, where he hit .383 with 26 homers.[19]

Ford's career was interrupted by a two-year stint in the Army, as the Korean War raged from mid–1950 to a stalemate in 1951 to an armistice in 1953. He served at Fort Monmouth, New Jersey, but didn't go overseas. Ford played service basketball or pitched, at first for the post team and shortly thereafter for a softball team, partly to keep in shape. Athletes were commonly given non-combat roles, perhaps as MP or at a desk job, and they were assigned to play their sport and make the service team better. Discharged in November 1952, Ford missed the Yankees' World Series–winning teams of 1951 and 1952.

From 1953, another World Series championship season, through 1960, Ford was the Yankees' ace. Casey Stengel, however, often pitched Whitey every fifth day. Ford, therefore, never experienced a 20-win season before 1961. The closest he came was in 1956, when he fashioned a 19–6 mark, made 30 starts, pitched 18 complete games, and posted a 2.47 ERA. On September 26 he lost his shot at 20 wins by falling to Baltimore, 1–0, thanks in part to Mantle missing Bob Nieman's two-out fly ball in the third, sending Tito Francona, who had singled, from first to third. Ford wild-pitched home the run, but Mantle felt terrible. Waiting in the clubhouse after the game, Mantle dreaded facing his friend. Ford, whose demeanor was calm whether he won or lost, clapped him on the shoulder, saying, "Forget it, Mick. Let's have a beer!"[20]

Ford's best was yet to come. In the 1960 World Series, Stengel chose not to pitch him in the opening game against the Pirates, a decision that meant Ford could not make three starts, if needed. Regardless, the little lefty pitched a pair of shutouts, winning game three, 10–0, and game six, 12–0. Bob Turley hurled 8⅓ innings and won game two, 16–3, with relief help from lefty Bobby Shantz in the ninth, but Pittsburgh won the World Series, Stengel lost his job, and Houk made the decision to pitch Ford every fourth day in 1961. The result: Ford enjoyed the best of his 16 seasons, going 25–4 with major league highs in winning percentage, .862, games started, 39, and innings pitched, 283, with an ERA of 3.21. Further, Luis Arroyo saved 13 of those wins, making Ford and Arroyo the best starter-reliever tandem in the major leagues.

A skilled, clever, and tricky hurler, Ford, a forceful presence on the diamond as well as in the clubhouse, enjoyed outsmarting his opponents, including with illegal pitches. He liked pickoff plays, and he would indicate to the infielder his plan by tossing the resin bag toward first, second, or third base, depending on the runner he wanted to trap. He seemed to plan where his next pitch would be hit, and he moved fielders accordingly. For example, Joe DeMaestri, a shortstop, said Ford would nod for him to move a couple of steps in one direction, and often the batter would hit the next pitch right at him. Also, Ford's curve was different. Ralph Terry, who threw a sizzling fastball and a fast curve, said most curve balls break in the direction of the spin, but Ford's broke down and away from the batter. When hitters looked for his curve, Ford would fire belt-high fastballs, and Yankee Stadium was big enough to keep most long balls in play. As Tony Kubek observed, Ford was a walking clinic with his knowledge of pitching.[21]

While Ford was earning his greatest success, Frank Lary, 31, was also enjoying the best of his 12 seasons. Lary, the talented, determined, down-home righty from the Deep South, produced a 23–9 record, starting 36 games, completing a major league best 22 games, hurling 275⅓ innings, and posting an ERA of 3.24. Lary, the Tigers' ace, won two fewer games than Ford and lost five more, but he didn't have Arroyo saving his bacon.

Ford and Lary had much in common, and each pitched his team to new heights. Ford and the Yankees won 109 games, and Lary and the Tigers won 101, making Detroit the only major league club, besides New York in 1954 (103 wins), to win 100 games and not win the pennant. In the end, the Yankees featured the slugging duo of Maris and Mantle and the pitching duo of Ford and Arroyo, and in the 1961 World Series, New York defeated Cincinnati in five games.

Lary was born and raised with six brothers on the family's 520-acre farm five miles west of Northport, situated across the Black Warrior River from Tuscaloosa and the University of Alabama. A Southern country boy rather than a Northern city slicker, Frank, whose chores included plowing

Frank Lary fueled the Tigers' pennant run in 1961 with his team-best 23-9 record. For the season, Lary won four of his six decisions against New York, the first three by 4-3 scores (author's collection).

and chopping cotton, learned the game from his father. Joe, or "Mitt," was a good semipro ballplayer, a crafty spitball pitcher, and a stern taskmaster who raised his sons to play baseball. Indeed, Mitt created a pitching mound in the front yard where he supervised his sons' pitching and catching lessons. Frank, a star football player in high school who was known far and wide for his punting, chose to play baseball at the state's most famous university. Before the Lary family saga was over, five brothers played baseball for the Crimson Tide, and Al and Ed also lettered in football. Frank, pitching in the College World Series as a sophomore in 1950, the year Whitey Ford debuted with the Yankees, led Alabama to a 9-2 victory over Bradley. But after the Tide lost to Washington State, 9-1, behind tall Gene Conley, later a Boston Celtics and Red Sox star, Lary and his teammates fell to Wisconsin, 3-1.

Once the 'Bama nine was knocked out of the double-elimination tournament, the 5'11", 180-pound right-hander with the sandy-colored hair, ruddy face, and slow drawl chose the Tigers over several other big league teams. At a Birmingham restaurant with Detroit scout Bill Pierre, Lary signed a Tigers contract that included an under-the-table payment hinted to be in five digits. He split the rest of the 1950 season between Detroit's two Class D affiliates, Thomasville, Georgia, of the Georgia-Florida League, and Jamestown, New York, of the PONY League, fashioning a combined 9–2 record.

Lary, like Ford, was drafted into the Army, and he was not sent overseas either. He was stationed at Fort Jackson, South Carolina, for a two-year hitch that involved handling routine base duties and playing service basketball and baseball. Also like Ford, who married his longtime girl friend, Joan Foran, on April 14, 1951, while still in Army, Lary married his hometown sweetheart, Emma Lou Barton, on July 22, 1951. Both pitchers and their wives raised three children, and both men valued spending time with their families.

Lary reported to Tigertown for spring training in 1953, the year Ford returned from the Army to the Yankees. Lary didn't shine as quickly as Ford, but instead spent two seasons pitching Triple-A ball. Without much coaching, the hard-throwing righty compiled a 17–11 record for Buffalo of the International League in 1953. Lary was invited to spring training with Detroit in 1954, but he had trouble getting the ball over the plate. Returning to the Bisons, he worked with catcher Al Lakeman and manager Billy Hitchcock, the ex–Tiger. Adjusting his delivery, Lary pitched well in the season's second half, posting a 15–11 mark, including a no-hitter. Called up to Detroit in September, he worked 3⅔ innings in three games, but earned no decisions.

Unlike Ford, Lary was not pitching for a pennant-winning team, but rather for mediocre Tiger teams from 1954 through 1960. He needed to improve his control and learn how to spot his pitches without losing power. His best pitch was the fastball, but he threw a good overhand curve and, later, a slider. In 1955 manager Bucky Harris said that Lary was often "high and wide" because he tried to throw too hard. Lary's first full big league season was a roller-coaster ride of wins alternated with losses, and he compiled a 14–15 record. He first defeated the Yankees on June 8, 1955, winning 3–1 in a matchup of fastballers, besting Bob Turley. However, Detroit's "bulldog," a comment from Casey Stengel, who found Lary to be an intense, hard-to-beat competitor, lost his next three starts, and so the season went. In 1956 Lary again got off to a slow start. His record was a dismal 4–10 after losing to Kansas City on July 1. At that frustrating low point, he added a knuckler to use as a changeup. Mostly throwing hard stuff, the Alabama native produced a sterling 17–3 mark for the remainder of the season, winning a league-best 21 times, the last eight in a row.[22] The Tigers roared to an AL-best 48–30 record in the second half, but they finished in fifth place at 82–72 overall, 15 games behind the World Series Champion Yankees, who were paced by Mantle's Triple Crown season and Ford's 19–6 ledger.

For the next four seasons Lary, unlike Ford, enjoyed mixed success, and the Tigers, lacking enough first-rate starting pitchers and without a strong bullpen, finished fourth in 1957, fifth in 1958, and fourth in 1959 (when the Yankees fell to third place), and plummeted to sixth in 1960. Lary's records were good, but not great: 11–16 in 1957, 16–15 in 1958, 17–10 in 1959, and 15–15 in 1960. Remarkably, when hurling against the Bronx Bombers before 1961, his ledger was 23–9, a mark that earned him the nickname "Yankee Killer," often causing writers to ask, "How do you beat New York on a regular basis?" The answer was partly psychological: Lary as well as the Yankees *knew* he could beat them. The gritty Southerner needed time and experience to build confidence after he appeared in the Motor City as a rookie in 1954, but within two years the intense competitor developed into one of the league's top hurlers.[23]

"I don't think I was any worse a pitcher when I was losing games the last few years," Lary told Furman Bisher of *Sport* magazine early in the 1961 season, "than I was when I was winning them in 1956." He was throwing the same pitches with the same motion. "I haven't changed my pitching style at all since I added the knuckle-ball." Lary said he threw the knuckler 8–10 times a game. His best pitches were the hard fastball and the overhand curve, and he liked using the knuckler to set up the big curve in a two-strike situation. The little right-hander with the big heart usually bore down more in big games, or in any game with runners in scoring position.

"You get by Mantle and a couple of other good hitters and those other fellows won't hurt you much," Lary claimed. "What I try to do is mix it up on him [Mantle], try to throw him something he's not expecting." Of course, that approach didn't make Lary any different from most American League pitchers, including, for example, the Tigers' Don Mossi, Jim Bunning, Phil Regan, and Terry Fox.[24] Lary, however, was cooler than most in the clutch, and he possessed the uncanny ability to rise to the occasion, a trait that appears in the best of athletes.

Former Tigers catcher Bob "Red" Wilson called Lary a power pitcher, indicating that he had a good two-finger overhand fastball, a good curve, a slider, and occasionally a little sinker, but he wasn't a control pitcher. "If you know you can't cut the corners," Wilson observed, "it makes it a little harder to get the guys out." Wilson had no solid answer about why his teammate often beat the Yankees, except that Lary "probably had a little more drive and a little more interest in beating the best club in the league. That's not to take away from his ability, but maybe the adrenalin wasn't running as well against other teams like it did against the Yankees."[25]

A quiet man with strangers around, Lary was funny around teammates. He and Norm Cash roomed together in 1961, and Cash was a goof-off and a cut-up too. Buddies called Lary a "cotton pickin', gee-tar strummin', red-clay Alabama farm boy," one who liked to mimic others. The Tigers knew him as "Taters," because he once wrote that term on a Pullman dining car menu, rather than potatoes. They called him the "Jonathan Winters" of the dugout, a witty fellow who might roll his pants up to his knees and mimic the bow-legged walk of Casey Stengel, or don a white shirt and white trousers with a Turkish towel around his head to look like the Bengals' longtime trainer, Jack Homel. "He's a droll fellow," remarked Bob Scheffing. But once he stepped on the diamond for a game, the oddball humorist became the Yankee Killer, able to beat them with his arm, his bat (he homered in the ninth inning of his 4–3 victory over New York on May 12, 1961), or his base running (he once beat a throw to second to avoid a double play).

"He's a good fielder and a hell of a competitor," said Scheffing, who, comparing Lary to Ford, pointed out that Ford pitched fewer complete games, received more runs scored, and benefitted from hurling at larger-dimensioned Yankee Stadium. On the other hand, Lary, who had less reliable relief support and usually less run support, pitched mostly in Tiger Stadium, the favorite road ballpark for longball stars such as Mickey Mantle and Ted Williams.[26]

Ford and Lary were seldom matched up by their respective managers, Houk and Scheffing, but they met for the first time in 1961 on Sunday, June 18, and the Yankees won a 9–0 rout, lifting Ford to his fifth straight of eight victories in June. Lary lasted 2⅓ innings and surrendered nine of the Yankees' 15 hits, including home runs by Skowron and Blanchard. But the season and the pennant race were far from over, and Lary was determined to bounce back as the Yankee Killer when the Tigers returned to the Stadium in the Bronx for a holiday twin bill on July 4.

Yankees Win in June

Following their sojourn to the Motor City, where New York lost two out of three to Detroit, the Yankees continued on their 16-game road trip, flying to Kansas City on Sunday evening for a four-game set at Municipal Stadium starting on Monday, June 19. This part of the long trip was special to Maris, because he lived in the suburb of Raytown, and many of his neighbors would be in the stands to watch him. "It is the one time that my wife can be at the ballpark to watch me play," Maris wrote after the season. "I know that when the game is over we can go home, together, and it is a pleasant feeling."[27] Maris the slugger liked Kansas City as his hometown, and Maris the young father loved to spend time with his family and friends.

Rollie Sheldon, the tall right-hander who was less than a year away from pitching for the University of Connecticut, faced Kansas City lefty Jim Archer in a pitching duel, and Archer came away the winner, 4–3. Sheldon, tiring in the ninth, threw a fat pitch to ex–Yankee Norm Siebern, whose ninth homer was an inside-the-park blast to center that tied the contest at 4–4. Houk called for Arroyo, but he surrendered the game-winning home run to pinch-hitter Wes Covington, a left-handed outfielder acquired from the White Sox in a multi-player trade nine days earlier.

Ignoring the loss, the Bronx Bombers won the next three games over Kansas City. On Tuesday Bill Stafford, who liked to throw his heavy sinker, lifted his record to 5–3 by spacing eight hits and winning, 6–2, while Jim Coates, called "Mummy" because of his deadpan expression, pitched hitless ball in the eighth and ninth to earn his third save. Stafford, who left three starts that season with leads that the bullpen didn't hold, tripled home the first run in the second frame, and the Yankees scored three more runs in the third. Maris belted his 26th home run in the fifth, and after Mantle and Howard singled, Skowron doubled home the last two runs. On Wednesday Bud Daley, a junkballer, recorded his fifth win, improving his overall ledger to 5–9 (1–1 with the Yankees), while Arroyo struck out Wes Covington for the game's final out, after catcher Haywood Sullivan touched Daley for a two-run homer. In Thursday's finale, Ford recorded his 12th win, tiring in the eighth and surrendering three straight hits. Arroyo came to the mound and stopped the rally after yielding Sullivan's two-run single. He gave up only one more hit, a single by ex–Yankee Jerry Lumpe in the ninth. Detroit (42–23) topped Washington that afternoon, 6–4, leaving New York (41–24) one game behind. That evening the Yankees took a chartered flight to Minneapolis for three games with the Twins.

Once again the Bombers lost the opener, falling 4–0 on Friday night, June 23, as Camilo Pascual, the Cuban right-hander who delivered his curves with varying speeds, improved his mark to 5–9 with a six-hit shutout. Sore-armed Bob Turley (3–4), perhaps the majors' best at reading and calling the opposing pitchers' pitches, hurled the first seven innings and yielded all four runs on nine hits. Rookie Hal Reniff, a stocky right-hander from Warren, Ohio, making his third appearance, finished the game. Harmon Killebrew led the Twins, going 3-for-4, driving in all four runs, and hitting his 20th homer, a two-run drive to left in the third inning. On Saturday the

Yankees captured a slugfest, 10–7, as Sheldon managed to up his record to 4–2 by lasting 5⅔ innings, Coates gave up two runs, and the stellar Arroyo blanked the Twins the last two innings. Skowron (number 15), Blanchard (number seven), and Howard (number two) hit solo homers, and Berra, Skowron, and Blanchard each drove in two runs. In Sunday's finale, the Yankees won, 8–4, as Stafford earned his sixth victory and Coates recorded the last two outs. Lefty Jack Kralick lost, working 6⅔ innings and yielding eight runs, including Bob Cerv's fifth homer and Ellie Howard's third, a three-run blast in the sixth that gave his club a 5–3 lead.

Boarding a jet for Los Angeles three hours later, the Yankees (43–25) still held second place, 1.5 games behind the Tigers (45–24), after the Bengals split their Sunday twin bill with the Indians.

In the final three-game series of the journey, the Yankees stumbled, losing two out of three to the tailenders at Wrigley Field, a scaled-down version of Chicago's Wrigley Field and frequently a home to Hollywood movies about baseball. On Monday, June 26, the gray-uniformed visitors won, 8–6, behind Ford, now 13–2, who yielded all six runs on six hits, including home runs by little Albie Pearson, his fifth, big Steve Bilko, his eighth, a two-run shot, and hard-hitting Ken Hunt, his 12th. Ex-Tiger Jim Donohue (1–2) took the loss when he walked Maris and Mantle in the top of the ninth, before the slugging Skowron connected for his 16th homer, a long belt to center field off right-hander Art Fowler, the former National Leaguer, that provided the game's final score. Arroyo helped Ford record his eighth victory of June with a scoreless ninth for his 16th save. Still, Daley took a tough 7–6 loss on Tuesday, and Turley fell to ex–Yankee Ryne Duren, 5–3, on Wednesday, leaving New York with a 44–27 mark. The losses left the Yanks 1.5 games behind the Tigers (46–26), who collected 16 hits to top the White Sox, 12–5.

Returning to New York on a late-night transcontinental flight, always an occasion for cards, drinks, pranks, and small talk about baseball, the Yankees worked out at the Stadium on Thursday and hosted the Senators for three games beginning on Friday, June 30. Ford won his 14th game on Friday night. On Saturday afternoon, the Bombers lived up to their nickname, winning a tense 7–6 battle behind yet another display of power, featuring Roger Maris' 28th home run in the ninth. The score was tied in the ninth, 5–5, when Dale Long, the journeyman slugger, socked his 12th home run off Coates. The tall right-hander retired two Senators, but after he allowed singles to ex–Tiger Chuck Cottier and ex–National Leaguer Danny O'Connell, Arroyo ended the inning on a grounder to third. Washington's Dave Sisler, the Senators' top reliever, replaced Joe McClain, and Tony Kubek greeted him with a single. Maris boomed the first pitch high and deep, just inside the foul pole, for a two-run homer and a walk-off victory. Arroyo was the winner, and Maris' homer lifted the ace reliever's mark to 3–3.

On Sunday, behind eight good innings from the rubber-armed Daley, now 6–10, and Arroyo's 17th save, the Yankees whipped the Senators, 13–4, fueled by five tape-measure home runs. Ellie Howard, averaging .355 in his best-ever season, slugged his fourth home run, a two-run clout into the upper deck in left off southpaw Pete Burnside in the second inning. Maris contributed two long homers. In the third, he slugged number 29, and the ball banged fair off the right-field foul pole, halfway to the stadium roof. He didn't move from home plate until the ball landed, making it a three-run homer. Afterward he said, "It was a hot day and I figured the ball was out of the park, no matter if it was fair or foul, so why run?" Maris trotted out his blast in the seventh after number 30 carried into the upper deck in right field. Bob Cerv, not to be outdone by his roommate, slammed a two-run double off the 457-foot-sign in left, a titanic drive that barely missed being a home run. In the eighth Mantle creamed a pitch that Tony Kubek said looked like it might be the first ball to leave Yankee Stadium, but instead, the two-run homer landed two-thirds of the way up in the upper deck in right. Following Howard's single, Skowron capped the Bombers' longball afternoon with his 17th homer. After the game, Ralph Houk sat in his office next to the clubhouse under the stadium, shaking his head and saying, "Did you ever see power like that?"

Writers were talking more about Ruth's single-season record, and after the game, one talked to Maris, who said that he never gave Ruth a thought. Houk wasn't surprised, remarking, "It seems like every hit Roger gets is a home run."[28]

Three victories over the Senators left New York (47–27) in second place, one game behind first-place Detroit (49–27), and Maris and Mantle, the biggest bombers, were in the media spotlight.

Facing the Tigers in the Bronx

Enjoying the league's off-day Monday, the Tigers flew into New York that evening to face the Yankees in a Fourth of July twin bill on Tuesday. Watched by a huge crowd of 74,246, the American League's two best teams split, leaving the standings unchanged. Detroit fell in the opener, 6–2, as Don Mossi, now 9–2, lost for only the second time. Handling the pressure, Frank Lary proved he could do it his way in the nightcap, earning his 12th victory against four losses, thanks to crucial relief help from Hank Aguirre and Terry Fox in a ten-inning, 4–3 thriller.

After several stories in the newspapers about managerial strategy, Scheffing responded to Houk's opening-game choice of his ace lefty, Whitey Ford, by using his best southpaw.[29] Through four innings Don Mossi pitched well, allowing singles to Howard and Skowron in the second, and in the fourth, Kubek's double and an intentional pass to Mantle. In the Tigers' fifth, Dick Brown reached Ford for his 11th home run, a blast to the left field seats.

The roof caved in on Detroit in the Yankees' fifth. Bob Cerv doubled to left center, Colavito mishandled the ball, and Cerv reached third base. Boyer grounded to Chico Fernandez, who booted an easy play, allowing the run to score. Trying to help his cause, Ford bunted, but too hard, and Mossi threw to second for the forceout. Richardson followed with a base

hit to left, and Kubek flied to center for the second out, but Maris singled to center to score the go-ahead run. Mossi passed Mantle on purpose, loading the bases. Howard boomed a triple to deep right, giving the Yankees a 5–1 lead. Foytack replaced Mossi, and Skowron greeted him with an RBI single for a 6–1 margin, but Cerv grounded out. Foytack retired three straight Yankees in the sixth, and Hal Woodeshick pitched two shutout innings, but too late. The Tigers scored the game's final run in the ninth when Colavito reached third on Mantle's error and scored on Boros' groundout to Boyer, but Ford, now 15–2, capped his five-hitter by fanning Wood. The Yankees (48–27) pulled into a virtual tie with the Tigers (49–28), but the afternoon was just beginning.

Scheffing sent forth Lary in the nightcap, and the Tigers' ace earned his stripes again, defeating the Yankees with his head, his heart, and his arm, 4–3. In the third frame, Cash drew a bases-loaded walk off a shaky Bob Turley (he made no more starts in 1961) to give the Bengals an early lead, and Colavito's RBI single in the fifth made it 2–0. In the Yankees'

Elston Howard, who had backed up Yogi Berra since 1955, became the Yankees' starting catcher in 1961 under Ralph Houk. Howard averaged a career-best .348, contributing 21 home runs and 77 RBI to the Yankees' high-powered offense (National Baseball Hall of Fame, Cooperstown, New York).

eighth, Lary threw a couple of pitches that didn't move enough. Kubek lined a fastball for a two-out double to right, and Maris, cracking a curve, homered just over Kaline's glove into the right field seats for a 2–2 tie. Arroyo was already gone, and Sheldon faced the visitors in the ninth. Bo Osborne, pinch-hitting for Mike Roarke, singled to center, and Scheffing sent Fernandez to run for the slower Osborne. Up next, Lary laid down a sacrifice bunt, advancing the runner. Left-handed batting rookie Dick McAuliffe, called up from Denver on June 22,[30] was playing shortstop but averaging .217. McAuliffe popped to short. Houk ordered Kaline walked, setting up a forceout at any base. The strategy failed when Bruton drew a walk, loading the bases. Colavito went to a 1–1 count, and sore-legged Fernandez, the "goat" after his error in the first game, saw Stafford again take a full windup.

A quiet, workmanlike pro who seldom made the headlines, Fernandez redeemed himself by stealing home, sliding head-first to score. Colavito popped out to short, but the Tigers led, 3–2.

The excitement, tension, and anticipation weren't over. In the Yankees' ninth, Lary was tired, and the Yankees reached him for the tying run. Skowron singled off Boros' glove, and Boros and Brown collided on Blanchard's foul popup toward third, giving him a second chance. He singled. Billy Gardner, a versatile infielder obtained from the Twins (for Danny McDevitt) on June 14 and subbing at third, flied out, sending Skowron to third. Batting for Sheldon, Hector Lopez dribbled one past Lary for an infield hit and a 3–3 tie. Lary closed the inning on Richardson's fly to center.

In the top of the tenth, the Bengals' chances looked good when Cash started with a walk, but Steve Boros hit into a forceout at second and Wood flew out to right. Brown, calm and focused, rose to the occasion and lashed a long drive to left that bounced into the stands, giving him a ground-rule double but keeping Boros at third. Lary, facing Stafford, took two strikes. Knowing his teammate at third was alert, Lary dropped a perfect bunt down the third-base line, scoring Boros with the go-

At Yankee Stadium on July 4, 1961, Chico Fernandez, Detroit's veteran shortstop, sparked the Tigers' holiday by stealing home in the ninth inning of the nightcap to help Frank Lary outduel the Yankees, 4–3 (National Baseball Hall of Fame, Cooperstown, New York).

ahead run. In New York's tenth, after Lary yielded a single to Kubek, Scheffing called for Aguirre, the tall southpaw, and Lary, grim-faced, walked off the diamond to a big ovation. Aguirre got Maris on a popup, walked Mantle, and retired Berra on a fly ball. Fox, Detroit's top reliever with a stingy 0.81 ERA, came in from the pen and ended the tension by getting Skowron to fly out.

In the clubhouse later, the Tigers (50–28), exhausted by the two games and preparing to leave on a late-night flight to Boston for three games, celebrated quietly, kidding each other, and talking about the win, the day's unusual highlights, and the Tigers' one-game lead over the Yankees (48–28). "Bob Scheffing got his split with the Yankees Tuesday," concluded Joe Falls, after mingling with players in the clubhouse, "and nearly a case of ulcers to go with it."[31]

Dick Brown homered in the first game and Roger Maris hit number 31 in the second, but power meant less than the pitching of Whitey Ford and Frank Lary and both teams' relievers in this crucial doubleheader at season's traditional halfway point. Maris called Lary "one of the greatest competitors I have ever faced."[32] Still, Maris had 31 home runs, Mickey Mantle had 28, Norm Cash had 24, and Rocky Colavito had 20. Cash was leading the league in batting at .365, with Ellie Howard next at .356.

Fans in New York and Detroit were excited about the dramatic contests, talking up their favorite teams and looking forward to more big games. Indeed, the *Free Press* started a new column the day after the New York–Detroit split, this one written by a staffer calling himself "Winn Pennant." Backed by the resources of Michigan's biggest newspaper, Pennant told the fans his assignment was to "keep the pot boiling for the Tigers and the cheers rolling."[33]

6

The Pennant Race Seesaws in July

Yogi Berra

Regardless of the 1961 pennant race, it turns out that Yogi Berra really didn't say everything he said (he did say that).[1] But it didn't matter, because the Yankees, the fans, and especially the writers loved Yogi for who he was, a down-to-earth, oddball character who was one of the greatest players wearing pinstripes during New York's "dynasty" years of 1949 to 1964.[2] In fact, his career was in transition in 1961. After more than a dozen seasons as the Bronx Bombers' All-Star catcher, Berra, 36, was asked by Ralph Houk to move to left field so that Elston Howard, another great all-around catcher, clutch hitter, and team-oriented personality, could become the regular catcher, not a platoon player, as New York's first black athlete had been since his rookie season of 1955. Houk wanted Howard's defensive prowess and potent bat in the lineup more often, and considering Ellie, as his team-mates called him, batted a career-high .348 in 1961, Houk made the best decision for the team. Berra knew it, and the future Baseball Hall of Famer (inducted in 1972) took his big bat to left field, platooning with right-handed hitting Hector Lopez.[3]

When the Yankees faced the Indians on Wednesday, July 5, after splitting the Fourth of July doubleheader with the Tigers, Lawrence Peter Berra was playing left field. Adults and kids knew him better as Yogi, the childhood nickname hung on him by a buddy who, when they saw an Indian fakir in a movie, thought his friend looked like a "yogi."[4] Berra, penciled into his accustomed fifth slot in the order, was hitting .277, not much below his lifetime average of .285 for 19 seasons. The rest of the July 5 lineup featured Bobby Richardson, the talented second baseman, leading off; Toby Kubek, the All-Star shortstop, batting second; Roger Maris, in right field, third; Mickey Mantle, in center, hitting cleanup; Berra, fifth; John Blanchard, catching and batting sixth; left-handed batting Earl Torgeson, released by the White Sox and signed by the Yankees three weeks earlier, subbing for Bill Skowron at first, and listed seventh; Clete Boyer, the timely-hitting third baseman, eighth; and Rollie Sheldon, pitching and batting ninth.

New York blanked Cleveland twice in the series, once with and once without Berra. Sheldon pitched a shutout, winning, 6–0, Maris went 3-for-4, slamming his 32nd home run in the seventh inning to cap the scoring, and Berra singled in four trips, knocking in a run in the first for a 1–0 lead. Gary Bell, the wise-cracking, fastballing right-hander who posted a 12–16 record in 1961, gave up five runs and eight of the Yankees' nine hits in four innings. Mantle's third-inning single made the score 3–0, while Sheldon, upping his ledger to 5–2, hurled a four-hitter.

On Thursday the Tribe fell, 4–0, as right-hander Bill Stafford improved to 7–4 with a two-hit shutout, and Berra rode on the bench. Howard caught and batted fifth in place of Berra. Skowron, back at first base and batting sixth, doubled in two at-bats. Bob Cerv, the Yankees slugger from rural Nebraska who had served time in Kansas City and expansion Los Angeles before returning to New York in a multi-player trade on May 8, 1961, batted seventh, but went 0-for-4. Howard provided the firepower with two solo home runs, his fifth and sixth of the year.

Berra wasn't needed as the Yankees improved their record to 50–28, leaving them half a game behind the Tigers. Detroit split a doubleheader with the Red Sox at Fenway Park on Wednesday, with Jim Bunning winning the opener and Bob Bruce taking the loss in the nightcap, but on Thursday

the Bengals won behind Phil Regan, aided by Terry Fox's seventh save. Winning two out of three in Boston left Detroit with a 52–29 record and a half-game lead on New York, at 50–28.

Berra, born on May 12, 1925, was the youngest of four sons of a working class family living in St. Louis. His father, Pietro, emigrated from a small town in Italy south of Milan, arriving in New York in 1909 and in St. Louis a short time later. After three years, by

Yogi Berra, the longtime Yankees catcher, answered Ralph Houk's request by playing mainly left field in 1961. Smiling in this picture, Berra proved he was still a clutch hitter by delivering 22 home runs and 61 RBI (National Baseball Hall of Fame, Cooperstown, New York).

prior arrangement, Berra brought over his betrothed, Paulina. The couple was soon married, and they settled in a St. Louis district derisively called "Dago Hill," made up of working class, Italian-American families. On the other side of Elizabeth Avenue, the Garagiola family raised a son named Joe, a close friend of "Lawdie," as the youngest Berra was called. Berra and Garagiola both played major league baseball, with Joe, also a catcher, later earning fame as a broadcaster. Like many young boys, they loved the national pastime. Berra and Garagiola were friends with contrasting appearances: Joe, six feet tall, athletic, and handsome, looked like an athlete, but Yogi, who grew to be 5'7" and 185 pounds, looked awkward, and his features included big ears, a broad nose, and a squat body. As a rookie in 1947, teammates teased the self-conscious Berra about his homely looks. Manager Bucky Harris even called him "Nature Boy" and "the Ape."

Despite the flak, Berra had learned the game well. In 1939 and 1940 the Gotham American Legion Post reached the playoffs, and Garagiola and Berra were the stars. Still, Berra worked, and his brother Tony contributed extra money to the family so their father would allow Yogi to keep playing baseball. After a tryout, the St. Louis Cardinals offered minor league contracts to the two friends, but Garagiola, who looked better in the workout, signed for a $500 bonus, while Berra was offered just a contract. Thanks to Legion coach Leo Browne writing to his old friend and the Yankees' general manager, George Weiss, the offer, including a bonus, was made. The 18-year-old Berra, with his quick reflexes, a strong arm, and fast feet, began his pro career with Norfolk of the Class B Piedmont League. Berra banked the $500 bonus, started the year earning $90 a month, and had a .253 batting average for the 1943 season. The Yankees never spent $500 better.

By the time spring training began in 1961, Berra's baseball odyssey had covered a light year in distance and time from his boyhood days in St. Louis. After the 1943 season, the young athlete enlisted in the Navy, later serving as machine gunner on a rocket boat launched from the USS *Bayfield*, an attack transport. While many big leaguers helped improve their service baseball squads, Berra learned gunnery, served off the coast of Normandy on D–Day, and finished his Navy duties at the submarine base in Groton, Connecticut. Returning to baseball in 1946, the year after World War II ended, Berra played for Triple-A Newark of the International League, where he averaged .314, hit 15 home runs, contributed 59 RBI, and displayed an erratic arm. Still, he made it to the Yankees in September, averaging .364 in seven games. In spring training of 1947, when he looked too awkward for the outfield, he was used behind the plate, where his skills worked better and his hitting gave New York a modest, unassuming, friendly rookie with power. Over the years, with the game on the line, pitchers preferred to face Mantle, not Berra.

Later, the St. Louis native received a great deal of help from former Yankee and Hall of Fame catcher Bill Dickey, hired by Casey Stengel when he took over as New York's manager in 1949. Stengel worked to boost Berra's confidence, and Dickey worked with him on the finer points of catching, including moving closer to the plate, stepping over the plate with his left foot when throwing to second, blocking pitches in the dirt, and using hard-to-steal signals. Stengel, who respected Berra's work ethic, sincerity, and heads-up style, liked his receiver and depended on him to handle the pitchers. In less than a season, Berra became one of the Yankees' brightest stars, dependable, if often comical. After being asked to do so, Bobby Brown, medical student, third baseman, and Berra's roommate, wrote a short speech for him to use in St. Louis on "Yogi Berra Day" in 1947. Instead of saying, "I want to thank everyone for making this day possible," the Yankees' catcher said, "I want to thank everyone for making this day *necessary*."[5] Indeed, he uttered so many incongruous phrases over the years that he became a baseball icon.

Away from the ballpark, Berra was a movie buff who liked the Marx brothers and Westerns. An avid reader of comic books, he had a knack for getting along with people ranging from star athletes to big-name writers to bellhops, cab drivers, and the man in the street. The many-time All-Star, who had a voracious appetite, crude table manners, and a hatred of being teased, gradually earned the respect and affection of most that met him or saw him in action. Teammates sometimes teased him about his fondness for comics, but Berra once replied, "Yeah, but I notice when I put them down, there's always guys around ready to pick them up."

By no coincidence did Berra's career span the Yankees' dynasty years. Berra won American League MVP honors for the 1951, 1954, and 1955 seasons, and he ranked fourth in MVP voting for 1952 and second in 1953 and 1956. Starting in 1950, he led the Yankees in RBI six years in a row. His 358 career home runs, with 305 hit when he was playing behind the plate, easily topped the total of any other catcher when he retired after the 1963 season. Whatever his lack of sophistication, Berra ranked with highest-paid Yankees by 1957, earning $65,000 in salary, not counting endorsements. Before his career ended, he was living with his beautiful wife Carmen and their family in a palatial home in New Jersey with a swimming pool. Casey Stengel once said, "Berra's house is so big your kid'll get lost in the backyard if you don't watch him."[6]

In 1961, when he was playing mainly left field, Berra ran well and made plays. "In the outfield," Tony Kubek recalled, "Yogi wasn't pretty, but he had an accurate arm and he got to more balls than you'd imagine." Catlike in his reflexes and blessed with great baseball instincts, Berra usually made the right play. "He was a great clutch hitter and a smart catcher," according to Kubek. "Basically, Yogi played like a guy who had great insight into the game."[7]

"For the 1961 Yankees," wrote biographer Allen Barra, "Yogi was a combination of mascot, good luck charm, and a walking piece of team history—one still capable of hitting a ball into the right-field stands in the late innings of a close game."[8] Berra was the old pro that Ralph Houk could use in left or behind the plate when he needed a clutch player in an important game.

Heading for the All-Star Break

After defeating the Indians twice on July 5–6, the Yankees hosted the Red Sox for single games on Friday and Saturday and a doubleheader on Sunday. The Bombers, behind Bud Daley, Whitey Ford, and Rollie Sheldon, won the first three games, losing Sunday's nightcap, 9–6, when the Bosox knocked around starter Ralph Terry, who suffered his first loss after five victories, and right-handed relievers Jim Coates and Tex Clevenger for all nine runs in the first six innings.

In the opener on Friday evening, the Bombers dumped their archrivals, 14–3, behind the effective hurling of Daley, who spaced eight hits using his sharp control and his assortment of breaking balls, and a 16-hit barrage that featured three safe blows by Richardson and two each by Mantle, Skowron, and Howard, whose three-run homer in the eighth which gave them a 14–3 lead. Maris laced a two-run single to cap the six-run second inning, and brought home another run with a grounder in the fourth that gave his club a 7–0 lead.

On Saturday, Ford yielded five runs on ten hits in six-plus frames, but he improved to 16–2 when Arroyo pitched shutout ball the rest of the way. The Yankees won, 8–5, launching four solo homers: Blanchard's ninth, Mantle's 29th, Kubek's fifth, and Skowron's 18th.

In Sunday's twin bill, the Yankees won the lid-lifter, 3–0. The first run came via second-inning doubles by Berra, playing left, and Howard, catching, and in the fifth, Berra's force play at second scored Maris, who had walked and took third when Mantle singled. Maris sealed the victory with his 33rd homer in the seventh. The blast came in New York's 81st game, placing him 14 games ahead of Ruth's 60-homer pace in 1927.

In the nightcap, Boston won, 9–6, behind the combined ten-hitter by Don Schwall (7–2), a 6'6" right-hander, once a star basketballer at the University of Oklahoma who threw a good sinking fastball, and southpaw Arnold Earley, who recorded his first save. The Red Sox racked up 13 hits off Terry, Coates, and Clevenger. Rookie Carl Yastrzemski, en route to a .266 season and a Hall of Fame career (inducted in 1989), went 4-for-5, and Jackie Jensen, Gary Geiger, and Pete Runnels each had two hits. Afterward, six Yankees got their gear together for the All-Star game.

The Tigers, after beating the Red Sox two of three on July 5–6, flew home to host the Angels for a four-game series. For Friday night's game, Bob Scheffing picked Hal Woodeshick to start, but the 6'3" lefty had nothing. Albie Pearson, at 5'5" the smallest outfielder in the majors, led off with a single, Joe Koppe, the ex–National Leaguer from Detroit, rapped a base hit, and muscular Ken Hunt, one of five Angels to hit 20 or more homers in the club's inaugural season, laced an RBI single for a 1–0 lead. After Woodeshick walked Steve Bilko to load the bases, Scheffing called on Paul Foytack. The veteran righty got George Thomas, purchased from the Bengals by the Angels 12 days earlier to line into a double play, and struck out Earl Averill, who hit 21 of his lifetime 44 homers in 1961. In the Tigers' first, Bruton led off with a single (Wood was dropped to seventh in the order), Dick McAuliffe, a left-handed batter who held his right wrist under his chin and his bat high, bounced into a force at second, and Kaline homered, his tenth, for a 2–1 lead. Billy Moran hit an RBI single to tie the game in the Angels' fourth. Facing Terry Fox in the eighth, Bilko smashed his 11th home run, and in the ninth, Averill capped the 4–2 win with his 13th homer, dropping Fox's mark to 3–1.

Fred Gladding made eight relief appearances for Detroit in 1961, all in July and August. Gladding won his only game of the season over the Angels on July 8, when he pitched a scoreless eighth inning, after which Steve Boros singled home the winning run (author's collection).

Against the Angels in a single game on Saturday and a double-header on Sunday, the Tigers won all three contests, two by one-run margins, to hang onto first place. Don Mossi pitched seven solid innings on Saturday, yielding five hits and two runs, but he departed with the score tied at 2–2. Rookie Fred Gladding, the 6'1", 220-pound fast-baller making his third appearance after being called up from Denver, pitched a scoreless eighth and won, 3–2, thanks to a two-out RBI single by Steve Boros in the Tigers' eighth and relief help in the ninth by Terry Fox (first out) and Hank Aguirre (last two outs). In Sunday's first game, Frank Lary won a brilliant three-hitter, 1–0. In the second inning, Norm Cash walked, and Boros was hit in the head by a fastball from Eli Grba, the first man picked by LA in the expansion draft. Boros was out for six days, Ozzie Virgil took his place, and Grba fanned Wood. Mike Roarke, catching due to the twin bill, singled to center for the game's only run. In the nightcap the Bengals won, 6–3, behind Jim Bunning's 8⅓ solid innings and Aguirre's seventh save. In the first inning, Rocky Colavito drew a bases-loaded walk, Cash grounded into a double play that allowed Bruton, who singled, to score, and Larry Osborne, filling in at third base, singled for a 3–0 lead After Bruton's two-run homer, his eighth, made the lead 5–2 in the sixth, Kaline walked and Colavito doubled home the Tigers' final run.

Detroit, with a 55–30 record, moved into the All-Star break holding a half-game lead on second-place New York, with a 53–29 ledger. Baltimore, at 48–37, occupied third place, seven games back, and fourth-place Cleveland (47–39) was 8.5 games behind. The White Sox held fifth place, 13.5 games below Detroit with a losing mark of 42–44, and Boston (40–45) was sixth, 15 games off the Bengals' pace. The American League had a two-team pennant race.

The First All-Star Game

The baseball All-Star Game dates to 1933, when Arch Ward, sports editor of the *Chicago Tribune*, advocated a "Game of the Century" between stars of the American and National Leagues. The first contest was held on July 6, 1933, at Comiskey Park, home of the White Sox. The game was designed to promote Chicago's Century of Progress Exposition, but Ward also wanted to promote baseball during the Great Depression. The event was so popular, drawing an attendance of 47,595, that it was staged again in 1934, at the Polo Grounds in New York, home of the NL's Giants. By the end of the decade, the "midsummer classic" was a baseball tradition.[9]

The first game featured American League favorites such as Babe Ruth, Lou Gehrig, and pitcher Lefty Gomez, all of the Yankees, shortstop Joe Cronin of the Washington Nationals, catcher Rick Ferrell of the Red Sox, and second baseman Charlie Gehringer of the Tigers. The National League's heroes included first baseman Bill Terry of the Giants, third baseman Pepper Martin, second baseman Frankie Frisch, and pitcher Bill Hallahan, all of the St. Louis Cardinals, and outfielder Chuck Klein and shortstop Dick Bartell of the Philadelphia Phillies. The superstar among these greats was Ruth, bulky and slow at age 39. Ruth fanned twice, but the famed showman thrilled the crowd with a two-run homer in the third inning to help the AL win, 4–2.

The interleague exhibition was held every year after 1933, except for 1945, when the game set for Boston's Fenway Park was cancelled due to wartime travel restrictions. The format of the game changed over the years from the original idea of the managers, both of whom piloted the previous year's pennant winners (except in 1933), selecting all of the players, and with each team having at least one player named. Starting in 1947, the fans voted on the eight position players, usually on ballots printed in local newspapers, and the managers chose the pitchers and reserves. That system worked well until a Cincinnati radio station promoted a ballot-stuffing plan to help the Reds in 1956 and 1957. Starting in 1958, the players, managers, and coaches made the choices until 1969. Beginning in 1970, fans again chose the starting lineups. In 1959 baseball decided to play two All-Star games to raise more money for the players' pension fund, for "old-timers" who played before the pension fund was created in 1947, and for youth baseball. The second game was dropped after the 1962 season, due to scheduling and other problems.

In 1961 the first All-Star exhibition was set for Tuesday, July 11, at San Francisco's Candlestick Park, where winds off the Pacific Ocean could be cold and tricky in the summer, and the second All-Star event was scheduled for Boston's Fenway Park on Monday, July 31. Hardly a surprise given the pennant race, the Yankees, with six players, and the Tigers, with five, dominated the American League All-Stars. The starting lineup featured ex–Red Johnny Temple, of Cleveland, second base; Norm Cash, Detroit, first base; Mickey Mantle, New York, center field; Roger Maris, New York, right field; Rocky Colavito, Detroit, left field; Tony Kubek, New York, shortstop; Johnny Romano, Cleveland, catcher; Brooks Robinson, Baltimore, third base; and Whitey Ford, New York, pitcher. For reserves the Yankees had Yogi Berra, listed as outfielder and catcher, and Elston Howard at catcher. The Tigers' reserves were Frank Lary, Jim Bunning, and Al Kaline. Interestingly enough, *The Sporting News* polled 20 contributing correspondents from major league cities. Cash led the AL voting with 235 of a possible 293 votes. On the other hand, Yogi Berra did not receive a single vote from the writers, while Stan Musial, the aging Cardinals great, received just one vote, though both longtime stars were chosen as reserves.[10]

The National League, managed by Pittsburgh's Danny Murtaugh, fielded a star-studded lineup including Dodgers speedster Maury Wills, shortstop; Braves slugger Eddie Mathews, third base; two Giants, the great Willie Mays in center field and slugging Orlando Cepeda in left; the Pirates' sensational Roberto Clemente, right field; the Cardinals' good-hitting Bill White, first base; the Braves' steady Frank Bolling, the ex–Tiger, at second base; and the Pirates' stellar Smokey Burgess as catcher. Braves ace southpaw Warren Spahn was pitching.

The AL All-Stars, managed by Baltimore's Paul Richards (Stengel of New York's 1960 pennant winners was out of baseball, and nobody asked Houk), lost in swirling winds to the NL's standout team in ten innings, 5–4. Mantle went hitless in three at-bats, and he was replaced in center by Kaline in the seventh. Maris singled in four official at-bats and he walked in the seventh, but the Giants' Mike McCormick retired the side. Cash, who had a sore foot (it was infected), doubled to right center in the ninth for his only hit, Chicago's Nellie Fox ran for him, and Kaline singled home the run. Colavito, hitless in four at-bats, reached on a grounder to third that the Cardinals' Ken Boyer threw away, and Kaline scored for a 3–3 tie. Ford pitched three innings, giving up one run on Clemente's second-inning triple and White's sacrifice fly. Lary replaced Ford in the fourth. After Mays was safe on Kubek's error, Paul Richards called for the Senators' sinker-balling Dick Donovan, but the NL took a 2–0 lead on Clemente's sacrifice fly.

The excitement continued. The AL got one run back on Harmon Killebrew's homer in the sixth, Bunning retired six straight batters in the sixth and seventh frames, but the Cubs' George Altman, batting for the pitcher, homered in the eighth for a 3–1 lead. In the ninth, the AL tied it by scoring twice, on Kaline's RBI single and on Ken Boyer's error on Colavito's grounder. In the NL's ninth, Berra moved behind the plate, the O's Jim Gentile took over at first, and Chicago's Nellie Fox played second, and the Orioles' Hoyt Wilhelm dazzled the NL stars with scoreless hurling. With two outs and Ken Boyer on via a walk, Richards subbed Elston Howard for Berra to handle Wilhelm's knucklers better.

In the climactic tenth, the AL scored once for a 4–3 lead on Nellie Fox's walk and Boyer's three-base throwing error on Kaline's grounder. In the NL's tenth, the Braves' Hank Aaron singled off Wilhelm, moved to second on Howard's passed ball, and tied the game when Willie Mays doubled to left field. Wilhelm, whose control was off, hit the Reds' Frank Robinson with a pitch, and Roberto Clemente singled to clinch victory for the National League.

Most players took the All-Star Game seriously, but by 1961, interest was waning. Still, the majority of big leaguers were honored by the recognition, especially with players, coaches, and managers picking the teams. Certainly Al Kaline felt that way, calling his first All-Star Game in 1955, when he played alongside Mantle and Williams in the outfield, one of his biggest thrills.[11] Norm Cash, making his first All-Star appearance, also considered it an honor.[12]

The players who didn't participate in the All-Star game had a three-day mid-summer vacation. In Michigan, July was a great time to go "Up North" to a lake. "When we got to the All-Star break," recalled Terry Fox, "not many of our players were usually picked for the All-Star team, so we'd go up to Houghton Lake, which is in the middle of Michigan. We'd be invited up there for two nights. We'd get in one night after the last game, and we'd spend the next day and another day, and we'd go home to Detroit. All the ballplayers were invited, so we got to associate more with family and everything."[13]

No Place Like Home

Before the All-Star game, Maris and his chatty roommate, Bob Cerv, were becoming inundated with autograph requests, both at the hotel and at any restaurant where they ate. Hating the "fishbowl" existence, Maris made a key decision. Cerv was his neighbor in Raytown, Missouri, and Cerv's family also stayed at home for the season. They had a friend, Julie Isaacson, who rented an apartment for them in the Queens, and the two moved there. Mantle's family lived in Dallas, and after Mantle was invited by Maris to join them, the three Yankees stars shared the one-bedroom apartment (Mantle later moved back to the Hotel St. Moritz). Mantle and Cerv had single beds in the bedroom, and Maris slept on a studio couch in the living room. Sharing $251 a month in rent, the three buddies spent free time watching TV, listening to records, and talking baseball. Nobody bothered them. With an unlisted address and phone number, they escaped the growing pressures of the pennant race, the home run derby, and the fans. When it was time to go to the ballpark, they rode together in Maris' new Oldsmobile convertible.[14]

Actually, the majority of big leaguers maintained homes away from their team's city, and a sizeable number of players preferred to keep their families at home. Frank Lary, Jim Bunning, and Billy Bruton were three Tigers whose families remained at home. Their homes were, for Lary, in Northport, Alabama; for Bunning, in Fort Thomas, Kentucky; and for Bruton, in Milwaukee. Steve Boros wasn't married, but stayed with his family in Flint.[15] Norm Cash and his wife Myrta lived with her family in Justiceburg, Texas, in the off-season, but they rented in Nankin Township (which today is Westland), 16 miles west of Detroit and an easy half-hour drive to Tiger Stadium. Charlie Maxwell rented a house for his family, Ann and the four children, in suburban Detroit, but the Maxwells maintained their home in Paw Paw, Michigan, where they had lived since 1950. By 1961 Al Kaline owned a house in Birmingham, northwest of Detroit, where his family lived year-round, but Kaline was the Tigers' biggest star and not likely to be traded.

Most of the married players rented an apartment for their family or lived alone by the week in a hotel not far from the ballpark, which was the case with, at first, Roger Maris, Tony Kubek, Bob Cerv, Bo Osborne, Jake Wood, and Bubba Morton. Indeed, players new to a team or who were not regulars usually rented. Mike Roarke and his wife Merry Sue rented near Grosse Pointe on the northeast side of Detroit in 1961, but in the off-season they lived in their home in West Warwick, Rhode Island. "When Mike was playing," Merry Sue said in 2013, "if you bought a home in the town you played in, you were traded or released shortly after that, so we never bought a house in those towns where you played."[16]

Off to the Races

There were two intense races after the San Francisco All-Star Game: the Tigers and the Yankees continued a seesaw battle for the pennant, and Maris and Mantle kept up the competition to break Ruth's homer record. It was the home run duel that fascinated most writers and fans.

The Yankees launched a ten-day, 11-game road trip, flying to Chicago to meet the fifth-place White Sox, and they won a night tilt on Thursday, July 13. In the first inning against future Hall of Famer Early Wynn, the 41-year-old ex–Indians' stalwart, Maris, with Richardson aboard, hit a two-run homer to deep right, number 34. Mantle followed with a longer blast to right, his 30th homer and the 350th of his storied career. The Yankees' 6–2 victory marked the second time Maris and Mantle hit back-to-back homers in 1961. Yogi Berra recalled that it may have been the first time he made his classic remark, "It's déjà vu all over again." Maris hit 16 home runs from June 10 to July 13, during which time he produced 37 RBI and a .368 batting mark. The slugger was currently batting .288, but he was worried about suffering one of his late-season slumps.

On Friday, Chicago's fireballing Juan Pizarro, the Puerto Rican lefty obtained in an off-season trade with Cincinnati, handcuffed the Yankees on seven hits for a 6–1 victory, though he surrendered Mantle's 31st homer. Rollie Sheldon, who gave up all six Chicago runs on nine hits in his 5⅓ innings, saw his record fall to 6–3. On Saturday the Yankees rallied to win, 9–8, in ten innings, with a huge boost from Maris, first, for throwing out Luis Aparicio trying to score from third base on a fly ball in the eighth inning, and second, in the ninth, his RBI double tied the game at 8–8. In the tenth, the Yankees won on Tony Kubek's RBI single. Arroyo, the fifth Yankees hurler, worked the last two innings and improved his ledger to 4–3. New York got homers from Howard (his eighth), a tape-measure shot off the left field roof at Comiskey, Maris (his 35th), and Cerv (his seventh). More important, Friday's win lifted the Yankees .003 percentage points above the Tigers, and Saturday's triumph gave the Bombers a 55–30 record, keeping them above the Bengals (56–31), who stopped the Twins, 2–1, behind Jim Bunning's four-hitter.

Flying back to Baltimore for what players of the era called the "Eastern swing," New York won twice, beating Baltimore on Sunday, July 16, and in what became a single game on Monday, as the second half of a twi-night doubleheader was rained out. On Sunday, Bud Daley won his eighth game of the season (he finished 4–8 for Kansas City and 8–9 for New York in 1961) with a four-hitter, outdueling hotshot south-paw Steve Barber, 2–1. The Yankees scored on Mantle's 32nd home run, a solo shot to center in the fourth, and in the ninth, his RBI double, scoring Kubek, who had doubled. In Monday's opener, the reliable Ford hurled another complete game (he recorded 11 in a major league-high 39 starts in 1961), blanking the Birds on six hits, 5–0. Mantle clouted his 33rd home run and Skowron added his 19th, both off right-hander Milt Pappas, another of Baltimore's "Kiddie Corps" pitchers. In Monday's nightcap, both Maris and Mantle homered, but a storm wiped out the game before it was official. As a result, both lost a home run, and in Maris' case, the four-bagger would have allowed him to tie Ruth in 154 games. Afterward, Maris joked about the "lost homer" with writers, but few believed he and Mantle were more interested in winning the pennant than in their home run "race."[17]

Bud Daley, obtained from Kansas City on June 14, 1961, posted an 11–17 record for the season. Daley, however, went 8–9 for New York, and the Yankees won the pennant by eight games over the Tigers (National Baseball Hall of Fame, Cooperstown, New York).

Traveling 30 miles to Washington, the Yankees dropped two out of three to the expansion Senators, and Maris, frustrated, went hitless in the series. His slump grew to 0-for-19 and his average dipped to .272. At Griffith Stadium on Tuesday, July 18, the Yankees won when Sheldon yielded three runs in six innings, but Arroyo (5–3) threw three innings of one-hit ball to earn the 5–3 victory. Mantle launched a two-run homer in the first inning, his 34th, tying Maris, and Senators catcher Gene Green knotted the score in the second with his 12th homer, another two-run belt. Gene Woodling put the Senators ahead in the sixth with an RBI double, and one inning later, Hector Lopez, batting for Sheldon, tied it with a sacrifice fly. Mantle broke the tie in the eighth with his 35th homer, Richardson singled home a run in the ninth, and Arroyo sealed the win.

In Wednesday's doubleheader the Yankees fell twice by scores of 8–4 and 12–2. Daley, now 8–11, lost the opener, yielding five runs on seven hits in five-plus innings. In the nightcap, rookie Al Downing, 20, a quiet southpaw making his big league debut, displayed his blazing fastball, but he got wild and surrendered five runs in the second inning. Rookie Hal Reniff, also shaky, gave up six runs on five hits in 2⅓ innings. Washington's Dick Donovan spaced nine hits for his sixth victory, Mantle hit four-bagger number 36, a bases-empty blow, and Maris went 0-for-4.

After a needed day off on Thursday, the Yankees ended the road trip by meeting the Red Sox at Fenway Park in another three-game set, winning the first two but losing on Sunday, July 23. On the Sabbath, Elston Howard gave the Yankees a 4–3 lead in the ninth inning with his ninth homer, a two-run wallop, but Daley, tiring, surrendered two runs, the game-winner scoring on Gary Geiger's single.

On Friday and Saturday the Yankees won a pair of slugfests, and Arroyo recorded both victories. On Friday night Ford lasted 4⅔ innings, Jim Coates pitched through the seventh, and Arroyo upped his mark to 6–3, allowing an unearned run in the last two frames. The Red Sox failed to homer, but Maris and Mantle homered back-to-back

Right-hander Rollie Sheldon didn't win against the Washington Senators on July 18, but the "Rookie from Class D" helped the Yankees by finishing with an 11–5 record in 1961 (National Baseball Hall of Fame, Cooperstown, New York).

for the third time in 1961. Maris slammed number 36, a bases-empty blast into the Red Sox bullpen in the first inning, and Mantle followed suit with number 37 for a 2–0 lead. The Bombers pounded Bill Monbouquette and two relievers for 13 hits and won, 11–8, including Berra's 12th homer, a two-run shot, and Blanchard's tenth homer, a pinch-hit, game-winning grand slam in the ninth. On Saturday the Yankees won, 11–9, but the chunky Arroyo blew a save by allowing two runs in the eighth inning for a 9–8 deficit. Still, he won when the Yankees scored three runs in the ninth, thanks to Blanchard's pinch-hit homer, his own double, Richardson's RBI single, and Kubek's RBI double.

New York's sojourn ended with the loss at Boston on July 23, but Detroit, after winning twice at Kansas City, took over first place with a 62–34 record, half a game ahead of New York's 60–33 ledger.

Home Runs, the Asterisk, and the "Chipmunks"

Before the trip ended, Maris and Mantle were confronted by a new aspect of chasing Babe Ruth's record, the so-called asterisk. Ford Frick, a graduate of Indiana's DePauw University in 1916, worked as a sportswriter, and he covered the Yankees for the Hearst newspapers from 1923 until he was selected as National League President in 1934. Voted in as baseball commissioner in 1951, he served two seven-year terms and retired in 1965. Frick was a personal friend of Ruth in the Roaring Twenties, and he believed Ruth's record should be protected. When the American League expanded its schedule to 162 games in 1961, nobody could predict the home run circus that would follow. On July 17, after speaking with several longtime writers, Frick held a press conference and recommended a "distinctive mark" be placed next to a new single-season homer record, if the old mark of 60 was broken in more than 154 games.[18]

As Maris biographers Tom Clavin and Danny Peary pointed out, Maris and Mantle were challenging Ruth's mark in a new era, including a new President, John F. Kennedy, a new Yankees manager, Ralph Houk, new baseball teams in the Angels and the Senators, a new age of televised journalism covering politics, news, entertainment, and sports, and Frick was "stuck in the past." In effect, the commissioner's statement to reporters meant that pretenders to Ruth's hallowed place in baseball history, especially Maris, not a lifelong Yankee (neither was Ruth), had to prove themselves worthy.[19] Frick had stated his opinion, but he had no authority to change record books. Writer Dick Young had asked about an "asterisk" during Frick's press get-together. In fact, no such change was made, but the myth of the asterisk persists today.[20]

Regardless, Maris had his critics, and their numbers seemed to increase by the week. The story is not new, but he faced repeated and similar questions in the clubhouse daily, particularly after the All-Star Game as home runs continued to fly out of ballparks. The supposed asterisk might as well have been well added to official records, because Frick's question kept being asked, "Are you going to break the record in 154 games?" Over the course of the summer, the sensitive Maris gradually lost his patience, his temper, some of his hair, much of his sense of humor, and almost all of his tolerance for fools bearing pens and clubhouse credentials. Maris, who enjoyed kidding with writers, as most ballplayers like to do, especially in the flush of victory, began to harden his views by the time the Yankees met the Tigers on July 4. The slugger wrote in his 1962 memoir, "I never knew when something I would say as a gag would get into the papers as if I meant it."[21]

As part of the new style in sports journalism, Clavin and Peary identified the gaggle of irreverent New York writers who went after Maris professionally and personally, almost as if hammering him with slanted words or partly-true stories was the sacred duty of sportswriters. The established system of reporting on baseball, or any other sport, glorified the deeds of ballplayers as well as the players themselves, and in New York, that meant worshiping at the Yankees' shrine. Writers like Dan Daniel of the *World-Telegram*, Red Smith of the *Herald Tribune* or Til Ferdenzi of the *Journal-American* occasionally made up quotations for stories—and most baseball scribes did the same. Writers did not, however, rip the players, or reveal secrets about their private lives.

Most people know the conversation of ballplayers is peppered with expletives, but writers "clean up" the language. Athletes, after all, are role models. Maybe that means honesty is prudently applied. The newer breed of writers, including George Vecsey and Stan Isaacs of *Newsday*, Maury Allen and Leonard Shecter, who had reported longer, of the *New York Post*, Phil Pepe of the *World-Telegram & Sun*, and Larry Merchant of the *Philadelphia Daily News* liked revealing the personal lives of players, especially Mantle and Maris, private guys who disliked their personal lives being invaded. Even so, matters concerning sex remained taboo. "We were irreverent," Isaacs said, "but we prided ourselves on honest, solid journalism."

Two writers, Jimmy Cannon, a friend of Hemingway, a lover of muscular prose, and a columnist for the *Journal-American*, and caustic Dick Young, of the *New York Daily News*, called them "Chipmunks," partly because they never stopped chattering. As the season moved into July, private lives of players were targeted by the younger writers, including many around the nation who imitated the Chipmunks' style, but lacked their talent. Some newer writers didn't, or couldn't, distinguish between cynicism and cruelty, or between articles written after an interview and stories based on gossip.[22] Writers in the new era of sports journalism loved going after the lives and idiosyncrasies of famous athletes like Mantle and Maris, because such stories sold more papers, accorded the writers more status, and, presumably, let readers see "real" baseball.

Bobby Richardson and Jake Wood

Robert Clinton Richardson, Junior, known to friends and teammates as Bobby, was a polished second baseman, a rookie in 1955, a "good-field, no-hit" infielder in 1957 and 1958, and a major contributor to the Yankees from 1959 to 1966. Jacob Wood, dubbed "Jake" as a kid playing sandlot ball, was a rookie at second base for the Tigers in 1961. While his baseball career also lasted until 1967, Wood never gained the iconic stature of Richardson.

"I've always said that the heart of the 1961 [Yankees] team was Bobby Richardson and Whitey Ford," recounted Tony Kubek. "Those were the guys you counted on, the guys who never were down if they had a bad day and who never pointed a finger. Bobby could go oh for a week and you'd never know it."[23]

Born on August 19, 1935, in Sumter, South Carolina, Richardson grew up in a Baptist family between older sister Inez and younger sister Willie Ann. His father was part owner and manager of the Richardson Marble and Granite Works in Sumter, and his mother was a homemaker. Bobby

grew up playing baseball with the influence of an older neighbor, Bobby Stokes, and his Edmunds High School and American Legion baseball coach, "Hutch" Hutchinson. Richardson, who testified that he accepted God at age 14, starred on the American Legion squad that won the state title in 1952. After graduating on June 12, 1953, he signed with the Yankees, who had scouted his progress. His minor league career was quite impressive at Class D Olean, New York, of the PONY

Bobby Richardson, the Yankees' standout second baseman, played 162 games in 1961, averaged .261, and helped anchor the best defensive infield in the American League (National Baseball Hall of Fame, Cooperstown, New York).

League in 1953, Class A Binghamton in 1954, and Triple-A Denver for most of 1955 and in 1956, following five games with New York in April and early May.

At age 19 in 1955, Richardson was called up by the Yankees after Gil McDougald was injured by a line drive, and he finished the season with New York. In his debut game against the Tigers on August 5, he drew a walk off Jim Bunning in the fourth inning and stole second. Mantle walked, and Berra, in the limelight of his career, slugged his 19th homer of the season to give the Yankees a 3–0 lead that Don Larsen preserved. In the seventh, Richardson singled for his first major league hit, but later he recalled being a "nervous wreck." He got into 11 games and averaged just .154, but he was a rookie trying to break into a lineup of All-Star infielders such as McDougald, Billy Martin, Jerry Coleman, and Phil Rizzuto. Richardson trained with New York in St. Pete in 1956, but he spent most of the season at Denver, where he averaged .328. The Sumter star made it with the Yankees in the spring of 1957, and several days before Martin was traded to Kansas City on June 15, the 5'9", 170-pounder took over at second base. He was named to the All-Star team (the first of eight times), but he was often platooned by Casey Stengel, who liked calling him "kid." Mainly riding the bench in 1958, he was such a clean-living person that the press dubbed him and his friend Tony Kubek the "Milkshake Twins."

Tony Kubek, the shortstop, and Bobby Richardson, the second baseman, hung around together on road trips. Kubek and Richardson were dubbed the "Milkshake Twins" because of their clean living styles (author's collection).

Richardson enjoyed his breakout season in 1959 when he batted .301 in 134 games, thanks to Yankees coach Bill Dickey. A Hall of Fame catcher (inducted in 1954), Dickey helped Richardson with his hitting, advising him to use a heavier bat and swing harder. "Lazy balls get caught," Dickey observed. The result: Richardson rapped more sharply-hit grounders and line drives for base hits.[24] Buoyed by his deep faith and his father's support, he played 150 of New York's 155 games in 1960. In the World Series against the Pirates, he earned the MVP Award with 11 hits, including two doubles, two triples, and a home run for a .667 slugging mark, and a Series-record 12 RBI. During his 12 seasons, Richardson, friendly, down-to-earth, and determined to succeed, averaged .266, but in World Series play he stepped up his game, batting .305. A short, heady, quick-moving fielder with a rifle arm, Richardson and Kubek, the versatile shortstop, made up one of the league's best double play tandems. Combined with in-season and off-season work in Christian ministries, Richardson was a faithful anchor of stability for the Yankees by 1961, when he played 162 games.[25]

Jake Wood, on the other hand, was beginning his big league career with the Tigers, though he, like Richardson, played 162 games in 1961. Wood, an African American native of Elizabeth, New Jersey, 40 miles north of Trenton, grew up as the second-oldest child, and the oldest son, in a close-knit family of nine children. His father Jacob and mother Roberta raised their sons and daughters to respect others, treat people right, and follow the rules. The Wood children attended integrated schools, and they played all kinds of outdoor games. He remembered stickball as his favorite along with football and basketball, but by the time he got to Jefferson High, he concentrated on baseball. His quickness, speed, and hitting ability led him to play shortstop, and, like Richardson, he excelled in American Legion ball. After graduation in 1955, Wood received a baseball scholarship to attend Delaware State, a black college in Dover, the state's capital. He excelled at shortstop during the 1956 season, but after a year and a half on the historic campus, the 19-year-old approached Tigers scout Rabbit Jacobson, who had encouraged him to go to college but also promised to sign him to a contract when he was ready. Wood signed, and he traveled to Tigertown in Lakeland for spring training in 1957.

Tall, willowy, and strong at 6'1" and 160 pounds, Wood was a thoughtful, hard-working, modest young man who aspired to play major league ball, but he quickly learned that being black made reaching his goal more difficult. For example, at Tigertown the white and black players slept in separate quarters in barracks that had been renovated from a World War II pilot training facility. Wood, quiet and reserved, had his eyes further opened to life in the segregated South when the team bus took him from Lakeland to the Tigers' Class D club at Erie, New York. Few restaurants were open to nonwhites, and one of his teammates had to bring him sandwiches that he ate on the bus. Ted Brzenk, from Milwaukee, one of Wood's white friends at Erie, called him "the best player I played with in the minor leagues." In 1959, when Wood was loaned in mid-season to Fox Cities, a

Senators club in the Class B Three-I League, he was shifted to second base because the deft Zoilo Versalles was the shortstop. Wood remained a second baseman. Playing for Charlie Metro at Denver in 1960, he made the All-Star team and averaged .305 with 12 homers and 76 RBI. An athlete with excellent speed, he led the league with 18 triples.

Wood got a major break when Bob Scheffing became Detroit's manager after the 1960 season, because Scheffing pushed the multi-player trade of Frank Bolling to Milwaukee on December 7. Wood, who fanned 126 times at Denver, had otherwise compiled a fine minor league record. Blessed with a positive attitude and a likeable presence, he needed the opportunity, and with second base open, he seized his chance. Improving his fielding and his hitting, he performed well in Lakeland and impressed Scheffing. Wood's main competition came from Chuck Cottier, a utility infielder who came to the Tigers from the Braves in the Bolling deal, but Wood was the better hitter. Reflecting the new decade, the Tigers had several nonwhite players, notably Bruton, Dominican infielder Ozzie Virgil, obtained from the Giants in 1958, Chico Fernandez, the Cuban shortstop who came from the Phillies in a multi-player swap after the 1959 season, and outfielder Bubba Morton, a good breaking-ball hitter who was getting his chance with Detroit after two summers of Triple-A ball, capped by his .296 season on the same Denver team as Wood.[26]

In Lakeland the Tigers trained a diverse team, and when they moved to Detroit, Wood, Bruton, and Fernandez were starters, with Virgil and Morton as reserves. While Wood remembered being accepted by ballplayers on the diamond, away from the ballpark he lived in an African American neighborhood near Livernois Avenue, and he never saw any teammates in social situations. That simply was not the custom of the day. Further, he expected to hear racial slurs from fans on the road, but he also heard too many "vile, negative comments" at Tiger Stadium.

Jake Wood didn't have the experience of the Yankees' Bobby Richardson, but Wood played his position well and contributed a .258 average with 11 home runs and 69 RBI in 162 games (author's collection).

He recalled, "If looks could kill, I died many a day in 1961."[27] Still, Wood was a hero to many black fans of all ages, including 14-year-old Willie Horton, later famous as the Tigers' slugging left fielder.[28]

Regardless, Wood became an integral part of the Tigers' infield, as Richardson already was for the Yankees. All through 1961, both were major contributors to their respective teams. During the July 4 Yankees–Tigers twin bill, Richardson, batting leadoff, went 1-for-5 and scored a run in the opener, but he was hitless in five trips in the nightcap. He was batting .235, but he improved to .261 for the season. Wood went 1-for-4 in the opener and singled once in five trips in the nightcap. He was batting .273, and for the season he hit .258, three points lower than Richardson. Wood led the league with 14 triples, and he hit 11 homers while driving in 69 runs, but he topped the AL with 141 strikeouts, his Achilles heel. Richardson, who didn't lead the league in any category, contributed three home runs and 49 RBI. Wood's on-base percentage was .320, and he scored 96 runs, fifth-most among the Tigers, behind Colavito's 129, Cash's 119, Kaline's 116, and Bruton's 99 runs. Richardson had an on-base percentage of .295, and he scored 80 runs, fourth-high on the Yankees behind 132 by Maris, 131 by Mantle, and 84 by Kubek.

Each second baseman was important to his ball club, but Richardson was playing his fifth full season, and Wood was a naive rookie. Richardson was experienced in big-game situations as well as in the World Series, and he had a major presence in the clubhouse and away from the ballpark. Still, Wood showed the potential to develop into an All-Star. His speed made him a threat to steal, and he zipped from first to third on a single. He not only stole 30 bases, tops for the Bengals, but he had the ability to stretch a hit for an extra base. Richardson, hardly a threat to steal, swiped nine bases, but he was caught seven times. He was an All-Star fielder, making 413 putouts, racking up 376 assists, making 18 errors, and participating in 136 double plays. Wood made 380 putouts, contributed 396 assists, made 25 errors, and turned 83 double plays. The Yankees won 109 games and helped pitchers with 180 double plays, while the Tigers won 101 times and made 147 twin killings. Richardson and Wood were at the center of most of the double plays.

Yankees Take First Place

Following the road trip that ended with a 5–4 defeat at Boston on Sunday, July 23, the Yankees returned to the stadium in the Bronx for two four-game sets, first with the White Sox, and four victories lifted them into first place. Beginning on Friday, the second series matched the Bombers against the Orioles, and surprisingly, Baltimore beat New York three out of four times, leading up to the second All-Star Game on Monday, July 31.

The games with the White Sox were filled with Yankees longballs. In the twin-bill opener on Tuesday, July 25, against six-foot lefty Frank Baumann, Maris hit home run number 37 high off the right-field foul screen with Richardson, who walked, on base, and Mantle followed with a shot, remarkably, off the left-field foul screen for the M&M Boys' fourth back-to-back homers. Maris also banged a solo clout in the eighth off right-hander Don Larsen, the ex–Yankee of "perfect game" fame, helping Ford win his 18th game, 5–1. In the nightcap the Bombers hit five homers to win, 12–0, as Stafford improved to 9–4 with a six-hitter. Boyer homered in the second frame following a single by Lopez. After two walks, Kubek singled, and Maris singled for a 4–0 lead. In the fourth, Maris belted number 39 for a 5–0 margin. Boyer homered again in the sixth, and after a groundout,

Bronx Bombers: Mickey Mantle holds up his jersey number 7 and Roger Maris holds up his jersey number 9, signifying the sluggers had 79 homers between them. Playing at Yankee Stadium against the White Sox on Tuesday, July 25, Maris hit home runs 39 and 40 in the nightcap of a doubleheader won by the Yankees, 12–0. The next day Mantle hit homer number 39 to help the Yankees win, 5–2. The "79" picture was one of thousands taken to highlight the Maris-Mantle home run race (National Baseball Hall of Fame, Cooperstown, New York).

Richardson's single, and Kubek's double, Maris hit number 40, a 440-foot rocket, making four home runs for Rajah in the twin bill. Mantle walked, and Howard hit number ten to cap the 12–0 rout. Juan Pizarro, who won 14 games in 1961, only lasted two innings, and three relievers weren't much better. Detroit lost at LA, and New York, paced by Maris' four circuit clouts, took a half-game lead in the AL. As it developed, the Yankees were in first place to stay.

On a roll, New York won single games over Chicago on Wednesday and Thursday by scores of 5–2 and 4–3, respectively. Sheldon spaced four hits on Wednesday, while his teammates socked four more homers. Facing ex–Tigers righty Ray Herbert in the first inning, Mantle hit number 39 with Richardson aboard, and Blanchard, catching, followed with his 12th homer for a 3–0 lead. In the fourth, Blanchard led off with another four-bagger, and two outs later, Boyer homered for a 5–0 lead. Sheldon gave up J. C. Martin's two-run single in the seventh, but that was it. On Thursday Chicago southpaw Billy Pierce yielded four runs in seven innings, and the M&M Boys led the attack, with Kubek's single, Maris' single, and Mantle's sacrifice fly in the first inning good for a 1–0 lead. Lopez's triple, followed by a throwing error, upped the margin to 2–0 in the second. Maris' RBI double and Mantle's run-scoring single gave New York a 4–0 edge in the third. Terry, the winner, tired in the ninth, and Arroyo, charged with one of Chicago's two runs, ended it on a double play grounder. The Tigers had an off-day, so the Yankees led the league by one game.

The third-place Orioles, however, were a different matter from the fifth-place Chisox, and their tough pitching slowed the Yankees. Baltimore's Hal Brown, the tall, skinny right-hander who was first signed by the Red Sox in 1946, hurled a six-hitter, three of them singles by Mantle and one by Maris, to win, 4–0, while Bud Daley gave up homers to Gus Triandos and Jackie Brandt. On Saturday Whitey Ford pitched a seven-hitter, and while he yielded four runs, he improved to 19–2 when Berra led off the eighth inning with the game's only circuit clout, his 13th, the winning run to the Yankees' 5–4 victory. On Sunday the Orioles swept a twin bill, winning 4–0 and 2–1. Steve Barber spaced seven hits to win his 12th game, 4–0, allowing Mantle one single and getting Maris, who pinch-hit with two outs in the ninth, to ground to second base. In the late game, Milt Pappas, with a save from Dick Hall, won his seventh game, allowing one run on five hits. Mantle tied the game at 1–1 with a bases-loaded grounder in the eighth inning, but Dick Williams cracked an RBI double in the ninth. Hall, the O's 6'6" right-hander with the herky-jerky motion, took over with the bases loaded, struck out Boyer on a questionable call, and got Lopez to hit the first pitch for a game-ending double play, upsetting Houk. That day, the

Tigers lost to the Twins, 4–0. Afterward, New York had a 1.5-game lead over Detroit, with the All-Star Game set in Boston for Monday.

Tigers Roar in July

The defending champion Yankees compiled a league-best 22–10 record in June, and they followed with a 20–9 mark in July, but the upstart Tigers, 19–10 in June, slipped to 16–12 in July. The third-place Orioles, after playing .500 ball in June (15–15), improved to 18–11 in July, partly due to victories against the Yankees (three wins in six games) and the Tigers (three wins in five games).

Before the first All-Star break, the lack of reliable secondary pitching caught up with Detroit. Following the July 4 doubleheader split with New York, the Bengals traveled to Boston for a day-night twin bill. Jim Bunning, pitching well, won the day game, 6–2, scattering seven hits and giving up both runs in the seventh inning. The Bengals turned seven hits into two three-run bursts. In the fourth, Bruton and Kaline bunted safely. Colavito followed with his 21st home run, a high drive over Fenway Park's left field barrier, the 37-foot "Green Monster" topped by a 23-foot high screen, for a 3–0 lead. In the fifth, after Bunning's single and Dick McAuliffe's double, Bruton bounced out, but Kaline doubled inside the left field line, scoring Bunning, and Colavito singled for the 6–0 lead that Bunning protected. In the second game, Boston collected 12 hits for an 8–3 victory. Sore-armed Bob Bruce, who had looked good earlier in the season, saw his record drop to 1–1. Bruce gave up five hits and four runs in four innings, and the Tigers trailed, 4–1. Bespectacled Fred Gladding, a burly right-handed reliever, pitched one scoreless inning, but erratic Bill Fischer, who posted a 3–2 record before being swapped to Kansas City on August 2, gave up six hits and four more runs. McAuliffe slugged his third homer and Colavito belted number 22, both solo blasts off Bill Monbouquette (8–6). Crafty veteran Mike Fornieles, the Cuban right-hander who went 9–8, earned his eighth save (of 15 in 1961) with 3⅓ scoreless innings.[29]

On Thursday at Fenway, Phil Regan raised his ledger to 8–4 with an eight-hitter, 3–0, thanks to the seventh save by Terry Fox, who retired Chuck Schilling on a popup to first with two on and two outs in the ninth. The win kept the Tigers half a game in front of the Yankees, as the Bengals flew home to Michigan to face Los Angeles four times before the All-Star interlude.

At Tiger Stadium on Friday, July 7, the Tigers lost to the Angels on two late home runs. In the eighth inning, big Steve Bilko, the minor league slugging legend who hit 313 round-trippers in 13 seasons, mostly at the Triple-A level, belted a bases-empty home run, and in the ninth, catcher Earl Averill hit a solo homer, both off Fox, who relieved Paul Foytack. Hal Woodeshick, the ex–Tiger who returned to Detroit in a trade with Washington on June 5, 1961, started, but with his control off, he gave up three singles and one run in the first. Foytack took over in the second, yielding one run on three hits while fanning eight and walking two in seven innings. It was the first loss for Fox (3–1), who hadn't given up an earned run in 12 previous appearances, earning him respect as the Tigers' most dependable reliever. Still, after the Yankees bombed Boston, 14–3, Detroit (52–30) fell behind New York (51–28) by half a game.

Unfazed, the Bengals defeated the Angels in three straight contests, once on Saturday afternoon and twice on Sunday, to regain first place. Saturday's victory started with Don Mossi, but Gladding earned his first win with a scoreless eighth inning, while Fox and Aguirre protected the 3–2 lead. Bilko hit a run-scoring double in the first, and Averill belted his 14th homer off Mossi in the seventh. Before that, Cash's RBI single tied the game at 1–1 in the fourth, and in the seventh, Bubba Morton, batting for Mossi, tied it again with an RBI single. In the tense eighth, Steve Boros' RBI single, following walks to Bruton and Cash, was the game-winner, thanks to the Tigers' bullpen heroics. On Sunday rugged Frank Lary, once jokingly called the "runt" of his family's seven sons, boosted his record to 13–4 by winning, 1–0, thanks to Mike Roarke's RBI single in the second, after Cash drew a walk and Boros was hit by an Eli Grba fastball. In the nightcap, Bunning (9–6) won, 6–3, over erratic Ryne Duren and five relievers. Bruton paced the Bengals with a single and his eighth home run, a two-run drive to right that gave Detroit a 5–2 lead in the sixth. Kaline walked, Colavito doubled him home, and, after Bilko belted his 12th homer in the eighth, the bullpen came through. The Tigers reached the All-Star break with a 55–30 mark, and the Yankees, at 53–29, trailed by half a game, an unusual position for New York.

Back in Detroit on Thursday, July 13, the Bengals worked out at Tiger Stadium, taking hitting and fielding practice, kidding around, and talking about the pennant race. So far the season was going well, but Bob Scheffing was concerned with the second-line pitching. Talking to *Free Press* scribe Bob Pille in Boston before the All-Star Game, Scheffing said, "We can't seem to win games with our secondary pitching." The manager was referring to the nightcap of the Fenway twin bill on July 5, when Bob Bruce failed to win his fifth straight start since being pronounced healthy in early June. Scheffing added, "When Phil Regan wins … we seem to run off five or six in a row." Bruce couldn't seem to find his groove. However, Bunning was going strong at the end of his latest effort, which Scheffing liked. He planned to try Woodeshick on Friday night against the Angels (but he failed to come through). As of July 6, the Big Three of Lary (12–4), Bunning (8–6), and Mossi (9–2) had contributed a 29–12 total to Detroit's 51–29 record. As if to confirm Scheffing's point, Lary and Bunning both won on Sunday against the Angels.[30]

After the Tigers returned to Detroit, Scheffing outlined his plans to start Lary, Bunning, and Mossi as often as possible. "All three are strong and they like hot weather," said the manager. Also, he figured on using Regan and Foytack, because they had proven to be Detroit's most reliable second-line hurlers. Scheffing was impressed with the performances of Fox and Aguirre out of the pen, and he saw a good future for hard-throwing Fred Gladding, who hailed from Flat Rock, Michigan. Of his pitchers, Scheffing liked Lary best. He praised the bulldog right-hander many times.

If he had one game to win, Lary would be his pitcher. "I'll take him over any pitcher in either league," the manager told Watson Spoelstra.

In other "Tiger Tales," Chico Fernandez had his tonsils removed, and doctors believed his bad throat had caused his recent leg problems. Dick McAuliffe, an explosive hitter, had become the team's top shortstop. Billy Bruton, using an old baseball weapon, was getting on base with drag bunts. Scheffing knew that Jake Wood fanned 73 times before the All-Star break, but the pilot said he would adjust. "I'd rather see Jake swinging than have him choking up on the bat or punching at the ball." Last but not least, Scheffing indicated that Larry Osborne was helping the Tigers off the bench, coming through with four pinch-hits in his last six trips to the plate.[31]

Against the Twins, Detroit split two games. On Friday, July 14, Lary, who gave up four runs on seven hits in seven innings, took his fifth loss against 13 wins. Southpaw Jack Kralick allowed ten hits, three of them to Mike Roarke. Dick Brown, batting for Fred Gladding in the ninth, doubled to

Paul Foytack, a Tigers mound stalwart since 1956, when he fashioned a 15–13 record, pitched mainly as a fourth starter in 1961. Foytack, recovering from torn muscles in his right shoulder, posted an 11–10 record, after going 2–11 in 1960 (author's collection).

left, following Roarke's single. Bruton grounded out to score the second run, and the Tigers lost, 5–2. On Saturday Bunning boosted his mark to 10–4 by hurling a four-hitter to win, 2–1, as Bo Osborne, starting because of Cash's foot infection, homered off Camilo Pascual in the eighth inning to pace the victory. But the Tigers suffered a major loss in the third inning when Brown, behind the plate, was hit on the end of his middle finger by a ball that caromed off the batter, injuring Brown's finger badly. "It was the worst split finger I've ever seen," Roarke recalled. "It looked like someone took a meat cleaver to Brown's finger."[32] The upshot was that Roarke did most of the catching until September.

Kansas City arrived in Detroit for three games, and the Tigers won all three, two in Sunday's doubleheader and another on Monday afternoon. Mossi hurled a five-hitter in Sunday's opener, boosting his record to 10–2 and winning, 11–1, as the Tigers reached Jim Archer and two relievers for nine hits. Fernandez went 2-for-4, and his RBI single in the second inning gave Detroit a 2–0 lead. Kaline belted his 11th home run, a bases-empty blow in the third, and Mossi, a left-handed hitter and hurler, chipped in with his first home run in the eighth. After two hits and an intentional pass, Colavito walked to force in another run, Cash doubled to clear the bases, and Wood scored the tenth run when the left fielder dropped Roarke's fly ball. In the nightcap, Regan boosted his mark to 9–4 by scattering 12 hits to win, 8–3, boosted by Colavito's 23rd and 24th home runs, Cash's 25th round-tripper, and McAuliffe's fourth four-bagger. On Monday, using Scheffing's pitching plan, Foytack upped his mark to 6–5 with 8⅓ good innings, and Fox recorded his team-high eighth save as the Tigers won, 7–4. The big blow came when Cash launched a grand slam off Joe Nuxhall in the first frame. Kaline singled twice while Wood and Colavito each knocked in one run. After the games of July 17, the Tigers, with a 59–31 record, held a half-game lead over the Yankees, at 57–30.

Pesky Baltimore came to the Motor City for a three-game series starting on Tuesday, and the Orioles won the first two. Lary started the first game and lasted six innings, but the usually tough right-hander allowed five runs on ten hits. Fox and Aguirre combined to hurl the seventh and eighth frames, and Bill Fischer pitched well for two innings but lost, 8–7, when he surrendered Jim Gentile's 23rd home run in the tenth. Detroit racked up ten hits off Chuck Estrada and three relievers, but All-Star Hoyt Wilhelm recorded the win by hurling the last four innings and permitting just the RBI single by Bruton that tied the contest at 7–7 in the eighth. On Wednesday Jack Fisher and Hal Brown (three IP) combined to allow six hits and stop Bunning, 4–2, a loss that dropped the Kentuckian's mark to 10–7. Gentile hammered his 24th home run, a two-run blast that gave the visitors a 3–1 lead in the third inning. Bruton added his ninth four-bagger, a solo belt in the fifth that cut the deficit to 3–2, but catcher Hank Foiles homered for the final margin.

The Tigers broke out their big bats against Steve Barber and three relievers on Thursday, winning, 15–8, despite a shaky performance by Mossi (ten hits and five runs in 3⅓ innings) but with adequate relief from Wood-eshick (4–3), who got the win, Fox, and Aguirre. Wood blasted his seventh homer, a two-run drive in the second inning, and Colavito connected for home runs number 26 and 27, the last a three-run blast to deep left that raised the lead to 15–6 in the seventh. Gentile and Foiles added solo homers in the ninth, and the bullpen preserved the win. As a result, Detroit, now 60–33, regained a half-game lead over idle New York (58–32). The pennant race was as tight as a rubber band when the Bengals left on a six-game road trip to Kansas City and Los Angeles.

In hot weather at Municipal Stadium on Friday, July 21, the Athletics' Jim Archer was able to outduel the Tigers' Phil Regan, 3–2, and when New York beat Boston, 11–8, the Yankees regained first place by half a game. Rain turned the Tigers' Saturday game into part of a twin bill on Sunday, but the Yankees beat the Bosox, 11–9, upping New York's lead to one game. Detroit caught up by winning twice on Sunday, with Foytack grabbing the opener, 6–4, and Fischer recording the victory in a late-game slugfest, 17–14. In the opener Cash homered, number 27, and drove in three runs. In the late game, both managers pulled out all the stops, using 17 players each, with Detroit calling on six pitchers, after Lary started and gave up six runs in two innings. The A's used seven hurlers, with Joe Nuxhall being the most effective reliever. As a result, Detroit, at 62–34, led the AL by .001 point after New York (60–33) lost to Boston.

The biggest blow came when Steve Boros collided with Frank Lary as they chased a bunt down the third base line in the nightcap. Lary hurt his leg, and Boros broke his left collarbone, knocking the third baseman out of action for up to six weeks. After staying overnight in a hospital, Boros flew back to Detroit, accompanied by Terry Fox, who was suffering an inflamed elbow for the third time in 1961. Fox was out indefinitely, and with catcher Dick Brown already on the Disabled List, the Tigers needed help. At the time Boros had 53 RBI and was hitting .273, the fourth-highest regular behind the sluggers, Cash, Kaline, and Colavito, so the loss was critical. Fox was the team's best late-inning reliever, making his loss another tough blow.

Bob Scheffing, like all managers, was used to juggling his lineup, and general manager Rick Ferrell made some deals to help the Bengals. Detroit reacquired catcher Frank House, the high school phenom from Bessemer,

Alabama, who originally signed with the Tigers in 1949 for a bonus of more than $70,000. "Iron Mike" Roarke, previously seen as good-field, no-hit, was thriving on daily work behind the plate and batting .292. But teams need more than one good catcher. House, just acquired from Baltimore for Harry Chiti, caught the nightcap on July 23 against the A's, belting a two-run triple in the 17–14 win. Also, the Tigers placed Boros on the DL and filled his roster spot by calling up Manuel "Pepe" Montejo, a 25-year-old Cuban right-hander with a 2–3 record and a 3.44 ERA at Denver, Detroit's top farm team.[33]

Newcomers or reserves like Regan, McAuliffe, Fox, and Roarke were helping fuel the Tigers' pennant race, so maybe, as manager Danny Murtaugh once said about the 1960 Pittsburgh Pirates, it was "in the cards for us to win."[34] Stated Bob Scheffing about the Yankees, "We'll have to outfight them and outpitch them. I believe we can do it."[35] Ralph Houk, meanwhile, was trying to outlast a rash of minor injuries to his pitchers, and as a result, the Yankees called up "sure-fire" rookie Al Downing, the team's first black pitcher.[36]

7

Fighting for First in August

The Second All-Star Contest

The Yankees and the Tigers wrapped up the month of July by sending their All-Stars to Boston to play the second interleague exhibition on July 31. All of the major league teams played contests on Sunday, so unlike the All-Star Game at Candlestick Park on Tuesday, July 11, the players involved did not have a day to rest or prepare. Regardless, the upshot on Monday afternoon was a tense 1–1 tie at Fenway Park that was perhaps more of a distraction from the pennant races than a celebration of the national pastime and baseball's greatest players. Still, a near-sellout crowd of 31,851 enjoyed the game, despite threatening weather and, later, rain.

For the American League, the lineup featured three Tigers batting in the first three slots, Norm Cash at first base, Rocky Colavito in left field, and Al Kaline in right field. Jim Bunning was the first of three AL stars to pitch three innings apiece, so four Tigers started the game. Bunning was followed on the mound by Boston rookie Don Schwall and Minnesota veteran Camilo Pascual, also right-handers. The AL's top players mustered only four hits, with the biggest blast coming off the bat of Colavito, who, facing Cincinnati's Bob Purkey, lofted a home run into the screen in left field, after Cash took a called third strike to lead off the home half of the first inning. Kaline singled twice and stole a base, so Detroiters racked up three of the AL's four hits and accounted for the league's only run. Further, Cash, who failed to hit safely, made two fine pick-ups of low throws, and one prevented a National League run, while Bunning hurled three hitless innings.

On the other hand, Yankees heroes played little part in the outcome. Mickey Mantle, batting cleanup, went hitless in three trips. Roger Maris, recovering from a pulled hamstring in his leg, pinch-hit for Indians catcher John Romano in the fourth inning and popped up to the second baseman. Whitey Ford, who might have pitched if the game had gone into extra innings, didn't appear. Elston Howard followed Romano behind the plate, but he went 0-for-2. In fact, Mantle and Howard were two of San Francisco junkballer Stu Miller's three strikeout victims in the ninth.

The NL All-Stars mounted only one threat. The 6'6" Schwall, having struck out the last two batters in the fifth with a runner on third, started strong in the sixth by retiring the Braves' Hank Aaron on a grounder to short. Milwaukee's Eddie Mathews walked on four pitches, but the Giants' Willie Mays, who made more than one spectacular play in center field, popped up to short right field for the second out. Schwall, working with a two-strike count on San Francisco's Orlando Cepeda, let one get away, and it hit Cepeda in the side. Cincinnati shortstop Eddie Kasko hit a high-bounding ball toward short, where Chicago's Luis Aparicio, playing medium depth, waited instead of charging the ball, and by the time he gloved the ball, he couldn't make a play. With the bases loaded, Bill White, the Cardinals' left-handed batting first baseman, smashed a grounder back at Schwall. The big right-hander tried to make the play, the ball caromed off his glove, and Aparicio saved the day by spearing the ball before it rolled into left field, preventing a second run. Still, the game was tied at 1–1. Schwall, unfazed, ended the inning by retiring ex–Tiger Frank Bolling on a fly to left, and the NL stars never threatened again.[1]

The closest the AL came to scoring again came in the ninth when Kaline led off with a single to right-center off Miller, the fourth NL hurler. Mantle struck out, but Kaline stole second on the play. Miller, relaying on his tricky array of slow pitches, fanned Elston Howard, with Kaline staying at second. With two outs, manager Paul Richards sent up Chicago's veteran slugger, Roy Sievers, but Miller fanned Sievers on yet another dancing curve. At that point, the rain, which had started midway through the contest, was coming down harder. The umpires called the game, making it the first tied contest in All-Star Game history.[2] Afterward, the players showered, changed, and packed their bags to leave for Boston's Logan Airport, flights to their homes cities, and a day of rest on Tuesday, before the major leagues resumed regular schedules on Wednesday.

Baseball, the Game of Inches

You often hear it said that baseball is a "game of inches," but Roger Maris believed it was a game where one-eighth of an inch mattered. To hit a home run, the batter has to swing with a slight uppercut, trying to get the right amount of loft on the ball. Maris explained when he met the ball solidly, the difference between a line-drive base hit and a home run was that eighth of an inch below the ball's midpoint where the bat connected and the ball jumped toward the stands.

Maris went through a home run "slump" in early August. Minnesota came to New York for a four-game series starting on Friday, August 4, and while the Yankees swept all four contests, Maris struggled at the plate. He usually disliked doubleheaders, partly because they made for a long day, plus he seldom contributed his best performances in twin bills. He did launch four home runs in a Sunday doubleheader against the White Sox at Comiskey on July 25, but that was unusual for him. In the August 4 opener against the Twins, he connected off Camilo Pascual, whom he called "the toughest right-hand pitcher in the league for me." Since the blast was a three-run shot, the home run lifted Maris to 101 RBI, and driving in 100 or more runs is a goal of every hitter. The Yankees won that game in the tenth, 8–5, when John Blanchard unloaded his 14th home run, a three-run shot that broke the tie. The Bronx Bombers won on Saturday, 2–1, thanks to a one-out single by Maris in the eighth, followed by Mantle's long triple off lefty Jack Kralick, but nobody on either team homered.

New York took a pair of cliff-hangers in Sunday's doubleheader by scores of 7–6 and 3–2, but Maris collected only two squib (his word) singles in 12 at-bats. Afterward, he posted a sign on his locker saying, "BAD DAY," with a number 1 under it—a joking way of saying he knew his afternoon was rough. On the other hand, Mantle enjoyed a banner day by hitting three home runs, numbers 41, 42, and 43, putting him two homers ahead of Maris' 41. Maris refused to feel bad, because Mantle performed so well and because the Yankees won twice, and in the end, the Fargo hero said, it was all about winning games and winning the pennant.

Maris was looking for his next homer when Los Angeles came to town for a four-game series starting on Monday, August 7. With the Yankees trailing in the third inning, 1–0, he came up with Bobby Richardson at third. Maris gave the bunt sign to Richardson, laid down a good bunt toward third base, and Richardson scored to tie the game. The Yankees won, 4–1, with a three-run rally in the eighth, kicked off by Maris drawing a walk. Kidding afterward with reporters, the down-home slugger later recalled that a couple of writers all but laughed in his face when he said the RBI bunt meant as much to him as a home run. Indeed, Ralph Houk told writers that Maris' bunt proved he was a team player, and Houk's statement made the next day's papers. By August, practically every comment that Maris made in the clubhouse was getting into the papers.

In Tuesday's game Maris hit a pitch that illustrated his point about an eighth of an inch. The Yankees and Angels were deadlocked at 4–4 in the tenth inning when Tony Kubek, another clutch hitter, led off with a double off reliever Art Fowler. Maris, hitless in four trips, teed off on Fowler's next pitch, hitting "a bullet line drive that got out to right field so fast that the fielder was handcuffed." The ball hit Lee Thomas in the chest, and he couldn't handle it, allowing Kubek to score and giving Maris the game-winning RBI. The Yankees improved to 73–37 with a three-game lead on the Tigers, who kept pace by beating the White Sox at Comiskey, 3–0.

Maris recollected, "If I had hit one-eighth inch lower on that ball I'm sure it would have gone into the upper deck." Thus, the eighth-inch gave him a clutch single, but not a home run. Still, he figured luck was with him all year: "Things were breaking right. Most of the time I was getting good loft on the ball." Luck is important, he wrote in 1962. "One of my favorite theories is if you have the skill and I have the luck, then I'm going to finish ahead of you." In other words, you need a certain amount of luck to take full advantage of your skill. Maris was pleased with his game-winning single, partly because his swing felt good.[3]

The crew-cut bomber proved he had both talent and luck all season long. After his home run off Pascual on August 4, the first round-tripper he had hit since the four clouts in the doubleheader at Chicago on July 25, he didn't reach the seats again until August 11 at spacious Griffith Stadium in Washington, one of the hardest parks for home runs. On that Friday evening, he blasted number 42 off lefty Pete Burnside in the top of the fifth inning, and the Yankees cruised to a 12–5 win. During the next week, Maris, always a streaky hitter, belted seven home runs in six games, capping his run by hitting numbers 47 and 48 at home against the White Sox on August 16 to lift the Yankees to a 5–4 victory. The win kept New York, with a 78–40 record, in first place by three games over Detroit (75–43), as the Orioles beat the Tigers in the Motor City. 8–2. Home runs were fueling the Bombers in 1961, as they slugged their way to a new team record of 240.

Tigers Need Relief

As the All-Star Game and the "dog days" of August approached, Bob Scheffing was juggling his pitching staff while relying on his Big Three—Frank Lary, Jim Bunning, and Don Mossi—plus spot starters Phil Regan and Paul Foytack. Bunning, the Tigers' second-biggest winner in 1961 with 17 wins behind Lary's 23, also lost 11 games as he compiled a 3.38 ERA in 38 games, 37 of them starts. Every pitcher loses some games that he doesn't finish, and Bunning may have felt that the good luck Maris experienced with hitting home runs didn't follow him to the mound.

In Detroit on Saturday, July 29, two days before the All-Star tilt, Bunning, who hurled an iron-man 268 innings (second for Detroit to Lary's 275⅓ innings) and entered the day with an 11–7 mark, looked strong for seven frames against the visiting Twins. The right-hander gave up two runs in the fourth, but the Tigers scored twice in their fourth, after Colavito was fanned by Jim Kaat, the 6'4" southpaw from Zeeland, Michigan. In the first frame, Kaat hit Norm Cash on the arm with a fastball, and in the fourth, Kaat threw at Cash again. Cash dodged but was hit in the back of the right thigh, and later he had to leave the game. Up next, Wood was safe on Zoilo Versalles' error. Chico Fernandez, playing third base (Steve Boros was still out with a fractured collarbone), and Mike Roarke followed with RBI singles, giving the Tigers a 3–2 lead.

The pitching duel resumed. In the eighth, Bunning, weakening, gave up a leadoff single to Bill Tuttle, the former Tigers flychaser. Julio Becquer, a left-handed batting first baseman purchased from the Phillies on June 1, batted for Kaat, but Bunning fanned the Cuban and retired Versalles on an infield popup, but walked Lenny Green. Bob Scheffing took a pilot's slow walk to the mound and asked Bunning if he was tired. Jim nodded, and Scheffing called for Pepe Montejo. Making his second appearance for Detroit since being called up from Denver, the right-handed Montejo lived off a sidearm fastball in the minors, but he had no good breaking pitch. The slim, 5'11" reliever tried to blow a 3–1 fast one by Killebrew, but the stocky slugger rode the ball deep into the upper deck in left for a 5–3 edge. After Allison singled, Scheffing

Jim Bunning started the 1961 season with a 7–6 record, but with the pennant race heating up, he hurled ten more victories after June 25 (author's collection).

Manny "Pepe" Montejo, the right-handed Cuban reliever called up from Denver in late July, provided the Tigers with a strong arm out of the bullpen. During his only major league season, Montejo pitched 16⅓ innings in 12 games, posted a 3.86 ERA, but recorded no decisions (author's collection).

called for Regan, who ended the inning. Colavito knocked in one run with a sacrifice fly in the eighth, but the Tigers couldn't score again.

The crushing 5–4 defeat was the second straight one-run loss to the Twins, after the visitors won on Friday night, 4–3, over Foytack, who hurled a complete game but saw his mark fall to 7–6. Saturday's defeat left the Tigers, now at 64–37, two games behind the league-leading Yankees, who topped the Orioles, 5–4, and improved to a 65–34 ledger.[4]

The Tigers gained half a game on the Yankees on Sunday afternoon, despite failing to score a single run before a paid attendance of 16,121, a crowd that lifted Detroit over the million mark in season attendance. Otherwise, if the day's results brought the Bengals any good news following a third straight defeat and the fourth in the last five games, it was learning the Yankees lost twice to the Orioles by scores of 4–0 and 2–1. Scheffing said a couple of days off for the All-Star break would help. "His boys looked like a team in need of a vacation Sunday," remarked Joe Falls, "as they gave another punchless performance in losing to the Minnesota Twins, 4–0."

Jack Kralick improved his record to 10–6 by scattering eight hits, all singles, although Wood solved the crafty southpaw's slants and deceptive changeups for two safeties. Lary, whose mark slipped to 14–6, lacked his usual control and stuff, and he never made it out of the second frame. The Tigers' ace surrendered two homers, Bob Allison's 23rd, a blast into the lower deck in left, and veteran Ted Lepcio's sixth, a two-run shot into the upper deck in left. For the Tigers, Fred Gladding worked 3⅓ innings and yielded just one run. Pepe Montejo, who had cost the Tigers on Saturday, hurled three scoreless frames, and he fanned Killebrew in the seventh, but

one day too late. Regan closed the game with a scoreless ninth, as Terry Fox, suffering an inflamed bursa in his pitching elbow,[5] was unable to pitch from July 20 to August 20.

The injury bugaboo hit Detroit again in the first inning when McAuliffe singled to center, but was caught off base as Bubba Morton, starting for Bruton,

Rookie Bubba Morton, a right-handed batter, helped the Tigers by averaging a solid .287 with two home runs and 19 RBI in 77 games. Morton was a dependable reserve outfielder who also provided right-handed pinch-hitting (National Baseball Hall of Fame, Cooperstown, New York).

popped a bunt to the pitcher. Kralick made the grab and fired to first to double off McAuliffe, who, sliding in headfirst, took a knee in the nose from Morton. Both Bengals left the game, McAuliffe with a broken nose and Morton with a sprained ankle, but both were expected to be ready after the All-Star break.[6]

While Scheffing and the front office contemplated one or more trades to offset injuries to catcher Dick Brown, third baseman Steve Boros, and reliever Terry Fox,[7] "Winn Pennant," the pen name for a *Free Press* writer, lauded a special family of fans. Pennant praised Ian Wilson, his wife Shirley, and their children, Linda, 12, and Dennis, 9. The Wilsons bought ticket number 1,000,000 on Sunday. The father, a maintenance supervisor at Chrysler Corporation's Highland Park Offices, indicated this was his family's second trip to Tiger Stadium, but not the last. Pennant named Wilson as the Tigers' "biggest fan." Unlike his wife and kids, Wilson had no favorite players, but instead he was rooting for all the Bengals. "They've got as good a chance as the Yankees have," remarked Ian. Concluded Winn Pennant, the Wilson family, living in East Detroit, loved their favorite team, win or lose, making them "pretty typical" fans.[8]

Resuming the Pennant Race

Following the All-Star break, Detroit got back on the winning track. After a 16–12 mark in July, the Bengals compiled a 22–9 record in August,

but at times the Tigers fell as much as four games behind the equally hot Yankees, who also went 22–9. Deciding to add bench strength, Scheffing approved a trade with Kansas City on August 2. At first the Tigers were going to sell hurler Bill Fischer's contract to the Athletics, but instead the two teams' general managers worked

Needing bullpen help, Detroit acquired veteran Gerry Staley on August 2, 1961. Pitching the last of his 15 big league seasons, Staley, once a star right-hander for the St. Louis Cardinals and the Chicago White Sox, had a 1–1 mark and saved two games for the Tigers (author's collection).

out a trade. The Bengals swapped little-used Ozzie Virgil, the Dominican infielder who integrated Detroit in 1958 but was hitting .133 in 30 games in 1961, along with Fischer to the A's for former Tigers infielder Reno Bertoia and veteran right-handed pitcher Gerry Staley, who first made the majors with the Cardinals in 1947 and hurled for the Reds and the Giants before going to the White Sox in 1956. Staley, 40, divided the 1961 season among the White Sox, the Athletics, and the Tigers with a 2–5 mark, including 1–1 in Detroit. Bertoia, a journeyman infielder who was one of seven big leaguers born in Italy, spent two seasons with Washington, peaking with a .260 mark in 1960. Moving with the franchise to Minnesota in 1961, he was dealt to Kansas City on June 1. Bertoia, who grew up in Windsor, Ontario, was a right-handed batter with a .244 average for ten seasons. The Tigers needed a third baseman and a pitcher, and Staley and Bertoia, both nearing the ends of their careers, were the best choices available.

Every athlete good enough to reach the majors, however, makes useful contributions in larger or smaller ways to his team. In Bertoia's case, while his batwork wasn't strong, he helped Jake Wood learn the mechanics of his position and feel more a part of the ball club. "One of the guys who was dear to me and took some time with me was Reno Bertoia," Wood said in 2014, as he reflected on the difficulties of adjusting to the big leagues as a rookie and a black man.[9]

The Tigers kicked off the season's hottest month by winning two of three from the visiting Senators, starting with a twi-night doubleheader split on Wednesday, August 2. Detroit won the opener, 4–3, behind Don Mossi, who, after a two-run first inning, allowed a total of three runs on eight hits, improving his mark to 11–2. A workhorse like Lary and Bunning, the big-eared southpaw hurled 240⅓ innings in 1961, third most for Detroit. He pitched 35 games, 34 being starts, and he led the Tigers with a 2.96 ERA. His ball club scored in the second when Cash tripled to center and Fernandez singled him home. Washington jumped ahead in the fifth, 3–1, when Marty Keough, the veteran left fielder, reached Mossi for his ninth (and final) home run of the year. The Tigers scored the winning runs in the sixth when Charlie Maxwell, enjoying one of his finest hours, batted for Mike Roarke. Facing Marty Kutyna, a right-handed sidearmer from Philadelphia, Maxwell slammed a three-run home run deep into the upper deck in right.

In the nightcap, however, the Tigers, after getting eight strong innings out of Paul Foytack, took a 2–2 tie into the 11th, when the bullpen failed. Phil Regan, who had rescued Hank Aguirre by getting the third out in the ninth, threw a one-out gopher ball to rookie first baseman Bud Zipfel, who hit his first homerun of the year for a 3–2 lead. Willie Tasby singled, and

Fred Gladding took the mound, but he gave up a single to Joe King and walked Gene Green. The erratic Pepe Montejo tried to stop the rally, but he gave up an RBI single to shortstop Bob Johnson and a run-scoring grounder to Chuck Cottier. In Detroit's 11th, ex–Cub Johnny Klippstein retired one batter to close out the win.

Roaring back on Thursday afternoon, the Tigers started a four-game win streak behind a clutch four-hit performance by Bunning as well as 2-for-4 days from Wood and Colavito. The slugging Bronx native, enjoying his best-ever season, singled home Wood in the first frame and led off the fourth with his 30th home run, a solo blast to left off right-hander Bennie Daniels, the ex–Pirate with the moving fastball and the shaky control. In the ninth, Bunning allowed a single to Zipfel before retiring the dangerous Gene Woodling on a fly ball to center. Swinging on a slider, Joe King lined a shot into the fortunate Bunning's glove as the tall right-hander was completing his exaggerated follow-through. Bunning whirled and threw to first for the game-ending twin killing. That same day New York fell to Kansas City, 6–1, so the Yankees' 67–37 mark left them 1.5 games above the 66–39 Tigers.

Detroit's ten-game home stand ended with a four-game set against Cleveland, and the Tigers won three out of four, losing the nightcap of the doubleheader on Sunday, August 6. Hurling on Friday night, Frank Lary dispelled concerns about his recently stiff elbow by spacing seven hits to win, 6–1. The Tigers totaled 11 hits, but they scored all six runs off 6'3" Barry Latman, who grew up in a Jewish family in Los Angeles. Latman departed in the sixth inning when Fernandez tripled, and Roarke brought him home with a sacrifice fly, boosting the lead to 6–1. Lary allowed one run in the second on Willie Kirkland's single, John Romano's double, and Vic Power's grounder.

The Tigers were cruising on Saturday, taking a 7–2 lead into the top of the seventh, when the Tribe's Woodie Held, once touted as the Yankees' shortstop of the future, led off with his 14th homer and Cleveland's third of the day off Regan, who was running out of gas. Regan, looking for his tenth victory, retired pinch-hitter Bob Nieman on a fly to center, but Johnny Temple, who already had two homers off Regan fastballs, drew a walk, and Don Dillard, a left-handed batter, rapped his second single. Tito Francona singled for the second run of the frame, and Scheffing called for Gerry Staley, who made his second appearance for the Tigers. Willie Kirkland, a left-handed slugger, met a Staley knuckler for a two-run double, and Bubba Phillips knocked in a run with a grounder, before Staley ended the inning. Scheffing called for the heady Bunning, who worked two hitless innings, the only game he saved all season. Kaline, who singled in the first and scored from first on Colavito's long double, had to take a breather in the dugout, as did several others, due to the heat and humidity. Always a gamer, Number 6 also belted a two-run double in the sixth that boosted the Bengals' lead.

The Tigers got another stellar performance out of Don Mossi in Sunday's opener, but in the nightcap, Foytack and four relievers couldn't maintain the winning streak. Mossi boosted his mark to a fancy 12–2 with a 2–1 victory, permitting three hits. Willie Kirkland drove his 22nd homer to right in the eighth inning, but the Indians mustered only two other hits, both singles. The Tigers scored in the first on singles by Bruton and Kaline and Colavito's grounder to third. The clinching run came in the seventh when popular veteran Frank House, drawing cheers for his play behind the plate, singled, took second on Wood's bunt, and tallied on Bruton's single for the deciding run. In the late game on the hot, humid evening, five Tigers pitchers gave up nine runs and 13 hits, making the up-and-down Montejo, who allowed nothing in his two-inning stint starting in the fifth, the only effective Bengals hurler. Bruton and Kaline both rapped two hits, Fernandez slugged a two-run triple, and Colavito added an RBI single and a sacrifice fly, but the Bengals turned ten hits into only five runs. For Cleveland, Mudcat Grant, a big right-hander, pitched a complete game, raising his ledger to 11–5, and the Tribe won, 9–5.

Regardless, the Tigers were proving resilient in the pennant race. For example, Colavito was helping with his glove as well as his big bat, making three running, one-handed catches against the Indians. Fernandez, displaying his old flash at shortstop, banged his third triple in five games. Bertoia was looking good at third base, although he lacked the punch at the plate of the injured Boros. Cash and Wood were prospering on the right side of the infield, and both continued to hit well. Cash was averaging .361, the exact mark that won him the batting title in 1961, and Wood was batting .262, a good figure for the speedy rookie. The weather in Detroit was so hot in August that on Saturday, after he singled and scored from first on Colavito's triple, Kaline took a whiff of oxygen in the dugout. Sunday's split gave Detroit a season series edge over Cleveland of 10–5. The Yankees, however, swept their doubleheader from the Twins, giving New York a 71–37 record and a lead of 2.5 games over Detroit, now with a mark of 69–40.

Scheffing, commenting on his pitching, said Lary, Mossi, and Bunning might have to win 60 games combined for the Tigers to take the pennant. The pilot added that Bunning and Mossi might take on an occasional inning of relief because, with Fox sidelined, there was no late-inning specialist, or "closer."[10]

Yankees Hot in August

The Tigers roared in August, but the Yankees, despite Ralph Houk being fined $200 and suspended for five days for his rhubarb with umpire Ed Hurley on Sunday, July 30, kept rolling toward the pennant. After a remarkable 20–9 record in July, the season's first hot, humid month, the Bronx Bombers played better in what ballplayers and writers alike call the "dog days" of August, racking up, like the Tigers, a 22–9 mark for a winning percentage of .710. All the while, the Mantle–Maris home run derby produced great excitement among fans and writers, and the Yankees played to near-sellout crowds. Indeed, Maris recalled that spectators at away games often booed their own team's pitchers if they didn't throw strikes to him or to Mantle, the cleanup hitter.

The booing of home-team pitchers started in Washington at a Friday night game on August 11, when Maris and Mantle homered in the same game, though not back-to-back. Highlighting New York's 12–5 rout, Maris victimized Pete Burnside for the third time in 1961, although the one-time Giant, who was signed as a free agent in 1949, tried to jam him inside. With the bases empty, Maris creamed one high and deep to right, and the ball cleared the 31-foot fence and hit halfway up the light tower behind the wall. In the seventh against Burnside, Mantle homered deep to right, with Richardson aboard via an error, and the clout boosted the Bombers' lead to 11–3. Of a day when Washington papers ran sports headlines like Mantle, Maris Here with Yanks, Maris wrote that the booing of opposing pitchers like Burnside was spreading: "This would soon become general as fans all over the league booed their own pitchers each time they walked either of us." Folks loved seeing the Yankees hit home runs, and after Friday's game, Mantle led in what Maris called "our personal score, 44–42."[11]

On Saturday the Yankees faced Dick Donovan, the 6'3" sinkerballer, and only Maris solved his slants. Maris lined his 14th double off the right field fence, a two-out drive, but Mantle flied out to deep right to end the first inning. Bill Stafford started for the visitors, and he allowed one run in the Senators' first on a pair of singles, a bunt, and an infield hit by cleanup batter Jim King, who went 3-for-4 on the day. Batting with one out in the fourth, Maris lofted his 43rd home run high over the right field fence, giving him homers in two straight days at Griffith Stadium, a first for him. Still, Donovan prevailed for the victory, allowing no other four-baggers. In the bottom of the seventh, Washington won when Gene Green, coming out on top for once against ace closer Luis Arroyo, connected for a grand slam for a 5–1 lead that became the final score. Green's 16th home run showed that the big blasts mattered most when they were game-winners, and aside from

Maris, the Yankees got only singles from Mantle, Boyer, and Stafford, whose record fell to 9–6.

In Sunday's doubleheader at Griffith, Washington's spectators enjoyed a hometown fan's favorite outing in 1961: the home team belted the Yankees, 12–2, but Mantle and Maris each delivered a home run. Washington started Bennie Daniels, the 6'1" African American from Tuscaloosa, Alabama, whose 12–11 record would make him the Senators hurler with the most wins in 1961. The big right-hander tossed a five-hitter and chipped in with two singles in five trips. Mantle homered in the ninth, a bases-empty blow to deep right that gave him a 45–44 edge over Maris in their personal rivalry. On the other hand, Washington knocked around Bud Daley and three relievers for 16 hits, paced by three each by Chuck Hinton and Bob Johnson. In the nightcap, Maris, with that one-eighth inch on his side, led a 12-hit assault with a single and his 45th homer, a two-run blow in the first inning off a sidearm slant from Marty Kutyna, while Jim Coates scattered nine hits for the 9–4 triumph. The most Mantle could do was draw a walk, while Maris, Bobby Richardson, John Blanchard, Hector Lopez, and Clete Boyer each collected two hits. New York's split with Washington gave the Yankees a 77–39 record and an edge of 3.5 games over Detroit, as the Tigers fell to the Twins, 13–5, dropping the Bengals' ledger to 73–42.

Not only were the fans excited about the home run race, but so were the teammates of Mantle and Maris. Reserve Joe DeMaestri, the longtime Athletics shortstop who arrived in the Maris trade on December 11, 1959, remembered how the Yankees on the bench enjoyed watching Mantle and Maris both having a fantastic year. "Every time they came up," DeMaestri observed, "we would stand up in the dugout to see who was going to hit the next one."[12]

In the Yankees' clubhouse, most reporters asked about the home run race. Maris and Mantle were tied with 45 four-baggers each, 16 games ahead of the pace set by Babe Ruth when he hit 60 homers in the 154-game schedule of 1927. Maris recalled expressing for the first time his hope that he or Mantle would break the Babe's record, but he told writers that it was too early with too many games left, 38, to think about breaking the single-season home run mark. Did he want Mantle to keep hitting longballs? Yes, because he was a team player, and he wanted Mantle to keep up his end of the slugging duo. In fact, with the dangerous "Switcher" batting behind Maris, hurlers could hardly pitch around him.[13]

In any event, many reporters whiffed on Maris. He was a big leaguer on and off the diamond. Later, although he was sometimes irritated and often answered an endless stream of questions with terse replies, Maris, a true everyman's hero, was what baseball needed during that famous homer-heavy season of 1961.

Unsung Heroes I

While the Bronx Bombers continued to win, due in large part to home runs from every position in the lineup as well as good pitching, the Yankees and the Tigers both received critical contributions from players who were less famous, but still important to each team.

For the Yankees, these lesser-known heroes included Hector Lopez and John Blanchard. For the Tigers, the unsung heroes were Bo Osborne and Mike Roarke. Everyone knows about the legendary Yogi Berra, who can be recognized from his first name, but how many remember Lopez, his left-field partner? Tigers fans remember stars like Al Kaline or Rocky Colavito or Norm Cash or Frank Lary, but not nearly as many will recall heroes like Mike Roarke or Terry Fox.

Hector Lopez, born in Colon, Panama, on July 8, 1929,[14] grew up playing pickup games of baseball with kids using a broom handle for a bat and a ball made of taped rubber. He dreamed of becoming a major league player, a hope fueled by watching Manuel, his father, pitch for local teams. He recalled seeing the Dodgers and the Yankees play an exhibition game in Panama in 1947, when the Dodgers trained in Cuba so that Jackie Robinson could play without being harassed in traditional sites such as the segregated cities in Florida. Lopez attended Rainbow City High in the Canal Zone, learned auto mechanics, and worked on the U.S. military base,

Hector Lopez, who made the majors with Kansas City in 1955, added a dependable right-handed bat to the Yankees when he arrived in a trade on May 26, 1959. Lopez endured an offseason in 1961, averaging .222, but he gave the Yankees a good reserve for the outfield as well as an experienced pinch-hitter (Author's collection).

but he was playing semipro ball by the time he graduated in 1950. Scouted and signed to an independent league in Canada, Lopez, quiet, respectful, and hard-working, ended up with the Philadelphia Athletics in 1953, after his contract was purchased from St. Hyacinthe in Quebec.

Lopez, who played well for Williamsport of the Class A Eastern League in 1953 and Ottawa of the Triple-A International League in 1954, went to spring training in 1955 with the Athletics, after the franchise shifted to Kansas City. Sooner or later, the 5'11" 180-pound Panamanian, a right-handed batter, played every infield and outfield position for the A's and later the Yankees. During his rookie season of 1955, he batted .290 with 15 homers and 68 RBI with sixth-place Kansas City. He also became friends with the team's other two non-white players, Vic Power and Harry "Suitcase" Simpson. Lopez kept a low profile off the field in segregated Kansas City, where he and Simpson shared an apartment. A good teammate, a clutch hitter, and a versatile glove man, Lopez flashed his power with the A's by reaching double digits in homers during four solid seasons, but KC was mired in the second division. "They traded most of their good ballplayers, and most went to the Yankees," Lopez recalled. "Kansas City was trying to build a ballclub, and they could get three or four players from the Yankees for one or two players."

Typical of such trades that helped the Yankees, Lopez was swapped to New York on May 26, 1959, with pitcher Ralph Terry in return for right-handers Johnny Kucks and Tom Sturdivant and second baseman Jerry Lumpe. On June 9, showing his clutch ability, Lopez sparked the Yankees to a 13-inning, 9–8 win over the visiting Athletics with a line single to right, driving in Yogi Berra with the game-winning run. In a game lasting over four hours, Lopez went 3-for-5 with one walk, and he saved the game twice. In the ninth, he tripled, and a few minutes later scored to tie the game when outfielder Whitey Herzog muffed Gil McDougald's short fly to right.

Lopez, always neat and well-liked, finished the 1959 season averaging .283, and he produced career highs with 22 homers and 93 RBI. In 147 games, he played 76 at third base, 35 in the outfield, and 33 at second base. He made 31 errors, but as Casey Stengel said about the win over the A's, his clutch hitting and versatility outweighed any fielding lapses.

In 1960, his first full season with New York, Lopez, the team's second non-white player after Elston Howard, helped the Yankees win the pennant with his timely bat and handy glove, averaging .284 with nine home runs and 46 RBI. In a story dated May 11, 1960, "The Lonely World of Hector Lopez," Stan Isaacs of *Newsday* detailed how Lopez left his home in Brooklyn, where his mother also lived, by ten o'clock in the morning for the hour-long subway ride to Yankee Stadium to be ready for batting practice at 11:30.

Following an afternoon game, Lopez, a major leaguer who was an outsider with his team as well as virtually anonymous in private life, rode the subway home, usually arriving after seven o'clock. Away from the intense pressure of the ballpark, he lived a quiet life, enjoying working as a carpenter and a mechanic. After the season, he returned to Colon and married his sweetheart, Claudette Brown, on November 30.

Before the wedding, Lopez played in the 1960 World Series, his first, but the Yankees lost in seven games to the Pirates. He got into three games. He started in left field in Game One at Forbes Field in Pittsburgh, and he singled once in five trips as the Yankees lost, 6–4. He didn't return to the lineup until Game Five, when he hit a pinch single for Bill Stafford in the seventh, but the Yankees fell, 5–2. In Game Seven, Lopez, pinch-hitting for Stafford again, singled in the third inning, but the Yankees lost, 10–9, on Bill Mazeroski's famous home run in the ninth. Lopez proved he could hit in October, averaging .429 with a 3-for-7 performance, but the soft-spoken, low-key, utility man didn't get many chances to contribute.

In 1961 Lopez endured a slump for most of the season. Playing in 93 games, he batted .222 with three homers and 22 RBI, his worst mark so far (he averaged .266 for his 12 seasons). The friendly Panamanian said it was tougher not to be a regular.[15] "Hector was never a spectacular player, but he was one of those guys you could always depend on when you needed him," said Ralph Houk, who was Lopez's manager for three of the Yankees' pennant-winning seasons in the 1960s. According to *New York Post* scribe Maury Allen, Lopez, thanks in part to a lifetime World Series mark of .286, became "a living legend in his home country of Panama."[16]

On Sunday, August 13, when the Yankees won the second game of the doubleheader at Washington, 9–4, and Maris socked his fourth home run in four games, Lopez started in left field. Hitting seventh, he went 2-for-3, clubbing a run-scoring double in the eighth inning as the Yankees rallied for five runs to take a 9–1 lead. Fans and writers may have overlooked Lopez's contributions, but his bat was usually potent for the Bombers.

For Detroit, a comparable but little-known utility player was Larry Sidney Osborne, better known to his teammates as "Bo." Like many of his contemporaries, Osborne, who attended West Fulton High in Atlanta, grew up playing team sports, notably football and baseball. The son of Tiny Osborne, a towering right-hander who pitched for the Cubs and the Dodgers in the early 1920s, Larry had baseball in his blood. Upon graduating in 1953, he was offered a football scholarship by Auburn University, but he signed with the Tigers and was sent to Class A Montgomery, Alabama, of the South Atlantic League. Mainly a first baseman, he could play third base, catcher, and the outfield. Stocky, strong, and agile at 6'1" and

205 pounds, the left-handed batter could, and did, hit with power at Detroit's minor league farms, but he never matched his averages or power after he reached the Tigers. For example, his first call-up to the Bengals in late 1957 resulted in a 4-for-27 performance, with one double and one RBI.

Osborne continued to chase his dream of being a major leaguer. Married to his high school sweetheart, Sandra Hosea, on June 24, 1955, after she graduated from West Fulton, he and his wife, a pretty brunette, lived in Atlanta during the offseason. The Osbornes rented in the Detroit suburbs for short stints in 1957 and 1958, and all of the 1959 season, when Bo stayed with the Bengals, hitting .191 with three home runs and 21 RBI in 86 games. Detroit decided Osborne needed more experience, and he was sent to Triple-A Denver in 1960. Rising to the challenge and swinging the team's biggest bat, Osborne battled Boston prospect Carl Yastrzemski all summer for the league's batting title. In the end, Osborne won the American Association's Triple Crown, averaging .342 with 34 home runs and 119 RBI. Returning to Lakeland in 1961, the versatile South-

Larry "Bo" Osborne, a slugger who could play first base, third base, and the outfield, gave the Tigers a reliable backup for Norm Cash. Osborne also added left-handed power off the bench (National Baseball Hall of Fame, Cooperstown, New York).

erner made the grade. Still, he struggled daily to unseat Norm Cash at first base. A team player, Osborne helped his club in several ways, but Cash hit for the league's highest average.

Like many other athlete-husbands, Osborne traveled to Detroit and lined up a place to rent before bringing his family, which later included three children, Larry, Jr., Tim, and Kimberly. Typical of families involved with pro ball, Sandra, a cheerful Southern belle, made friends with other baseball wives. Those who were younger and newer to the major leagues, like Sandra, became close friends with others sharing the same experience, such as Merry Sue, the wife of Mike Roarke, Shirley, the wife of Terry Fox, and Myrta, the wife of Norm Cash. Asked if Larry competing with Cash for playing time hurt the two men's friendship, Sandra Osborne said it didn't. She described Cash as a down-home, friendly person, and her husband was the same.

Almost all of the wives had babies or toddlers to care for, Sandra commented, but they all enjoyed getting a babysitter, "dressing up," and going to games at Tiger Stadium, where the wives sat together in a section of reserved seats behind third base. When the team was on the road, the wives busied themselves with children, leisure activities like reading, watching their favorite TV programs, getting together for lunch with other baseball wives, and, when the time came, meeting their husbands at Metro Airport when the Tigers returned. Sandra remembered that one of the game's thrills, which happened more often to the big stars, was when kids and adults knocked on the door or came up to them in restaurants to get autographs. In fact, the wives became celebrities too. She concluded, "We were so typical of that era. We were married for 55 years and had three children … all adored watching their dad play baseball."[17]

Despite the fact that they were friends, Osborne, doing his job, pushed Cash hard. Nobody wishes that a friend or teammate will get injured or sick, but if that happens, ballplayers call it "breaks of the game." Baseball is a team sport, but every player is out for himself as well as for the team, because if not, the less talented, those who perform less well in the clutch, or those who let emotions get in the way of playing hard every day, end up in the minors or out of uniform.

Osborne gave his team a good season in 1961, but similar to other non-regulars like Hector Lopez, he enjoyed his big hits and his good days in spurts. For example, the big first baseman went 10-for-41 as a pinch-hitter, not quite a .250 average, but still a good mark for hitting off the bench. At one point, starting with a pinch-hit single on June 24 in the Tigers' 6–4 victory in Washington, and continuing through his single in Detroit's 8–3 loss at Boston on July 5, Osborne went 4-for-6 (including one double) as a pinch-hitter, a sizzling .667 mark.

When Cash suffered an infection in his foot and sat out two days against the Twins in Detroit on July 14–15, Osborne played well at first base. On July 15, Bunning was hurling a four-hitter and the score was tied at 1–1 in the eighth inning when Osborne, who walked once, faced the stellar Camilo Pascual. Getting a good fastball, he rocked the Cuban right-hander for a solo home run that gave the Bengals a 2–1 victory. The win kept Detroit virtually tied with New York in the tightening pennant race. Osborne was hitting .281 at the time, but he got fewer opportunities in the last two months of the season. Playing first base on August 31, he produced his only RBI of the month, driving in a run on a groundout that gave Detroit a 2–1 lead over Chicago. When the year was over, he hit .215 with two homers and 13 RBI. Considering that a big leaguer with the experience of Lopez batted .222 in 1961, Osborne was a useful player for the Tigers, pinch-hitting as well as playing 11 games at first base and eight more at third base.

Home Run Chase and the Pennant Race

In the Bronx on Tuesday, August 15, the White Sox took the opener of a three-game set, 2–1, behind a four-hitter by fastballing Juan Pizarro. Roger Maris singled and hit number 46, but it wasn't enough to keep Whitey Ford's mark from slipping to 20–3. In Wednesday's tilt, Maris, swinging a hot bat, slammed home runs number 47 and 48 and produced four RBI, lifting his team to a 4–4 tie going to the ninth inning. The Bombers won, 5–4, when Bob Cerv, pinch-hitting with the bases loaded for winner Ralph Terry (9–1), who hurled the last four innings in relief of Rollie Sheldon, was hit with a pitch by reliever Warren Hacker. In Thursday's finale, Bill Stafford delivered a seven-hitter, improving his record to 10–6 after the 23rd save by Arroyo, who hurled a shaky ninth but persevered. Maris had a quiet day, going 0-for-4, but in the first inning, Mickey Mantle slugged an RBI triple off Frank Baumann. New York scored three times in the fourth, and Mantle made it 5–0 in the sixth with a bases-loaded grounder. Arroyo surrendered three runs before fanning pinch-hitter Bob Roselli on his sinking, curving screwball. The win lifted New York to a 79–40 ledger and a four-game lead over Detroit, after the Bengals lost at home to the Orioles, 3–1, when Paul Foytack spaced seven hits but got little help from his friends.

On Thursday night, the Yankees players and team personnel boarded a Cleveland-bound flight at Idlewild Airport (renamed John F. Kennedy International Airport on December 24, 1963, following the assassination of the President). The Bronx Bombers were flying on a 13-game odyssey that would end on August 31, to be followed by a three-game showdown with the Tigers at Yankee Stadium. By the time the trip ended, the Yankees had defeated the Indians three out of four, lost two of three to the expansion Angels, beat Kansas City three straight, and lost two of three to the Twins for a 13-game record of 8–5. Starting on August 15, the Tigers played eight games in the Motor City, seven games on the road, and three more at home. The Bengals wrapped up the month's schedule by defeating the White Sox, 8–2, on Thursday, August 31, and the victory left Detroit with an 86–47 record and 1.5 games behind New York, now 87–45.

On Friday night, August 18, at Municipal Stadium on the shores of Lake Erie, the Indians beat the Yankees, 5–1, as Florida-born African American Mudcat Grant, backed by ten safeties, won his 12th game with a three-hitter. Jim Coates started slowly for New York, yielding three runs in the first inning, capped by Bubba Phillips' two-run homer to left. Coates lasted into the third, when Woodie Held, the quick-handed shortstop who swung a big bat, lined a two-run triple for a 5–0 lead. Bud Daley replaced Coates and worked 4⅓ scoreless frames, and Al Downing hurled a hitless ninth, but too late. The only Yankees' run came in the fifth when, with two outs, Ellie Howard slugged his 12th home run to deep center. The only other hit allowed by Grant was Kubek's one-out single in the ninth, but Maris struck out and Mantle flied out to end it.

The Bombers won the remaining three games. Ford won his 21st on Saturday, thanks to a third out in the tenth inning by Arroyo, Ford's savior in 1961. New York rook a 2–0 lead in the fourth on two walks, Howard's double, Boyer's double play grounder, and Ford's base hit. The game's only four-bagger came when All-Star catcher John Romano hit number 18, a solo blast off Ford in the fifth. The Indians tied it at 2–2 in the eighth on Ford's bases-loaded wild pitch. In the Yankees' tenth, Billy Gardner doubled, Maris grounded out to first, Mantle looked at a third strike, Berra was walked intentionally, and Howard singled for a 3–2 lead. In the Tribe's tenth, Ken Aspromonte socked a two-out double, but Arroyo ended it by retiring Piersall on a grounder.

The Yankees won twice with their biggest bats on Sunday. In the opener, Mantle took Jim Perry downtown in the first inning with his 46th round-tripper, a three-run bomb into the right field seats for a 3–0 lead en route to a 6–0 victory, and Ralph Terry boosted his record to 10–1 by hurling a three-hit shutout. Mantle went 3-for-4 and drove in four runs, and Maris cracked his 49th home run, a two-run drive good for a 5–0 lead in the third. In the nightcap, Bill Skowron supplied the power, belting his 21st home run, a two-run blow in the second frame off Gary Bell, who lasted 5⅓ innings as his record fell to 8–13. Rollie Sheldon spaced eight hits to win his ninth game, Mantle chipped in with a bases-loaded walk and an RBI single, and Berra added a run-scoring single in the eighth, boosting the lead to 5–1. Afterward, as the team showered, packed, and took a bus to Hopkins Airport for a late-night flight to Los Angeles, the Yankees (82–41) held a three-game bulge over the Tigers (79–44), after Detroit split a twin bill with Boston.

On the West Coast the Yankees didn't fare as well against the eighth-place Angels, but Maris got welcome news from home. On Monday, August 21, his wife Pat delivered their fourth child and third son, Randy. Before hearing that welcome news, Maris, Mantle, and Berra went to a movie studio and made a cameo appearance in *That Touch of Mink*, a romantic comedy starring Cary Grant and Doris Day. On Tuesday it was back to baseball for all the Yankees. That evening in the Spanish-style architecture of Wrigley Field, they lost the opener, 5–4, even though Maris smashed his 50th round-tripper over the center field wall into the street, a two-run blow off right-hander Ken McBride in the sixth that cut the Angels' lead to 3–2.

When Maris clubbed number 50, he joined eight previous sluggers, including Mantle with 52 in 1956, who had hit 50 or more homers in a season. Ruth, of course, led those longball hitters, having cracked 54 twice (1920 and 1928) and 59 once (1921), in addition to his 60-homer season. The Bambino, who totaled 714 career home runs, actually hit more home runs in 1927 than any other American League team, but Maris hit 50 before September, and not even Ruth achieved that milestone. Besides the Babe, the other big belters were Hank Greenberg with 58 in 1938, Jimmie Foxx with 58 in 1932 and 50 in 1938, Hack Wilson, who set the NL record of 56 in 1930, Ralph Kiner with 51 in 1947 and 54 in 1949, Johnny Mize with 51 in 1947, and Willie Mays with 51 in 1955. Of those famous hitters, Maris is the only one not enshrined in the Baseball Hall of Fame.

Over the next two days the teams split two games, with the Yankees riding Maris' bat to a ten-inning, 8–6 victory on Wednesday. The game's only home run came in the sixth when Skowron homered for the 22nd time, a two-run blast off ex–Yankee Ryne Duren that cut the Angels' lead to 6–5. The Bombers tied it with an unearned run in the eighth, and the teams remained tied through the ninth. In New York's tenth, Maris, with Billy Gardner aboard, boomed a triple that hit inches below the top of the center field wall off ex–Tiger Jim Donohue, giving New York a 7–6 lead. The rookie right-hander, shaken by the blast, proceeded to walk Mantle. Lefty Ron Moeller came from the pen, but wild-pitched home the final run. The rubber-armed Arroyo, the fourth Yankees hurler, tossed three scoreless innings and improved his mark to 11–3.

In the finale on Thursday, the Yankees lost their third West Coast series of 1961 to the Angels, falling 6–4. Neither team homered, but LA combined six hits with nine walks off four Yankees pitchers to score six runs, while the visitors tallied four runs off three walks and 13 hits. Mantle singled once, and Maris contributed a sacrifice fly to score New York's first run. On the same day that Detroit topped Cleveland, 6–0, the Yankees, sporting an 83–43 ledger, saw their lead over the Tigers, now improved to 81–45, shrink to two games.

Unsung Heroes II

In 1961, John Blanchard would have been the regular behind the mask on any American League team except the Yankees. New York, the league's perennial pennant-winner in the 1950s, started out with Berra and Howard doing most of the receiving, often including doubleheaders. Every team, however, needs a backup catcher and a bullpen catcher, and the latter, the

third-stringer, mainly warms up the
pitchers and, if an injury occurs, fills in
behind the plate.

Blanchard, a 6'1", 193-pounder in
his prime, grew up in Minneapolis, and,
like Roger Maris and many other youths,
played the three big team sports of the
era, football, basketball, and baseball.
Blanchard, scouted by 12 major league
clubs, signed with the Yankees in 1951,
right after graduating from Central
High, where he was all-conference in
all three sports. The Yankees gave the
third baseman-outfielder big bucks:
$30,000 and a guarantee of $5,000 a
year for five years. A left-handed pull
hitter with good power and adequate
defensive skills, Blanchard played much
of the 1950s in the Yankees' farm system. Bill Dickey, the Hall of Famer who
worked with Yogi Berra on the finer
points of catching, converted Blanchard
to catcher in 1952. Three years later,
Blanchard was called to New York, and
he played one game on September 25,

John Blanchard enjoyed a remarkable season for the Yankees in 1961.
The left-handed batter wasn't a
regular behind the plate, but he
strengthened the Yankees with his
.305 average, 21 home runs, and 54
RBI (National Baseball Hall of
Fame, Cooperstown, New York).

1955. He was hitless in three trips, walking once, against Boston's George
Susce in an 8–1 loss. At home in the offseason, Blanchard often played with
a team that practiced against the NBA's Lakers.

Blanchard, friendly, witty, and hard-working, was drafted and spent
two years in the U.S. Army. He served the latter part of his hitch in Bavaria,
Germany, where he played some service ball, a staple of pro athletes in the
1950s. After completing his military stint, he married hometown sweetheart
Nancy Carey on March 12, 1955. But for that season, the Yankees had Berra,
rookie Elston Howard, and longtime backup Charlie Silvera. Blanchard,
after four games at Triple-A Denver, played most of the year at Binghamton
of the Eastern League, where he hit .281, produced 112 RBI, and displayed
good power with 34 homers. For New York, the 26-year-old Howard came
through with a .290 season, contributing 10 homers and 43 RBI. Backing
up Berra, Howard caught nine games, spending most of his time as a reserve
outfielder.

The Yankees, always with a stockpile of talent during the years before the draft began in 1965, had no room for Blanchard. Instead, he spent all of 1956 catching for Binghamton. During 1957 and 1958, he was sent to Denver, where he batted .310 and .291, respectively, producing a two-season total of 37 home runs. Houk, a catcher himself, managed Denver for three seasons, starting in 1955, before returning in 1958 to New York as a coach. Blanchard played under Houk in 1957, and when he was finally called up to the Yankees in 1959, Houk coached him for two seasons before taking over for Casey Stengel in 1961. Stengel largely ignored Blanchard, who appeared in eight games in the outfield and once at first base in 1959. Mostly warming the bench, the Minneapolis native, often frustrated, batted .169 in 1959 and .242 in 1960. Altogether, he played in 102 games during his first two full seasons.[18]

Nobody knew it at the time, but facing so much failure, first, to make the Yankees, and second, to play more games, if not become a regular, Blanchard, like many pro athletes in similar situations, did more than a little drinking. But he denied having a problem. To teammates and friends, he was happy-go-lucky and a dedicated player. Even though he was a reserve, Blanchard loved being a Yankee. But as many other players learned from experience, being a major leaguer isn't all great and glorious. "If I went 0 for 4, I drank to forget it," he later told Tony Kubek. "If I was 4 for 4, I drank to celebrate. I had a problem when I played, but I didn't admit it."[19]

Still, Blanchard often proved to be the right man with the powerful bat at the right time, notably in 1961, the best year of his career. In one three-game stretch in late July, he connected for four straight home runs, the first two as a pinch-hitter. On Friday night, July 21, against Boston at Fenway Park, Maris, Mantle, Berra, and Blanchard all homered to spark the Yankees' victory. Blanchard, batting for Clete Boyer in the ninth inning, blasted the winning home run, connecting off Mike Fornieles with the bases loaded to bring the Bombers from behind for an 11–8 win. On Saturday afternoon against the Red Sox, Blanchard, again batting for Boyer, slugged a long home run to right field off Gene Conley to tie the game in the ninth inning at 9–9. Luis Arroyo, a .280 hitter in 1961, doubled, Bobby Richardson singled for one run, and Kubek doubled to provide the winning margin of 11–9. Blanchard didn't play on Sunday, and Monday was an off-day. On Tuesday against Chicago at Comiskey Park, Blanchard caught and went 2-for-4, both homers. Mantle, facing Ray Herbert in the first with two outs and Richardson aboard, drove his 39th home run deep into the right-center field bleachers. Blanchard followed with his tenth four-bagger for a 3–0 lead. Leading off the fourth, Blanchard again homered off Herbert, boosting New York's lead to 4–0. The bases-empty shot to deep right gave him four home runs, the first two as a pinch-hitter, in four consecutive plate appearances over three games, surely a major league record for timely clutch hitting.

When the season was over, Blanchard, looking forward to his second World Series, had a career-best .305 average with 21 home runs and 54 RBI, which he achieved playing in 93 games with 275 plate appearances. Of such money players are championship teams made, and Blanchard may remain the most underrated Yankee ever. "I always wanted to be a Yankee when I was growing up," he said more than once. "That is all I ever wanted to be."[20]

For the Tigers, Mike Roarke played an equally valuable role, but unlike Blanchard, who was a big-time power hitter but a good catcher, Roarke was a big-time catcher but only a decent hitter. Tall and strong at 6'2" and 195 pounds, "Iron Mike," a 31-year-old Tigers rookie in 1961, took over behind the plate when starter Dick Brown suffered a split finger on July 15. After Brown's injury, Roarke entered the game, his 33rd of the

Mike Roarke, Detroit's rookie catcher who took over for six weeks when the regular, Dick Brown, was injured in mid-July, steadied the Tigers' pitching staff with his excellent receiving (National Baseball Hall of Fame, Cooperstown, New York).

season, and he finished up behind the plate. Afterward, he caught 55 games, including doubleheaders on July 16, July 23, and August 2. Iron Mike was batting .276 when Brown was hurt, and gradually his average slipped until he was batting .223 at the season's end. Yet like other Tigers reserves, including Bo Osborne, Bubba Morton, and Charlie Maxwell, Roarke enjoyed his key hits in bunches, a familiar routine for any big leaguer who is not a regular but awaits the opportunity to come off the bench.

Roarke, a native of West Warwick, Rhode Island, starred in football and baseball at Boston College before graduating with honors in 1952. Like Blanchard, Roarke was a child of the Great Depression, and pro baseball became a way to achieve a good income for his family as well as meaningful recognition by using the natural athletic skills that he honed as a young man. Roarke, like Blanchard, excelled at football, basketball, and baseball, but his best opportunity came with a pro baseball contract. "As an athlete, his talent is almost limitless; as a leader, he is a model for his teammates; as a gentleman, he approaches perfection," commented assistant football coach Bill Flynn for the college's student newspaper in 1951.

The Boston Braves signed Roarke to a minor league contract, but he had been drafted, so after a few games, he entered the Army. The Korean War was winding down in 1952, but many eligible adult males were drafted into the armed forces throughout the 1950s. Those were the times of Eisenhower, the Cold War, and fears of Communist expansion, so a strong, well-prepared, potent military as well as a major defense budget characterized the federal government.

Roarke returned from his Army tour of duty in February of 1955, went to spring training with the Braves, and launched his minor league career, which carried him to the Triple-A level by 1957. There he languished during four long seasons, largely due to his "good-field, little-hit" reputation. At the major league level, the Braves, like the Yankees, fielded two good catchers, Del Crandall backed up by Del Rice. The Braves won National League pennants in 1957 and 1958, winning the first of two World Series against the Yankees in seven games in 1957, and losing the 1958 fall classic to the Yankees, also in seven games.

Roarke lived with the frustrations of a multi-talented athlete trying to make the majors. He played well behind the plate, but posted a .246 mark for eight minor league seasons. Big Mike peaked at first-place Denver in 1960, starring with others who made the Tigers, including Jake Wood, Steve Boros, and Larry Osborne. Roarke's performance, batting .255 with eight homers and 40 RBI, made him an American Association All-Star. A quiet team player, Roarke, who was up with the Tigers for the first month of the 1960 season, took his wife of three years, Merry Sue, and their child to the Motor City to live what became the great adventure of their lives.[21]

Homers and Pennants: The Pressure Builds

Taking yet another late-night jet flight that arrived in the dawn's early light at Kansas City, the Yankees beat the last-place A's three times. The series highlight for thousands of folks, including many friends of Maris' family, came on Saturday, August 26, in the sixth inning when Rajah, with all eyes in a crowd of more than 32,000 glued to him, pounded his 51st homer, a blast into the right field seats at Municipal Stadium that was his only hit in a three-game series seen by standing-room-only crowds. Stafford improved to 11–7 with a three-hitter, and the Yankees, fueled by ten hits, including two singles and two walks by Mantle, won, 5–1.

The biggest show was Maris returning home, and one thoughtless writer put his address in the local paper. The next morning Roger's street in suburban Raytown looked, he said, "like the Los Angeles Freeway." Baseball always attracts countless fans, autograph collectors, and camp followers who want a piece of major leaguers, especially the big stars, but 1961 was turning into an unprecedented media-fan circus. Reported Joe King, "the M & M combo was subjected to a ceaseless chase by autograph hounds, friends, and friends of friends wherever they went." Maris stayed at home in Raytown with his family, but the lobby of the Muehlebach Hotel, housing the Yankees, was jammed with sight-seers, autograph seekers, and others curious about the celebrities made so famous by an increasing torrent of newspaper and magazine stories.

After grabbing the series finale on Sunday, 8–7, thanks to home runs by Howard and Berra, Ford's 22nd win, and another save by the intrepid Arroyo, the Yankees, watching the scoreboard daily, knew that Detroit had defeated Washington twice, cutting New York's lead to two games.

Afterward, the Yankees took an evening jet to Minneapolis, bound for a welcome day off on Monday followed by a Tuesday tilt with the Twins. Maris, upset about the fiasco of his address being printed in the paper, stayed behind until Monday, enjoying his first chance to visit Pat and his infant son, now home from the hospital. The proud father recalled that his four days at home refreshed him, despite the circus atmosphere at the ballpark. "I honestly believe that those four days had a lot to do with making it possible for me to go on," Maris wrote, "and keep striving to reach the sixty home-run level. It was a good break in the pressure-packed season."[22]

Maybe a nice break for Maris, but from the first game of the Yankees' West Coast trip until the final day of the season, the home run duel made the biggest headlines in baseball. Otherwise, the newspapers were full of stories about the European crisis over Berlin, as the East Germans began building a high wall to separate East Berlin from West Berlin on August 15. In the backdrop hovered a possible conflict with the Soviet Union, and President Kennedy and his top advisers carefully considered their options. On the home front, the papers featured news about a threatened strike against the Big Four auto makers in Detroit, despite the high seven percent unemployment rate. Most people were still enjoying the nation's great love affair with the automobile, and by 1961 compact models were growing in popularity. Small cars such as Chevy's Corvair, Plymouth's Valiant, and Ford's Falcon attracted many buyers, but the German-made Volkswagen was still popular. In addition, most people used consumer products such as transistor radios, direct-dial telephones, color TV, and stereo record players. For the majority of Americans in all walks of life, the new decade felt like a new beginning.

On Tuesday afternoon at Metropolitan Stadium, the Maris-and-Mantle home run derby opened to another sellout crowd in another city filled with fans and tourists hoping for a glimpse of the nation's biggest sports story.

Camilo Pascual blanked the Yankees sluggers, allowing just four singles and showing the paid audience of 40,118 a win. Maris was 0-for-3 with a walk, Mantle singled once in four trips, and the Twins' Earl Battey ripped the only extra-base hit, a two-run double in the sixth that made the final score 3–0, as Ralph Terry slipped to 11–2. Yankees' eyes kept glancing at the scoreboard, after Detroit beat Washington on Monday, 7–3. But on Tuesday, the Tigers lost a squeaker to the White Sox, 4–3, and the Yankees, at 86–44, held a game-and-a-half lead.

On Wednesday, August 30, Bill Stafford hurled his own four-hit shutout, shutting down the Twins' sluggers—Harmon Killebrew, Bob Allison, and Jim Lemon—but Mantle and Howard thrilled an outpouring of 41,357 with a long home run each. Mantle starred, singling home one run in the fourth inning. In the seventh, the Switcher drove one of Jim Kaat's slants deep into the left field seats for a 2–0 lead. Maris, who didn't homer, contributed an RBI single in the eighth. Howard finished the scoring in the ninth, belting a Ray Moore fastball deep to right field for his 14th homer. For New York, the best news came when Detroit lost to Chicago, 7–4.

The month ended on Thursday, and on "Ladies Days," the Twins' ace, lefty Jack Kralick, scattered 11 hits and proved tough enough with runners on base to notch his 12th victory, 5–4. All of the Yankees' runs came on homers: Mantle slammed his 48th, a solo blast to left in the fourth inning, and Skowron, one out later, hit number 24, also with the bases empty. Facing the hard-throwing Kralick in the sixth, with Mantle on second after a single and a steal, Hector Lopez, flashing his power, connected for his third home run, a drive that cut Minnesota's lead to 5–4, the eventual final score. The Twins scored all five runs off Rollie Sheldon and Jim Coates in the third, with Sheldon giving up RBI singles to Killebrew and Allison. When Coates took over, Lemon launched his 13th home run, and the loss left the Yankees with an 87–45 mark.

Also on August 31, the Tigers hosted and defeated the White Sox, 8–2, behind Paul Foytack's best game of the season. The savvy right-hander, relying mainly on breaking balls after tearing muscles in his pitching arm in 1960,[23] improved to 10–8. Bruton belted his 16th homer in the first inning, a two-run shot off Frank Baumann, who, with three relievers, allowed 14 hits. The biggest blow came in the fifth when Norm Cash, enjoying his career season, ripped into Russ Kemmerer for homer number 32, a towering drive that thrilled a crowd of more than 25,000 and lifted Detroit to a 7–2 lead. The Bengals, now at 86–47, trailed the Bombers by just 1.5 games.

After Thursday's contests, both teams boarded late-night planes bound for their rendezvous with destiny at Yankee Stadium, where they would play single games on the first three days of September. Those games would mark the turning point of the season for both teams, but nobody knew it.

As New York and Detroit entered September, the month in which the legendary Ruth had connected for 17 of his record-setting 60 homers, including five off last-place Red Sox pitchers in a three-game series on September 6–7, 1927, the Maris–Mantle home run extravaganza remained baseball's biggest story.[24] Regardless, the Tigers–Yankees showdown would be the single biggest series of the remarkable 1961 American League season.

8

The Yankees Win the Pennant

Getting Ready for the Bronx Bombers

For the week leading up to the showdown three-game series with New York at Yankee Stadium, to start on Friday, September 1, Bob Scheffing had rotated his starting pitchers so that he could use his "Big Three" against the Bombers, leading off with Don Mossi.[1] Scheffing's plan was to follow on Saturday with Frank Lary, the "Yankee-Killer." Commenting on the right-hander, Mike Roarke told Watson Spoelstra for *The Sporting News*, "Lary throws everything hard, like the hard slider and the hard curve. His fast ball has a tendency to move more than anyone else's on the staff. Lary gets the ball over with his good stuff." The Bengals' manager planned to wrap up the series with Jim Bunning on Sunday. Roarke, who caught the Kentucky sidearmer often, observed, "Bunning changes speeds on his curve as well as I've ever seen."

Scheffing commented on his ball club's readiness to meet the Yankees. For example, Cash, with 32 games to go on August 28, had boosted his average to .370. Washington manager Mickey Vernon, who won American League batting championships in 1946 and 1953, said, "Cash will win it easily." Colavito blasted seven home runs in the seven-game road trip to Cleveland and Washington, and his 122 RBI as of August 31 left him two behind the leader, Jim Gentile, with 124. Scheffing also credited Al Kaline and Billy Bruton for their outstanding outfield play as well as their hitting prowess. Kaline, a premier hitter, scored his 100th run when he hit his 17th homer on August 28. Dick McAuliffe, who averaged .300 in an 18-game stretch at third base, was playing well on the left side of the infield, and Chico Fernandez was "sharp" at shortstop for the last two months, following his recovery from a leg injury.[2] Finally, Steve Boros and Dick Brown would return to the active list on September 1. Boros participated in throwing and pepper drills on the sideline, but no batting yet. Brown had taken batting practice, though his injured but recovering finger kept him from gripping the bat properly. Further, Hank Aguirre started the season strong, but recently the lefty was working on improving his delivery.[3]

Mossi made his previous start on Sunday, August 27, in the opener of a twin bill at Washington's Griffith Stadium. Winning his 14th game on the fourth try, Mossi (now 14–3) was inspiring several veterans to perform better, notably Paul Foytack, Ron Kline, and Gerry Staley. Detroit won, 4–1, and Mossi, so calm that he was dubbed "The Sphinx," missed a complete game by one out. To date the 6'1" southpaw had held Maris to a career mark of .174, and Mickey Mantle, batting right-handed against Mossi, hit .289, with three homers in 137 plate appearances.[4]

Against the Senators, Mossi, who liked pitching hitters low and away, gave up five hits heading into the last of the ninth, and the Bengals led, 7–1. Listed third in the batting order, Bob Johnson, a right-handed shortstop-second baseman acquired by the Senators after he averaged .205 for Kansas City in 1960, doubled to left. Mossi fooled Gene Green with a slider, and he popped up to second base. The Tigers' lefty got a pitch in on Willie Tasby's hands, and he bounced one toward third, but Dick McAuliffe made a bad throw, leaving Tasby safe and Johnson on third. Bearing down, Mossi induced Harry Bright, a right-handed batting catcher who spent his first three seasons with the Pirates, to ground one to shortstop, and Chico Fernandez, seeing no chance to double up the speedy Tasby, rifled the ball to first, but the run scored, making it 7–2.

Mossi, tiring from the near–100 degree heat in the District of Columbia, gave up a single to rookie Bud Zipfel, the one-time Yankees prospect who went 3-for-4, and Tasby tallied to make the score 7–3. Mossi delivered a low curve, and Zipfel, not known for speed, stole second. Chuck Cottier, who had started the season with Detroit, singled to make it 7–4. Scheffing ambled out of the visitors' dugout, spoke to Mossi, and signaled for Terry Fox, making his second appearance since coming back from a sore arm on August 20. With the pitcher due up, Mickey Vernon used Gene Woodling. A clutch left-handed batter, the ex–Yankee singled off Fox. Billy Klaus, the one-time Red Sox shortstop, ran for the aging Woodling. Scheffing, with speedy rookie Chuck Hinton up next, called for Gerry Staley, who made his sixth appearance in a Tigers uniform (in his 45th game of the 1961 season). Staley, a savvy right-hander with a tricky knuckler, earned his first save for Detroit (and third of the season), fanning Hinton to end it, 7–4.

The Tigers won going away, and Rocky Colavito, facing Bennie Daniels in the sixth inning, smashed his 35th home run, upping Detroit's lead to 6–1. The Tigers totaled seven hits off Daniels and two relievers, Norm Cash led the way with a two-run double to center field in the first, and McAuliffe followed with a triple off the right field wall that made the score 3–0. Jake Wood slammed an RBI triple in the fifth, and Billy Bruton hit a sacrifice fly to make the lead 5–1.

Detroit won the nightcap, 10–1, when Foytack (9–8), a workhorse since 1955 who usually won in double digits, pitched a seven-hitter. The Bengals backed Foytack with a 12-hit assault paced by three home runs by Colavito, numbers 36, 37, and 38, giving him four clouts in one day, plus two hits each by Wood, Kaline, and Cash.

The Tigers took the fourth game of the series on Monday behind long-time National Leaguer Ron Kline, whom the Bengals had purchased off waivers from the Angels on August 10. Kline, a 6'3", fastballing right-hander who started his career with a 0–7 record as a Pittsburgh rookie in 1952, worked 6⅔ innings and recorded the 7–3 win. Fox, the late-inning specialist who could cut the plate's corners, finished the seventh and added two score-less innings for his ninth save. Kaline belted his 17th homer in the first inning, and Colavito followed with his number 39. In the sixth, Wood belted his 11th home run, a grand slam into the upper deck in left that lifted the lead to 7–1.[5]

Terry Fox, a 6'0", 175-pound right-hander with good control, was signed by the Double-A Atlanta Crackers after trying out in his hometown of

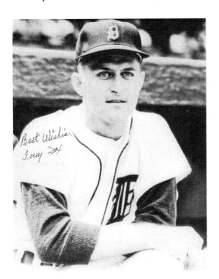

Terry Fox pitched out of the bull-pen for the Tigers in 1961, fashioning a 5–2 record with a team-high 12 saves. Fox and lefty Hank Aguirre provided Bob Scheffing with a strong one-two punch in late-inning relief (author's collection).

Chicago in 1953, the year he graduated from high school. Atlanta offered $250 a month for a C-ball contract, and Fox began his career in 1954 with New Iberia of the Evangeline League. He spent two years with Iberia, going 13–4 and 21–12, mainly as a starter, and the Milwaukee Braves bought his contract after the 1956 season. By 1959 he climbed to Triple-A Sacramento of the Pacific Coast League, where he was converted to relief. He went 12–9 in 53 appearances for Sacramento in 1960, and the Braves called him up in September, but he had no decisions in 8⅓ innings pitched over five games.

During the 1956 season at Atlanta, where he posted a 4–8 ledger, Terry took his wife Shirley for a picnic outing during a day off, and while polishing his car, he hurt the bursa in his right (pitching) elbow. Talented, determined, and quick to learn the tricks of his trade, he spent the rest of his career improving his techniques and his control and working around periodic soreness. By the time he reached Milwaukee in 1960, Fox, like many other hurlers of his era, was getting cortisone shots for his arm. "I'm just trying to express," Fox explained in 2013, "that without those shots, I don't know how well I would be able to continue to do as well as I did."

Fox proved to be a friendly, down-to-earth, and hard-working big leaguer. He thrived on a good fastball and a deceptive curve, plus the ability to spot the ball at clutch times. Following his trade to Detroit in the Bruton-for-Bolling deal in 1960, Fox began to shine out of the Tigers' pen.[6]

By that time, youth baseball leaders in the Motor City were wondering why Cash and Colavito couldn't walk up to the plate in "normal" fashion, rather than twirl bats or do warm-up exercises. Cash, for example, enjoyed swirling a pair of bats over his head, or sometimes swinging two bats behind his back like the Indian clubs that fans ordinarily saw in a circus. The small fry who copied Cash, pointed out Lyall Smith, often got disastrous results, "like strained backs, bruised heads, and battered torsos—not to mention an occasional backward flip that is completely unrehearsed." Colavito's loosening-up exercise was figured to have originated with a Bavarian

Rocky Colavito, the Tigers' popular slugger, entertained Tigers' fans with his batting warm-ups before each trip to the plate (author's collection).

pretzel-twister and carried over the Alps generations ago, where the Colavitos picked up the trick. The main idea was for the batter to push out his chest until his shoulder blades almost touched, and the bat, held behind the back on both ends, was slid down from the neck to the waist so as to create a flexible posture. In any case, Colavito slugged four homers in one twin bill, and the bat tricks of Detroit's two hammering heroes were popular with fans of all ages.[7]

Scheffing's choice for the Saturday game against the Yankees was Frank Lary. The Alabama ace last hurled at Tiger Stadium on Tuesday, August 29, against the White Sox, fashioning an eight-hitter but losing, 4–3, on a day when unsung heroes delivered big blows. After Colavito's first single and McAuliffe's two-out walk off ex–Bengals journeyman Ray Herbert, Chico Fernandez laced an RBI single to left, and Mike

Roarke hit a run-scoring double, giving the Tigers a 2–0 lead. Lary gave up three Chisox runs in the fifth inning. In the sixth, Colavito doubled and Fernandez blasted a triple, his fourth, but the visitors scored the winner in the seventh when Fernandez booted Roy Sievers' two-on grounder. Herbert improved to 9–12 and Turk Lown earned his ninth save. Lary, who singled, felt wiped out after his long day in the sticky heat.

Scheffing's selection to face the Yankees on Sunday was Jim Bunning, who lasted seven innings and yielded four runs to Chicago on August 30, but the Tigers lost, 7–4. Gerry Staley began the eighth, but he walked Luis Aparicio and gave up a triple to Roy Sievers. Scheffing called for Hank Aguirre, who had worked only 2⅔ frames in August, and the tall lefty yielded two runs on two singles plus a poor pickoff throw to first base. Terry Fox ended the inning, and he added a scoreless ninth, but too late. Strong-armed Juan Pizarro, the White Sox's fastballing ace, hurled a five-hitter, upping his mark to 11–5. Billy Bruton cracked his 15th homer in the fifth, and Reno Bertoia hit number two in the ninth, but both were bases-empty blows. Colavito, who didn't hang on to a fly in short left by Nellie Fox, argued with umpire Hank Soar, but Soar won. Rookie speedster Floyd Robinson swung Chicago's biggest bat, going 3-for-5 and driving in three runs, and Pizarro, adding insult to injury, singled in another run.[8]

Foytack, improving his mark to 10–8 on Thursday, won his third straight as the Tigers rolled over the White Sox, 8–2. Foytack had walked only four batters in his last three games, and he was throwing strikes on breaking balls when he was behind in the count. The Bengals rapped 14 safeties off Frank Baumann and three relievers as Detroit's lineup tuned up for the Bronx. Wood, batting leadoff, hit a single and an RBI double. Bruton, number two, opened the scoring with his 16th homer, a two-run shot in the first, and he added a single. Kaline, batting third, rapped two singles and a double in five trips. Colavito, the cleanup man, knocked in two runs, one with a single and another with a sacrifice fly. Cash, the number five hitter, socked his 32nd home run in the fifth, a skyrocket that bounced off the third deck. Bertoia, playing third base and batting sixth, hit a run-scoring single in four trips. Fernandez, listed seventh, singled once. Roarke, catching and batting eighth, contributed two singles, and Foytack, joining the fun, singled.[9]

The victory righted the Bengals' ship, as they had lost twice to the White Sox after winning five in a row and ten of their last 11 games. The Yankees fell to the Twins, 5–4, on August 31, so as Detroit's personnel packed before taking the bus to Metro Airport, the Bengals had an 86–47 record and trailed the Yankees by 1.5 games. Every man in the comfortable club-house under Tiger Stadium knew the next three games in New York meant winning, or losing, the pennant. Remarked Billy Bruton, the team's elder statesman, "If the Yankees win the pennant it will be because they've outplayed us and not for any other reason." Concluded Norm Cash, "All the rest of us have to do is be as good as our pitching." The Tigers to a man were confident.[10]

Bronx Showdown

When the national anthem was sung on Friday evening, September 1, at the triple-decked stadium in New York, the Yankees were lining the top steps of the home dugout on the first base side (a switch made in 1946), caps in hand, and the Tigers were standing in the visitors' dugout behind third base. Watching the flag in center field, every player wearing New York's famed white pinstriped uniforms as well as those in the Tigers' gray flannels adorned by the block letters DETROIT knew what was at stake.

This aerial picture of Yankee Stadium in the 1960s shows the "House That Ruth Built" from the third base side (National Baseball Hall of Fame, Cooperstown, New York).

Joined by dozens of writers from New York and around the nation, the noisy crowd of 65,566 realized the game's importance.

Looking around at the storied stadium, the players, fans, and reporters could sense history in the making. Ruth, Gehrig, DiMaggio, and other greats had created fabled careers in the old ballpark renovated with covered triple decks running from left center around behind home plate all the way to right center. The center field bleachers were uncovered, but left field, facing west toward the Harlem River separating the Bronx from Manhattan, was the "sun field" where those like Gene Woodling had lost a fly ball or two in the afternoon sunshine. More than 70,000 fans could jam the stadium, and more than 160,000 were expected to see the three games. The 457-foot fence in left-center was where home runs turned into doubles, or outs, but down the line in right, hitters like Maris and Berra saw the 296-foot sign as an inviting "short porch." Mantle, batting right-handed, liked the 301-foot distance just inside the left field line. Otherwise, the dimensions were some of the league's longest, with center field at 461 feet.[11] Yankee Stadium, the home to so many championship ball clubs, was a fitting place for the league's two best teams to meet.

On the day of the game, Harold Rosenthal, a veteran writer with the *New York Herald Tribune*, summarized the Yankees' situation. Ralph Houk's main problem was whether his pitching would stand up to the Tigers' challenge in the remaining games, including four in Detroit during the middle of September. Would Whitey Ford, admittedly weary on the recent two-week journey, bounce back? Would younger hurlers like Bill Stafford, just turned 22, and Rollie Sheldon, 24, maintain their edge in the "fiery competition" against Detroit? The consensus in the Yankees' dugout was that Houk had done a first-rate job juggling his pitching staff. Yogi Berra, the team's elder statesman, was adamant on this point. Two expected starters, Bob Turley and Art Ditmar, were lost early,[12] but Houk patched, cajoled, traded, and wheedled (Berra's terms) his way to victories, aided, of course, by the Maris–Mantle home run barrage. Still, Mantle was slumping, and many of his teammates, like Bill Skowron, got hot when Mantle was hot. Regardless, Houk figured his team's experience was a big factor: "The pressure is on them … not us."[13]

Actually, a great deal of money was involved in the home run chase and the pennant race. Frank Scott, once a front office employee of the Yankees who became one of the first business agents, had contracts with almost all of the Bombers, including Mantle and Maris. Scott said that if either New York star, or any big hitter such as Norm Cash, Rocky Colavito, or Harmon Killebrew, broke Ruth's record, it could mean more than $250,000. Scott, who found most players were bewildered by the financial end of sports, made deals for a growing list of friends. Taking ten percent, he signed Casey Stengel to a book deal that paid $200,000, making Scott a fee of $20,000, more money than most major leaguers earned in 1961. While in Detroit, Scott talked business with several Tigers stars. The slugger who broke Ruth's mark could sign for a magazine series, a book deal, and likely a movie. Scott also had promises of $5,000 from a suit maker, $25,000 from a toothpaste company, and $10,000 from a shirt manufacturer, and he figured on a whole line of kids' wear, sweatshirts, caps, and jackets. "There's practically no end to the thing," Scott said, adding, "Roger and Mickey know it too."[14] Maris, who grew up in the Depression, was careful with money, and he wanted security for his family.[15] In any event, even when reading about big bucks for product endorsements or salary increases, most fans figured baseball wasn't about money, but such was a naive view of the national pastime as business.

As usual, what happened off the field affected what happened on the diamond. Tony Kubek remembered that Bob Cerv, Maris' roommate in the Queens, noticed that Maris had white spots on his head. They looked in the bathroom mirror, and Maris had a skin rash as well as a place where hair had fallen out of the back of his head. Maris went to see a doctor, who advised him to stay out of "pressure situations." Maris laughed. Also, the day before the Tigers arrived on September 1, Luis Arroyo received a letter threatening to kill him if he pitched. Arroyo, worried, told Ralph Houk, and the Yankees' front office arranged to have more police in the crowd. But if a person was deranged enough to shoot a player, would extra police help? Of course, the Labor Day weekend games would be played, and Arroyo was determined to pitch, if needed.[16]

Taking the mound in a pressure-packed, chips-down atmosphere on Friday night, Mossi pitched the best game of his life through the first two outs of the ninth inning, when the roof fell on the southpaw. Deceptive, baffling, and changing speeds, the

Don Mossi pitched one of his finest games on September 1, 1961, but the Tigers fell to the Yankees, 1–0, on what Mossi called one "lousy curve" (author's collection).

Sphinx dominated the Yankees' lineup, especially Maris and Mantle, who both went hitless in four trips. After finishing fruitless turns at bat, Mantle tossed his helmet and bat in disgust, and Maris mumbled on his way back to the dugout. Entering the ninth, the Yankees had five hits, including Clete Boyer's double down the left field line leading off the eighth, but Mossi set down the next three hitters in order.

Kaline gave one of his better performances, going 3-for-4, starting with a two-out, line-drive triple to left center in the first inning, a ball that bounced off the fence near the 457-foot marker, but Colavito, who went hitless in two trips and drew two walks, followed with a roller to Kubek at short. With the temperature above 90, Ford matched Mossi pitch-for-pitch through two outs in the Tigers' fifth, when Ford pulled a muscle in his hip. Mike Roarke, who singled, waited at first. Houk called for Bud Daley, and facing the smooth lefty, Jake Wood grounded out to third.

The turning point for the Tigers came in the top of the eighth. With Daley's breaking balls still prevailing, Wood lined to Berra in left, but Bruton worked the lefty for a walk. Up next, Kaline lined one down the left field line for an apparent double. Berra backhanded the ball off the wall in left, and, throwing from the ear, like the catcher he was, made a great peg to Bobby Richardson, who tagged out the sliding Kaline. With Bruton at third, Houk called for an intentional walk to the dangerous Colavito. Cash, equally tough with a runner in scoring position, popped out to Ellie Howard, the catcher, ending Detroit's best chance. Kubek later called Berra's catch and throw one of the "pivotal plays of the season," and it cut the heart out of the Tigers' rally.

In the ninth, the 34-year-old Arroyo retired Steve Boros and Chico Fernandez on grounders, and Roarke took a called third strike. In the Yankees' ninth, Mossi, tiring but still tough, got rid of Maris on a fly to Kaline in right, and he slid a third strike by Mantle, who was caught looking. But Howard lined Mossi's first pitch for a base hit to left, and Berra, also first-pitch hitting, singled to right. With a 1–1 count, Moose Skowron shot a hard bounder between short and third, and Howard scored, giving the Yankees a crucial 1–0 victory and a 2.5-game lead over Detroit. Later, Skowron recalled that former Yankee Frank Crosetti, reading Mossi's pitches from the third base coaching box, whistled for a breaking ball, and Skowron got his big bat on a curve.[17]

Mossi, who pitched his heart out, walked into the visitors' clubhouse, head down, and slumped onto a round wooden stool in front of his wire-encased cubicle. At first nobody spoke. Slowly, he pulled off his left shoe, dropping it. His teammates came, one by one, starting with Roarke, Kaline, and Colavito. They made quiet remarks, like, "We let you down in your greatest and guttiest game." Mossi, speaking softly, explained that he had located his pitches where he wanted them, the fast one, the curve, the slider, but he threw a "lousy curve" a little too high to Skowron, and that was the game. Talking to Lyall Smith, Mossi said he got Mantle and Maris mainly on sliders. Other talk centered on Kaline's triple to the fence in left-center in the first frame, but Phil Cavarretta, coaching at third, said the relay from Mantle to Kubek was good, and he didn't think Kaline had a chance for an inside-the-park homer. Listening, Mossi dropped the other shoe.[18]

In retrospect, Arroyo racked up the crucial win, Tigers batsmen left eight runners stranded, two Bengals were picked off first, and Kaline was cut down trying to stretch a single into a double.[19] All who watched the game realized that not only was Skowron a big hero but so was the ageless Berra. More important, the victory, which Houk called "the toughest game we've played all year," meant the Yankees would hold onto first place, even if Detroit won the last two games.[20]

Tigers fans from New York made up a sizable portion of the huge crowd. Those rooters wanted the young, energetic, high-spirited Bengals to win, and thousands "shouted themselves hoarse at every Tiger sally." The crowd was big, sprawling, and colorful, and several folks told Detroit writer Jean Sharley they were "anti-Yankees." Few were hometown Detroiters, and afterward, these fans, mostly Dodgers loyalists who hated all things Yankee, boarded the El at 161st Street and headed for home, dismayed but looking forward to Saturday's contest.[21]

On Saturday afternoon, a boisterous crowd of 50,261 turned out on another broiling day to see the Bronx Bombers battle "Yankee-Killer" Frank Lary. Hometown fans saw the circuit clouts they loved, and true to his streaky form, Maris slugged numbers 52 and 53. Facing Ralph Terry, the Tigers jumped to a first-inning lead. Kaline, now 4-for-5 in the series, singled to left, and Colavito took Terry downtown with a long blast into the left field seats for a 2–0 edge, a blow that caused Papa and Mama Colavito, seated behind the Tigers' dugout, to cheer and hug each other. In the Yankees' second, Skowron lined a two-out double to center, and Mantle, who led off with a walk, scored to make it 2–1. In the fourth, Maris doubled to center, a hit that made him, he wrote, feel like his swing was back in the groove. After a passed ball sent Maris to third, Mantle, signaling to his teammate, surprised the infield and dragged a bunt toward second base, tying the game. The season's two biggest sluggers were team players at heart. Lary and Terry both persevered into the sixth, when Maris, batting with two outs, broke the tie by slamming a full-count slider into the right field seats, giving his club a 3–2 lead.

With Detroit batting in the eighth inning, Scheffing pulled out all the stops. Chico Fernandez flied out to right. Stepping up for Roarke, who had two singles in Friday's contest but was hitless on Saturday, Charlie Maxwell fouled out to the catcher. Lary, always a battler, hit a two-out single to left. Wood was due up, but Scheffing, playing the percentages, called for Bo Osborne and his left-handed bat. Terry, working carefully, walked Osborne, advancing Lary into scoring position. Houk called for Arroyo, and the 34-year-old stopper entered yet another tension-packed game. Instead of Bruton, Scheffing went to George Alusik, a right-handed hitter who was called up on August 1 from Denver, where in 1960 he produced a .329 season with 26 homers and 106 RBI. Tall, lean, and strong, Alusik, not used to pennant-type pressure, peered through his glasses as Arroyo threw a screwball by him for strike three. In the Yankees' eighth, Frank House moved behind the plate, Reno Bertoia, who ran for Osborne, went to second base, and Bubba Morton replaced Maxwell in right field, a move that sent Kaline to center.

Luis Arroyo, the Yankees' standout reliever who was named the American League's "Fireman of the Year" in 1961, defeated the Tigers with his arm and his bat. In three straight clutch performances from September 1–3, Arroyo won the first game, saved the second, and won the finale (National Baseball Hall of Fame, Cooperstown, New York).

Lary started the eighth by getting Boyer on a routine fly to left, but the Yankees broke the game open quickly. Arroyo, hitting .273 in limited appearances, singled to center. Richardson followed with a single to center, Arroyo chugged around to third base, and on Kaline's throw to third, which arrived late, Richardson took second. Kubek singled through the drawn-in infield for a 5–2 edge. With Maris at bat, Scheffing called for Hank Aguirre. The southpaw, who had disposed of Maris on a pop fly in the ninth inning of Detroit's 4–3 victory over New York on July 4, pitched carefully to him, not knowing Mantle could hardly swing a bat. On a 3–2 count, Maris slammed a fastball for his 53rd homer, his second of the day. The big crowd roared and applauded as he trotted around the bases for the final lead of 7–2. In the ninth, Arroyo retired Kaline on a roller to short and completed the save by fanning Colavito and Cash. Detroit fell 3.5 games behind New York, and the Yankee-Killer fell short. Lary's career mark against the Bombers slipped to 26–10, but this loss was huge. Detroit's clubhouse was more somber than it was after Friday's loss.[22]

In the jubilant Yankees' clubhouse, Arroyo was largely overlooked while Maris posed patiently for photographers. Backed into his cubicle, Maris, crew-cut, sharp-chinned, and tight-lipped, had no escape. Following directions, he looked left and smiled. He looked right and smiled. Flashbulbs popped, and the anxious writers waited. One cameraman told him to "hold up five fingers on one hand and three on the other, Roger. For 53, you know." Now with seven homers needed to tie Ruth's 60, the ultimate slugger seemed calm. But when a clubhouse boy brought a paper cup with crushed ice, Maris' hand shook slightly. The home run leader was playing in the shadow of Ruth's record and the quarter-million or more dollars estimated to go with the prize, reported Lyall Smith. As the questions continued, Maris kept answering. Finally, he capped the crowded session by saying, "I got a belt out of both homers. But especially on Frank Lary's. He's got me out plenty of times. He's hard to crack up."

Questions and answers continued. Did Maris know both were home runs as soon as he hit them? No, he replied, with a tight smile, but they were home runs. In fact, both were high, arching shots that traveled well over 300 feet to the right field seats. Also, Houk told the writers that Mantle hurt his left forearm badly in the sixth inning, trying to check his swing. Mantle, his arm packed in ice, said little. Houk would decide on Sunday morning if he could play.[23]

Sunday brought one more day with stifling heat, and the irrepressible Yankees prevailed once more. Well before game time, Mantle, with his injured left forearm, went to Houk, who had Maris penciled in to play center field. Mantle, pumped up, asked for the chance to play. He proved in batting practice that he could hit, booming one off the frieze-adorned facing of the third deck in right. Houk, smiling, wrote Mantle into the lineup. Indeed, true professionals want to play the game, even when hurting, and Mantle was ready to add to the lore about his storied career.

Facing Bill Stafford, the Tigers scored when Colavito hit an RBI single to left, following Wood's single, Bruton's forceout and steal of second base, and a foul fly out by Kaline. In the Yankees' first inning, Mantle came up with Maris on first after a two-out single. On a 3–2 pitch from the stout-armed Bunning, the sore-armed Mantle, using Cerv's 36-inch bat, took a "nice, easy cut," launching a 400-foot home run deep to right field for a 2–1 lead. Mantle had no sooner reached the dugout when Berra hit Bunning's next pitch for his 19th homer, and the crowd of 55,676 let out another huge roar. Bunning, regrouping, matched Stafford out after out into the fifth, when Richardson hit an RBI single. In the Tigers' sixth with two outs, Cash slammed his 33rd home run to deep right, cutting the gap to 4–2. Two innings later, the Tigers scored off Arroyo as Bruton singled, Kaline singled him to third, and Colavito grounded into a double play.

The Tigers, trailing 4–3, came up to bat in a do-or-die ninth. Facing Arroyo, McAuliffe led off with a walk, Fernandez took a third strike, and Dick Brown, in his first game since July 15, topped one in front of the plate, but Arroyo's throw bounced off Skowron's glove. Morton, batting for Terry Fox, who had blanked the Yankees in the seventh and eighth, walked to load the bases, and Reno Bertoia came in to run. Wood, in the biggest at-bat of his life, met a screwball for a single to left that scored two runs and a Tigers' 5–4 edge. Arroyo, bearing down, retired Bruton on a pop to short-stop and Kaline on a grounder to third, setting up New York's last shot.

With Staley on the mound and House behind the plate, the first Yankee up was Mantle, whose arm was iced between innings to reduce the pain. Staley, who threw low stuff the players called "grounders," bounced the first ball. On the next pitch Mantle, unable to grip the bat tightly with his left hand, swung and connected for his 50th homer, a magnificent drive that carried more than 400 feet into the third row of seats in right center for a 5–5 tie, igniting a roar of deafening noise. "You knew then," wrote Joe Falls, "that it was almost inevitable that the Yankees would come on to win. This [homer] had given them the momentum, turned them aflame."[24]

Berra singled into short right, and Scheffing walked to the mound and called for Ron Kline. Arroyo, who won (his second win of the series) due to slugging heroics, bunted, sacrificing Berra to second. Scheffing ordered Skowron intentionally passed, setting up a possible double play. Boyer became the second out on a fly to right, giving Elston Howard his biggest at-bat of the year. On an 0–1 count, Howard crashed a drive into the left field seats, recording his 15th circuit clout, giving the Bombers a series sweep, and sending the pro–Yankees crowd into a frenzy.[25] After Howard's clutch blast, Maris later wrote, "We could almost see the pennant waving in the breeze."[26]

The exhilarated Yankees celebrated joyously and loudly in their club-house, the dispirited Tigers showered, changed, and got ready for a flight to Baltimore and a twi-nighter on Labor Day, and the players, fans, and writers reflected on the results. Pointing out that Detroit now trailed New York by 4.5 games, Lyall Smith observed, "They left here at twilight Sun-day—sadder, wiser and disillusioned to the extent that they somberly admit their pennant bubble has burst."[27]

The losses ripped the Tigers. One discouraging point was that Frank

Lary, who had beaten New York 26 times since 1955 and had won in the Bronx on July 4, could not win. Jean Sharley, sent by the *Free Press* to observe the reaction of the fans, concluded the weekend meant "there isn't any Santa Claus," but all the Tigers could do was regroup, because the Yankees would travel to Detroit for a four-game series in the middle of September.[28] Winn Pennant offered a similar opinion, encouraging Tigers fans to look forward to the Yankees' arrival in the Motor City on September 15. Until then, Pennant would run special standings daily to show what could happen "if the Tigers pull off a miracle and take those four big games."[29]

Down but not out, the Bengals, professionals all, thought long and hard about their season that night as another big jet carried them to Baltimore to meet the third-place Orioles.

The Yankees' Home Run Show

The Bronx Bombers, who would win ten more games in a row, hosted the Senators, and since most of the writers figured New York had the pennant in hand, Maris and Mantle became an even bigger story. "Every time they stepped on a field," explained Tony Kubek in *Sixty-One*, "even just to take batting practice, they got great ovations. When the game was over, the security guards ran onto the field with ropes, creating a path so Mickey and Roger could make their way from the outfield to the dugout without being mobbed. I've never seen anything like that before or since."[30]

On Labor Day, Mantle sat out and nursed his ailing forearm during the doubleheader, and the Yankees swept the Senators by scores of 5–3 and 3–2 while Maris, playing center, went 0-for-4 in both games. Rollie Sheldon worked seven innings in the first game, giving up eight hits and three runs, and Hal Reniff pitched two hitless innings to boost his mark to 2–0. The Yankees rode to victory on Blanchard's solo home run, his 16th, off Bennie Daniels in the eighth, and Clete Boyer's RBI single that made it 5–3. In the nightcap, Bud Daley (now 10–16) and Pete Burnside (1–7) both hurled complete games, and Cerv's triple and Boyer's sacrifice fly in the seventh inning gave the Yankees the winning margin of 3–2. As if only Maris and Mantle mattered, the *Daily News* headlined the game story, "Maris (0-for-8), Mick Idle, But Yanks Win Pair."[31]

Maris, despite his two homers against the Tigers, was annoyed when he was booed and insulted by Yankees fans while he played his position in center. Afterward, surrounded by the usual crowd of reporters, Maris lost his temper and knocked the fans, forgetting to add that many in the near-sellout crowds supported him. Although out of character, he was quoted as saying, "They are a lousy bunch of front-runners, that's what they are. Hit a home run and they love you, but make an out and they start booing. Give me the fans in Kansas City every time."[32]

On Tuesday Maris regretted what he said, but booing in the Bronx increased as he took another 0-for-4 collar. The Yankees won, 6–1, as Mantle returned to the lineup and hit number 51 off Joe McClain, Howard hit number 16, and Jim Coates won his tenth game. In the series finale on Wednesday, Ford improved his record to an impressive 23–3 with a five-hit shutout, and Maris, rebounding, slugged number 54, a solo clout off former Pirate Tom Cheney. He started the scoring with his longball to deep right in the fourth inning, Mantle drew a walk, and the remarkable Blanchard, batting fifth and playing left field, unloaded his 17th homer, his first of his two that day. Howard singled, and Skowron belted his 24th homer for a 5–0 lead. Capping the score, pull-hitting Bob Hale, acquired off waivers from Cleveland on July 28 and now Skowron's backup, connected for his last major league home run—and his only Yankees homer. Maris, happier today, admitted he was embarrassed about his previous day's remarks. Also, Cerv noticed more of Maris' hair falling out. By now all of his teammates realized the tremendous pressure Maris was facing.[33]

At the same time, the Tigers slumped, dropping three straight to the Orioles. Only the finale was close, as Mossi saw his record slip to 14–5 with yet another one-run defeat, 1–0, thanks to Jackie Brandt's RBI single in the sixth inning. Chuck Estrada blanked the Bengals and raised his mark to 12–8 with a three-hitter, and Steve Barber recorded his first save by getting the last out in the ninth, retiring Cash on a grounder. Detroit, with an 86–53 record, suddenly trailed 93–45 New York by 7.5 games. The pennant race was over, but the excitement over home runs was growing.

Cleveland came to the Big Apple, and the Yankees swept the five-game series. In the opener on Thursday, September 7, with Houk's usual lineup in place, Maris enjoyed a 3-for-3 day, starting with an RBI single in the first inning off Dave Stigman, a tough lefty. Boyer tripled in the third, and he came home when shortstop Woodie Held made a bad throw. Facing Stigman with two outs in the fourth, Maris pounded a fastball high and deep for his 55th home run and a 3–0 lead. He singled in the sixth, later scoring on a bases-loaded walk. The Yankees scored twice in the eighth for the final 7–3 margin, and Maris' sacrifice fly scored the first of the two runs.

After he hit number 55, Maris was pleased and proud when Mantle told the writers, "I'm rooting for him. Let's everybody root for him. I want to see him do it and I'm sure he will."[34]

On Friday New York triumphed again, this time 9–1, as Bill Stafford won his 13th game by spacing seven hits, plus he connected for a triple leading off the fifth inning. After Richardson grounded out, Kubek lofted his seventh homer off hard-throwing Gary Bell. Maris flied out to left, but Mantle followed with his 52nd home run, boosting the lead to 6–1. The Yankees totaled nine hits and crushed Cleveland, a pennant contender until early June. Making more homer headlines, Mantle's clout gave him and Maris a combined total of 107 four-baggers, tying the record set in 1927 by Ruth and Gehrig, who hit 47, when the Babe out-homered every other AL team.

Maris broke that teammates record on Saturday by launching his 56th home run off a fastball by Mudcat Grant, and the Yankees won, 8–7, boosted by solo blasts by Blanchard, his 19th, and Howard, his 17th. Altogether in 1961, the three hitters who handled catching duties, Howard (21), Blanchard (21), and Berra (22), totaled 64 homers, only 30 of the four-baggers were hit when those players were behind the plate. This time, celebrating "Whitey Ford Day," New York won by scoring four runs in the

Bill Stafford, the Yankees' right-hander from Catskill, New York, compiled a 3–1 record as a rookie in 1960. Stafford blossomed under Ralph Houk's leadership in 1961, fashioning the first of two straight 14–9 seasons, victories that were critical to New York winning the pennant both years (National Baseball Hall of Fame, Cooperstown, New York).

ninth inning, capped by Skowron's sacrifice fly. At this point Maris had 56 home runs in 143 games, leaving him 11 games to tie Ruth's record for the 154-game schedule of 1927, and Ford Frick was saying nothing.

Maris was frustrated by the twin bill on Sunday, September 10, his 27th birthday, because while the Yankees won by scores of 7–6 and 9–3, he collected just two singles. In the opener, the birthday boy, blessed that day by priests in Fargo and Kansas City, capped a six-run rally in the second inning with a two-run single, making the score 6–2. Cerv, his friend, roommate, and protector, provided the winning margin with his RBI single in the eighth. In the nightcap, while Mantle homered for the 53rd time and Howard hit number 18, Maris singled in three trips and drew one walk. Howard's four-bagger in the seventh raised the lead to 9–2, and Bud Daley pitched a five-hitter to improve the Yankees' mark to 99–45.

New York now held an 11.5-game bulge over slumping Detroit (87–

56), and the Yankees' sweep of the Indians created the biggest margin by the Tigers or the Yankees over the other in 1961.

The Bronx Bombers carried their home run extravaganza on the road to Chicago. After winning the rain-shortened opener on Tuesday, September 12, for their 13th win in a row and 100th for the season, the Yankees lost the next two, and neither Maris nor Mantle homered in the series. Ralph Terry hurled six innings for his 14th win against two losses on Tuesday, and his teammates piled up 14 hits to win, 4–3. Rain through the contest finally caused it to be called with two outs in the sixth inning.

Maris, who walked and singled in four plate appearances, told reporters afterward that since the Yankees won their 13th in a row, it didn't bother him that he lost two at-bats and two chances for home runs to the rain. Writers weren't satisfied. Asked about being called out on strikes by Hank Soar in the second inning, Maris said he tried to lay off bad pitches, but Soar "called them strikes time after time." Asked about Maris, Soar replied, "Bad calls? What bad calls?" When they spoke the following night, Maris and Soar both denied saying what appeared in the papers. In *Roger Maris at Bat*, Maris said that he disliked such uproars in the papers. "Too often, however, writers are trying to create excitement and juggle words to make a better story."[35]

Maris lived that experience indelibly, but he was resilient. By mid–August, however, he was largely confined to the Queens apartment when the Yankees were home or to his hotel room on the road. He was hardly the first, as stars like Mantle knew, but the intense scrutiny of Maris' every move in the fall of 1961 was unprecedented. "Everywhere I went I knew eyes were on me," Maris said. "When I went out to eat, when I walked into the hotel lobby, as soon as I appeared on the field there were always eyes, eyes, eyes."[36]

In Detroit the stars like Cash, Colavito, Kaline, Lary, and Bunning were living a lesser version of this media-frenzied season, without the endless attention that Maris attracted. Fans in Detroit and Michigan were mainly praising them as heroes, rather than berating them for daring to try to match a legend like Ruth. The shadows of Ty Cobb and Hank Greenberg didn't affect the Tigers, except perhaps Kaline, who wasn't hitting as many home runs as expected.

After rain in Chicago on Wednesday, the Yankees' series ended with a doubleheader on a chilly Thursday, and the visitors lost twice, breaking the 13-game win streak. Mantle, feeling ill, went hitless in seven at-bats in the twin bill, leaving him averaging .320 with 53 homers. Maris singled three times in eight trips, giving him a .273 mark with 56 longballs. As the Yankees prepared for a flight to Detroit, Mantle knew he had only an outside chance at Ruth's mark in 154 games, but Maris, optimistic, still hoped to break the record within Ford Frick's deadline.

Tigers Lose Their Roar

The winding road home to the Motor City was a difficult one for the Tigers. Major leaguers are paid to give their best effort every day, and these Bengals were resilient, but they no longer felt the same confidence they had when they stepped off the flight at Idlewild on Friday, September 1. When a player's team had won 11 of the past 14 games but lost three straight to the Yankees with their World Series–tested veterans all making contributions, it didn't make any Tiger's step lighter or day brighter.

Instead, the third-place Orioles inflicted three straight tough defeats on the sinking Tigers. Baltimore swept the doubleheader on Labor Day, September 4, and the twin losses crushed Detroit's fading pennant hopes. In the opener, Jack Fisher, the burly right-hander from Frostburg, Maryland, scattered nine hits and lasted into the ninth inning, when Hoyt Wilhelm and his knuckleballs saved the game by recording the last two outs. The Tigers took an early lead on Kaline's RBI double in the first inning, and Cash slugged his 34th home run in the fourth. The Orioles rallied for four runs in the fourth, capped by a two-run homer off the bat of former Tigers catcher Charley Lau. On a day when he needed his best stuff, Paul Foytack instead surrendered all six runs on seven hits in 5⅓ innings, dropping his ledger to 10–9. In the nightcap, which was suspended after eight innings due to a Baltimore law that no inning of a game could start after 11:59 p.m. ex–Tigers southpaw Billy Hoeft, who had enjoyed his only 20-win season for Detroit in 1956, won, 4–1, but not until Tuesday. Wilhelm saved this victory, too.

The pressure of September affected the largely untested Tigers. Only three players, Cash, who played as a reserve for the White Sox during their pennant-winning season of 1959, Bruton, who played for the first-place Braves' clubs of 1957 and 1958, and Mossi, who was a rookie when Cleveland won the flag in 1954, had experience playing for a pennant contender. The month of September, when the Yankees had played clutch ball almost every fall since 1949, hurt Detroit. "If the roof fell in on the Tigers in New York," observed Lyall Smith, "then the whole house starting shaking here in Baltimore."[37] "The Tigers," concluded Hal Butler, Cash's biographer, "who had been at or near the top all season long, had folded at the most crucial time of all."

The folding wasn't over. To complete the ninth inning of Monday night's suspended game, Wilhelm earned another save on Tuesday. The stocky North Carolinian did allow Dick McAuliffe's one-out single, but he nailed Bertoia on a fly to right and slipped a third strike by Bruton. Thirty minutes later, Don Mossi took the mound and delivered a sterling performance, but the Orioles won, 1–0, behind the often-wild Chuck Estrada and his three-hitter, plus a save from Steve Barber. Mossi, almost like his last effort in the Bronx, spaced five hits, but again his teammates scored no runs, and he endured a second straight 1–0 loss. Brooks Robinson, the "Human Vacuum Cleaner" at third base, led off the sixth inning by doubling to left field, Dick Williams grounded out, and Jackie Brandt singled for the game's only run. For the Bengals in the ninth, Colavito hit a two-out single to left and took an extra base when Brandt made a wild throw. Manager Lum Harris signaled for Barber, and after warm-ups, the hard-throwing lefty ended it by getting Cash to hit a grounder to Jim Gentile at first.

On the same Tuesday that Mantle launched his 51st home run to lead New York to a 6–1 win over Washington, the Tigers' sixth straight loss dropped them 7.5 games behind the league leaders. Joe Falls led off his story about the defeat by saying, "Anybody got a Lions' schedule?" Observing that the collapse of the Tigers hardly matched the fall of the Roman Empire or the end of the Third Reich, Falls said the fall happened mercifully quicker, in five days, starting with Mossi's 1–0 loss on September 1.[38] In six losses to New York and Baltimore, Detroit scored 11 runs, including one on a wild pitch, one on a double play, and two on errors. Still, Lyall Smith figured Mossi's loss to the Yankees was the turning point in the pennant chase. "If the Tigers won it," the Detroiter observed, "they would not have been sure of a flag. But I'm convinced they still would've been in the race for it."[39]

Were the Tigers' fans more disappointed than the Bengals themselves? Don't count on it. Ballplayers know who made the big hits, big pitches or big plays when such were needed. They know who picked up big hits with runners in scoring position. They know who pitched tough in the clutch to the best of his ability, game after game. They know who led the way, even through difficult losses and the hard times recovering, mentally, from those losses, because no team wins every game. Still, fans pay for tickets, and in a time when most of a franchise's money was still earned from admissions, the players, the team executives, and the writers listened to the folks, many of whom wrote to complain, not praise. As losses mounted, Lyall Smith talked of receiving a bag of letters, larger by the day, at the *Free Press* offices. Taken together, Smith saw a theme from the "wise men" who wrote to blast the team and the manager. The mail's gist was that the 1961 Tigers had just a "ghost of a chance to make a decent showing in the pennant race." How could folks expect a team with "prima donnas" like Kaline and Colavito and rookies like Boros, Wood, Roarke, and Fox to "make a run for anything except the customers' money under false pretenses?"

Writing with his usual wit and sarcasm, Smith pointed out that the Tigers were the surprise team of the American League, but they needed more of "some things" before they could win a pennant. Still, the Yankees already had won ten games more than they had the previous year at this time. Thus, the Tigers deserved credit for the race they ran, not "sour-grape kicks" from fans. "Now if the trashman will empty the waste basket," Lyall said, doubtless with a chuckle, "the senders of the post–Labor Day Epistles can consider themselves answered."[40]

The light returned in Boston on Saturday, September 9, when Detroit won the third game of a four-game set behind the hurling of Ron Kline, capped by Kline's own RBI single, but they lost the other three games. Following a tough 8–7 loss to Boston on Sunday, when Mossi failed again to win his 15th game despite Bruton's 17th homer and Colavito's 41st longball, the Tigers rode home on a chartered jet to Ypsilanti, near where B-24 Liberator Bombers were built in World War II. Ypsi is home to Eastern Michigan University, and the airport is 35 miles west of downtown Detroit, within easy driving distance for fans and families of the Tigers' personnel.

Regardless of Detroit's record of 1–9 on the road trip, Tigers fans numbering more than 8,000 turned out at Willow Run Airport that Sunday evening to greet their heroes. One big sign carried a heartfelt welcome, GO TIGERS, GO—WE LOVE YOU IN SEPTEMBER AS WE DID IN MAY. Merle Alvey's Dixieland Band, the group that entertained at Tiger Stadium during night games, played "As the Saints Go Marching In," while Cash, Colavito, Kaline, and other Tigers stepped down the jet's ramp. An improvised platform was raised on a truck, and Bob Scheffing, speaking with a microphone, promised, "We'll win some more games for you." On behalf of the Bengals, Colavito and Jim Bunning thanked the fans. Bob Reynolds, sportscaster of radio station WJR, the organizer, introduced Scheffing and the players to the crowd.[41]

Showing confidence in the manager, Detroit's owner, John Fetzer, tore up Scheffing's contract and gave him a two-year deal, with a $10,000 raise to $40,000 annually for 1962 and 1963. "The thing that impressed me about Scheffing," Fetzer observed, "is that he is willing to put his trust in young players."[42]

Taking the diamond at the friendlier confines of Tiger Stadium after a welcome day off on Monday, Detroit hosted Kansas City, winning the first two out of three. Frank Lary, back in form, fashioned his 20th victory in the opener, 3–1, and Dick Brown hit his 13th homer, the second since he was disabled on July 15. On Wednesday Bunning won a five-hit shutout, 8–

0, improving his ledger to 16–11. Colavito and Cash backed Bunning's outing with home runs, Colavito's 42nd and Cash's 35th, giving a scattered crowd of 2,785 partisans plenty to cheer about.

Before an embarrassingly small paid audience of 2,269 on Thursday, a date that had been declared "Rocky Colavito Day," Foytack, on a roller coaster ride all season, slipped to 10–10 when the Tigers lost, 5–2. In ceremonies before the contest, the Tigers and Colavito's fans gave him a 1962 Ford Thunderbird along with a pair of rifles, since the slugger enjoyed hunting near his home in Temple, Pennsylvania, in the off-season. "The Rock," as in the old Cleveland chant, "Don't Knock the Rock," really wanted to win that game, hopefully with a homer. Instead, Detroit's leading longball hitter made a leaping catch against the left field screen to rob Deron Johnson of an extra-base hit, and he singled in the second inning, but alas, that was his only hit in five trips.

Lasting only two innings, Foytack coughed up four of the A's five runs. Three relievers, rookie Ron Nischwitz, a lanky 6'3" lefty up from Denver, sidearming Manny Montejo, and Hank Aguirre gave up one run between them, but it didn't matter. Dick Brown singled and homered for the 14th time, and Jake Wood added two singles, but the Bengals totaled only eight hits. With his club trailing 5–2 with two outs in the ninth, Colavito, after undulating through his pre-batting gyrations, stepped up to the plate. The Bengals had two runners aboard. Colavito, with a chance for heroics on the day Detroit honored him, flied out to center, ending the game.[43]

Anticlimax in Motown

The Yankees arrived in the Motor City late on Thursday, September 14, for the two teams' final series. Starting at the doubleheader on Friday, the hyped-up atmosphere at Tiger Stadium was a notch or two below the excitement fans had felt when the teams faced off in the Bronx two weeks earlier. Indeed, many of the Bengals had long since resorted to humor to deal with their discouraging downturn. Nobody suffered more than Mossi. Bob Scheffing patted him on the back after his one-run loss in Baltimore, the eighth time the southpaw had started and yielded one run in 1961. "Good game, Don," the manager said. "You can count that one on the credit side when you go in to talk contract." Even though Mossi doubted that sentiment, he replied, with a faint smile, "Don't worry. My wife's keeping track of them."[44]

Baseball, whether it is a game determined by eighths of inches, a kids' game played by talented big boys for major bucks, or a game celebrated as the national pastime, lasts for a full season, and in 1961 that meant 162 games. Professionals give those games their best shot, and the Tigers were every bit as professional as the Yankees when they listened to the national anthem before the twin bill at Tiger Stadium on Friday, September 15. The regular season had just over two weeks remaining, the Yankees were in the driver's seat, and they soon proved it.

Maris remembered the media hoopla in Detroit. The Yankees were hoping to clinch the pennant. When the first game started, he knew something was different. Leadoff man Tony Kubek stepped in the batter's box, and cameramen began strolling on the field like, Maris wrote, "they were coming out of the woodwork." Photographers were lined up behind the third base and first base lines when he came up to bat. "I knew they were there to get some unusual pictures of me at bat, or possibly a home-run swing … if any."

Maris didn't have a good night, but Skowron's homer broke the major league team record of 221, and the Yankees loved it. The Bombers lost the nightcap, and afterward, Maris supposedly "sulked" in the trainer's room.[45] His brother Bud, who came to the game, joined him. Writers demanded that Houk produce Maris for interviews, but Houk refused. After Saturday's game, when the crewcut slugger again sat in the trainer's room, teammates convinced him it was better to do the usual "press conference." Accepting their judgment, he spoke with reporters, trying to answer the endless stream of questions. In *Roger Maris at Bat*, he quoted what the Detroit writers said and mentioned the obscenities shouted by several of the crudest fans.[46]

A large crowd turned out on Friday afternoon, 46,268 to be exact, but most disliked seeing Whitey Ford space eight hits and win, 11–1. Mossi worked 6⅓ innings, but he showed neither the stuff nor the control that had baffled the Yankees in the Bronx. The visitors led, 5–1, in the seventh inning after Bobby Richardson hit a one-out RBI double. Scheffing summoned Aguirre, who ended the inning. Afterward, Montejo, allowing three runs, and Nischwitz, giving up two more, weren't much relief. The Tigers failed to deliver a single extra-base hit, but the power came from Berra, who slugged his 20th homer, a two-run blow, and Skowron, whose 25th was good for three runs. Maris, frustrated, was 0-for-5, and Mantle banged a double off the 440-foot sign in center.

In the nightcap on a cool evening, the Tigers roared back for a 4–2 victory as Cash and Boros stroked home runs to pave the way. Facing Bud Daley in the second inning, Colavito singled to left, but Cash fanned and Boros flied out to Blanchard, playing left field. Brown followed with a double to left, with Colavito holding at third. Ralph Houk called for an intentional pass to Wood, bringing up Ron Kline, the pitcher. Daley hit Kline with an inside pitch, forcing home the first run, but Fernandez, batting leadoff, fanned to end the threat. In the third inning, Daley walked Kaline and retired Colavito on a fly to center, but Cash plowed a fastball into the upper deck in right, giving the Tigers a 3–0 lead. Boros, back in the groove after returning to the lineup at Yankee Stadium, followed with his fifth home run, a drive into the upper deck in left. Suddenly the Bengals had a 4–0 bulge, and Kline, pitching steadily, was retiring the big bashers with ease. Clete Boyer, hitting just .229, led off the fifth with a solo home run, number ten for the expert glovesman, but most fans had come to see the M&M Boys. Maris and Mantle singled in the eighth, the only hits for each slugger (Mantle also walked twice), and Maris scored on Boros' error. Kline ended the inning on Skowron's fly, and he added a perfect ninth, giving Detroit the victory.

Surveying the twin bill, the standings were unchanged, and the Yankees, sporting a 101–48 record, held a huge, 10.5-game bulge over the 90–58 Tigers. The home run show continued, and the Bombers, after Skowron's four-bagger, set a major league team record of 222, passing the old mark of 221 set by the New York Giants in 1947 and matched by the Cincinnati Reds in 1956. Also, the Yankees' magic number for winning the pennant was reduced to four games, meaning they could take the flag by beating Detroit on Saturday and Sunday. But the season wasn't over, and Frank Lary had no intention of letting the Yankees win at "The Corner."[47]

On Saturday afternoon the fans saw the stuff of legend when Lary and the Tigers won, 10–4, but Maris launched his 57th home run high over the 360-foot sign in right center, a skyrocket that bounced off the facing of the roof. Maris slammed a low, outside fastball with Kubek on base, but the Tigers thumped the Yankees, 10–4, although, Joe Falls pointed out, for Detroit the victory "mainly soothes their pride and delays the Yankees' formal clinching [of the pennant]." New York's magic number remained at four, but the traveling Yankees lost their fourth game in the last five. Cash unloaded his 37th home run as well as a long triple, driving home four runs, and the sizzling Kaline enjoyed a perfect day, going 4-for-4, including a double and a sacrifice fly, raising his average to .323. Showing his many skills, Kaline made a leaping catch of Mantle's liner to the top of the right field wall. Dick Brown, back at full strength, added three hits, a single, a double, and his 15th home run. Altogether, the Tigers raked Ralph Terry and three relievers for 17 hits, the last three off rookie Al Downing, the Yankees' first black hurler. Afterward, Lary was smiling as his mark against the Bombers improved to 4–2 for 1961 and to 27–10 lifetime.

Maris, however, couldn't seem to win with the press, no matter how well he played. The ball he blasted off the roof bounced back on the field, and Kaline retrieved it, tossing the ball toward the New York dugout for Maris to have for his trophy case. When Maris hit number 57, Detroit's partisan crowd reacted with varying degrees of indifference, derision, and cheers, starting with a ripple of boos and finally ending with a round of applause. "There were cheers," observed Lyall Smith, "but not the full-throated kind." In the visitors' dressing room afterward, Maris, surrounded by two dozen reporters, talked freely. On one hand, he admitted hearing a lot of obscene comments from the crowd. "Believe me, it's hard to take." On the other hand, Maris said, "I'm proud of every home run I hit, whether I ever break Ruth's record or not."

Finally, sitting on a stool in front of his locker, the crewcut Yankee, looking weary and admitting he was tired, said he was looking forward to October 2: "That's the day the season is over." The writers straggled off, one by one, and at last Maris was left with his teammates to shower, dress, and head for the Hilton Hotel, where they could eat and wait for the next day's baseball circus.[48]

On Sunday afternoon, Maris went 2-for-4 and walked twice. In the 12th inning, batting against bullpen ace Terry Fox, Maris stepped out, took off his cap, mopped his brow, and watched some geese flying overhead. The plate umpire waited. Stepping back in, the slugger teed off on a low, outside fastball for his 58th home run.[49] The two-out, two-run blast lifted the Bombers to a 6–4 victory and tied him with two famed sluggers, Detroit's Hank Greenberg, who hit 58 home runs in 1938, and Jimmie Foxx, who hit 58 homers in 1932 with the Philadelphia Athletics. Fox, who came in for Jim Bunning to open the ninth with a 4–4 tie, pitched well until Maris unloaded in the 12th. The 400-foot homer reached the bleachers beyond the right field pavilion. Afterward, Maris, surrounded by a throng of writers, said, "It's the greatest thrill I've ever had in baseball." The Yankees hero said he always hoped for good seasons, but nothing like this. "If I never hit another home run, I'll always remember this one."

Maris just missed another longball. He drew a walk off Bunning in the first inning, fanned in the third, and received another base on balls in the fifth, as Detroit's All-Star right-hander pitched carefully to the left-handed batter. In the seventh, with Kubek aboard via a two-out single, Maris smashed a drive off the top of the new right field screen (installed in 1961), missing a home run by inches, but he legged out a triple as Kubek scored for a 4–2 Yankees lead. The diehard Tigers scored twice in the eighth, first on Wood's RBI single and again when Luis Arroyo tried to pick Wood off, but threw it by Skowron, and the speedy Wood raced around to score for a 4–4 tie.[50]

For the visiting Yankees, holding a 102–49 record and a 10.5-game lead, the home run derby enjoyed one night off before flying to Baltimore, while the Tigers, now 91–59, rested on Monday before hosting the Angels for two games. For the Yankees, most writers, and many baseball fans, the burning question was whether Maris, with 58 circuit clouts, could match or break Ruth's single-season record, with the 154th game set for Wednesday night in Baltimore. For the Tigers, after Tuesday the ball club would board yet another flight for the remaining ten games. The season's finale would come at Minneapolis against the Twins, winding up on Sunday, October 1. The home run chase was alive, but the Tigers were playing mainly for pride.

Baltimore and the Babe

As the Yankees took the field at Memorial Stadium on Tuesday, September 19, the carnival atmosphere they faced in Detroit followed them to the land of Crabcakes, the Preakness, and the NFL's beloved Colts. After lounging around the team's hotel on Monday evening, the Bombers met the Orioles in a twi-nighter. Tuesday's opener was all Steve Barber, who fired one of his league-high eight shutouts, a 1–0 four-hitter, and the O's handed Whitey Ford his fourth loss. Richardson, Howard, Skowron, and Boyer each singled, but that was it for the Bombers. Mantle, suffering the ill effects of a "heavy cold," was dizzy and didn't play,[51] and Maris, again with photographers on the foul lines, drew a one-out walk in the first, as did Howard, but Skowron bounced into a double play. Afterward, the visitors failed to launch a threat. New York won the nightcap, 3–1, behind steady Bud Daley, who scattered five hits, two by Brooks Robinson. Berra's RBI single in the third inning put his team ahead, but Ron Hansen's home run tied it. In the fourth, Skowron provided the final lead with his two-run home run, number 27, and Daley finished the job. The big news was that the Yankees clinched a tie for the pennant. Further, Berra batted cleanup for the ailing Mantle, while Maris managed one single in five at-bats and, according to the commissioner, had one more game to tie Ruth.

On this trip to Baltimore, Maris, who was usually besieged by autograph seekers, celebrity groupies, writers, and photographers, even in the team's hotel, stayed at the home of his buddy from their Kansas City days, Whitey Herzog, who was traded to the Orioles before the 1961 season. Herzog drove Maris to the park daily. On Wednesday, before game 154, Herzog remembered his friend being quite nervous. In the clubhouse, Maris paced, smoked Camels, picked up stuff to keep his hands busy, walked through the tunnel to the dugout a couple of times, smoked, and paced, but he was ready at game time. Baltimore had rain that morning, but it stopped, and a stiff wind was blowing in from right, bad news for a lefty-swinging slugger.

The Yankees won, 4–2, and Maris, bearing down, thrilled the evening crowd of 21,032 with one homer, but he couldn't hit two. Batting in the first inning, he hit a drive into the wind, but right fielder Earl Robinson caught it near the warning track. Boyer singled home a run in the second, and in the third, Maris unloaded his 59th home run, a one-out, bases-empty, 380-foot smash off Milt Pappas. The four-bagger made the Bombers' lead 2–0, and now only Ruth had more home runs in one season than Maris. Berra, replacing Mantle, belted his 21st home run, Blanchard singled, and Howard doubled to make the lead 4–0. At that point, Dick Hall took over, ended the rally, and worked five more innings. Maris, going for longball number 60, hit a towering fly to deep right in seventh, but, held up by the wind, the ball was caught. Afterward, Maris, his voice not much above a whisper, said, "The damn ball just died." In the ninth facing Hoyt Wilhelm's knucklers, Maris tapped to the pitcher, but the Yankees clinched their 26th pennant.[52]

Maris' teammates were disappointed, and Whitey Herzog recalled most of the Orioles were pulling for Maris.[53] Talking later to the reporters, Rajah's words were quiet and resigned, but his eyes showed relief, disappointment, and heart-felt pride. Ball players like to win, but they like to see their teammates do well, and they respect opposing performances too. Most big leaguers appreciated Maris' pressure-packed season more than did the writers or the fans.

Still, the home run show wasn't over. Regardless of what the commissioner said, a season is a season, and it wasn't Maris' fault that Ruth's home runs came in a 154-game schedule. Late that night, as the Yankees' champagne-toasting pennant celebration moved into high gear at the hotel, Maris, looking pale, stayed for a while, answered another barrage of questions, and left early for bed. Determined to succeed, the reluctant hero was still going for 61.[54] At the same time, Mantle's only appearance in Baltimore came when he batted for the pitcher in the ninth inning of the opener on Tuesday, and he struck out.

On Thursday morning Maris was ready to play ball, but Mantle stayed in bed. The *New York Herald Tribune* reported the kind of favorable cover that Yankees stars often received in those days: Mantle's "sniffles" was complicated by "a penicillin rash."[55] That morning Maris received a telegram from Jimmie Foxx, who had been critical earlier. The slugging Hall of Famer stated: "Congratulations on your 59th home run. You have broken my record and Hank's. May God give you strength with which to break all records." Greenberg, serving as a commentator on national TV, saw the game and agreed.[56] In any event, Maris wasn't resting on his laurels.

9

Home Runs, the World Series, and Heroes

Baltimore, the Orioles, and Awards

New York's last game in Baltimore on Thursday, September 21, felt like anticlimax for the Yankees. The home team was sponsoring "Oriole Appreciation Night." Not only did Baltimore's players receive gifts before the game, but Maris was surprised by a huge trophy, inscribed, "Presented to Roger Maris for his sportsmanship while achieving the ultimate respect and admiration of all Oriole fans." Maris was grateful. That afternoon he learned that the Maryland Professional Baseball Players Association had named him as "Sultan of Swat," an award symbolized by a $2,500 jeweled crown named after Babe Ruth that was first presented in 1957.[1]

The Orioles won, 5–3, but the Yankees played no regulars except Maris, who agreed it would look bad if he sat out, and Bobby Richardson, who walked leading off but departed in favor of Joe DeMaestri after one inning. John Blanchard caught and batted cleanup in place of Mickey Mantle, and Maris, exhausted, went 0-for-4, but none of it seemed to matter. The Yankees owned the pennant, and the Orioles improved to 90–65, but they were 4.5 games behind the idle second-place Tigers. Jack Fisher upped his mark to 10–12 by permitting just three hits, but one was a pinch-hit homer by Tony Kubek in the eighth inning. Bill Stafford, who gave up all five runs on eight hits in his seven innings, slipped to 13–8.

The Yankees had Friday off before they traveled to Boston for two games, starting on Saturday night. Maris, who needed a break, knew that he had eight games left, five against Boston and three against Baltimore, in which to hit two home runs for a new single-season record. A team with enormous pride, the Yankees were thinking about the World Series. On the other hand, the Tigers were playing for pride—and for next year's contracts. Regardless, home runs still mattered to everyone around baseball, the players, the fans, the writers, and, of course, Maris.

Where Have You Gone, Mickey Mantle?

Boston was surrounded by World Series–type hoopla on Saturday. Before a noisy, partisan crowd of more than 28,000, the Yankees beat the Red Sox, 8–3, fueled by Whitey Ford's 25th victory, his last regular-season win, and Mantle's 54th and, as it developed, final home run of his second 50-homer season. In the first inning Richardson was hit by a pitch, and Kubek bounced out to rookie right-hander Don Schwall, as Richardson advanced to second base. Maris grounded to first, but 6'6" reserve Don Gile couldn't handle it, and both runners were safe. With two outs, Mantle unloaded a long home run that carried deep into the right field seats, and the Yankees led, 3–0.

Ford gave up an RBI single in the first inning to Jim Pagliaroni, a big right-handed batting catcher in his first full season with the Bosox, a solo homer in the second to Don Gile, the third-year first baseman-catcher, and a bases-empty clout in the fourth by Carl Yastrzemski, the ballyhooed replacement for Ted Williams, but that was it. Jim Coates came in from the pen in the sixth and allowed two hits in three innings, and Luis Arroyo pitched a hitless ninth. Maris walked leading off the fifth and later scored on a throwing error by third baseman Frank Malzone for a 4–3 lead. The Yankees scored twice in the eighth, capped by Maris' single, and Howard and Bob Cerv clinched the victory with home runs in the ninth.

On Sunday the Yankees lost, 3–1, as Bill Monbouquette, who liked to deck an opposing hitter after the opposing pitcher threw at one of his team-mates, lifted his mark to 14–13 with a five-hitter. Skowron slugged his 28th, and final, home run in the fifth, and four Yankees singled: Billy Gardner, who came in for Richardson in the third, Maris, who also walked once, Blanchard, who replaced the ailing Mantle in the sixth, and Howard. Ralph Terry worked six innings and Arroyo took over in the last of the seventh. Hard-hitting Malzone singled, Jackie Jensen, struggling in his comeback year, sacrificed him to second, and Pete Runnels and Jim Pagliaroni both doubled for the winning 3–1 margin. Bob Cerv tore cartilage in his knee, and his season was over.

The big stories were Maris and Mantle, first, because Maris failed to connect for a four-bagger, and second, because Mantle also failed to connect, plus he was feeling poorly. A near-capacity crowd of 30,802 backed Maris all the way, and they bid him farewell for the season with a standing ovation after the slugger flied out to left field in his final appearance. Before the game, he had predicted he wouldn't hit number 60, saying, "I can tell you I'm not going to do it; I just don't feel strong." Mantle came close to his 55th circuit clout when he drove a liner to the right field corner, but Jensen made a sensational running catch to prevent a home run.[2]

In his time off the diamond, Mantle, who usually liked the bright lights of Broadway, spent most of the summer in the Queens apartment with Maris and Cerv. After Labor Day, Mantle returned to the ritzy Hotel St. Moritz (at $125 a night). Cerv, the Yankees' 6'0", 240-pound strongman, said that Mantle played by house rules all summer, except once, when he brought a girl to the apartment. "We ran 'em out," Cerv explained, "and pretty soon, about a couple of weeks later, that's when he left. Labor Day, he said he had enough of this life. Went back to Times Square."[3]

Mantle pinch-hit once in Baltimore, but otherwise stayed on the bench. Maris wrote, "He was feeling dizzy, and although in uniform, it was doubtful if he could even pinch hit."[4]

Regardless, Mantle traveled with the Yankees to Boston. In his first at-bat in Saturday's game, he socked a three-run homer, number 54, the most he ever hit in a season. He singled in the seventh and he was replaced by a runner, rookie Tom Tresh, who in turn gave way to John Blanchard, who played right field. As usual, Maris, a fine defensive outfielder, moved over to play center. In Sunday's loss Mantle was 0-for-3, flying out to deep right in the sixth. In bottom of the inning, Blanchard trotted out to right field, with Maris again taking center. On the flight back to New York, Yankees broadcaster Mel Allen recommended that Mantle see his doctor, Max Jacobson, and, for whatever reason, Mantle listened.

On Monday, September 25, a day off in the schedule before the Yankees hosted the Orioles for two games starting on Tuesday, Mantle visited the doctor at his office on 79th Street near Central Park. It turned out to be one of his greatest mistakes. Doctor Max, or "Dr. Feelgood," often treated celebrity patients such as actress Elizabeth Taylor and playwright Tennessee Williams. One of Jacobson's most potent shots contained amphetamines, what ballplayers and others called "speed," an addictive stimulant that usually made the user feel like he or she had endless energy.[5] But in Mantle's case, the needle caused severe pain in his hip, and he woke up in the morning with a fever. Merlyn had arrived from Texas, and she asked, "What happened to you?" The reply, "Nothing much. I just got sucked dry by a vampire."[6]

On Tuesday evening, Merlyn Mantle and Pat Maris sat beside each other in a box next to the Yankees dugout. Mickey, feeling lousy, nevertheless started in center. But after he drew a base on balls from Baltimore's Jack Fisher in the bottom of the first inning, Hector Lopez came in to pinch-run. Mantle made it to the clubhouse and watched the game on TV. Fisher retired Berra on a fly ball to end the frame, Lopez took over in right field, and Maris played center. In the end, Bud Daley pitched the first six innings, Blanchard's RBI single in the sixth tied it at 2–2, and Rollie Sheldon hurled the last three innings and recorded his tenth, and final, victory by a score of 3–2. The Yankees scored the go-ahead run on singles in the seventh by Billy Gardner, playing second base, and Tom Tresh, the recruit shortstop who took over for Tony Kubek, followed by Jackie Brandt's error on Lopez's fly ball to center.

The game's big story came when Maris connected for number 60 off Fisher with the bases empty in the third inning, cutting the Orioles' edge to 2–1. Fisher, who had given up Ted Williams' career-ending 521st home run in 1960 in Williams' last-ever at-bat at Fenway Park, worked the count to 2–2 and threw Maris a curveball up in the zone. The intense slugger got good wood on it, pulling the pitch high and deep, and the ball struck the façade on the upper deck, five feet fair, bouncing back to the field. Maris watched until the ball landed fair. Satisfied, he put down his head, and, the way big hitters of his era finished a home run, jogged around the bases to the roar of a crowd of 19,401, a small turnout considering the chance to see baseball's top home run hitter tie the Babe's record.

Maris, who, unlike Mantle, never liked being a celebrity, was stunned: "As I trotted around the bases I was in a fog. I don't remember running around the bases. I don't think anyone said a word to me. If they did, I didn't hear it." When he reached the dugout, Maris, ever modest, was congratulated by his teammates. Outfielder Earl Robinson picked up the ball, tossed it to the infield, and umpire Ed Hurley threw it into the dugout. "The fans were still roaring," Maris said. "I stood and waved my hat, but I was in such a daze that I didn't really know what I was doing."[7]

Afterward, Mantle showered, changed, and went with Merlyn back to the St. Moritz for another rough night battling sickness, and Maris spent hours with writers, answering question after question. In the end, Maris said, "This is easily the greatest thrill of my life." The quiet hero stood in front of dozens of cameras with tearful Claire Ruth, the Babe's widow, and kissed her cheek, saying, "I'm glad I didn't break the record in 154 games. This record is enough for me."[8]

The next morning, September 26, Mantle was missing in action. He felt ill and couldn't report to the stadium. When he didn't show up, the Yankees sent a doctor to examine him. Later, Mantle was taken to Lenox Hill Hospital with a temperature over 100 degrees. That night the team's physician, Sidney Gaynor, removed an abscess in the right hip, "like a boil," Gaynor said afterward, only under the muscles.[9] Years later, Mantle said the surgeon "lanced the wound, first cutting a three-inch star over the hip bone, then letting it drain. It left a hole so big you could put a golf ball in it."[10] Biographer Jane Leavy indicated that the unasked question about Mantle was why he didn't go first to the team's physician for his ailment. Quoting

Clete Boyer, Leavy concluded that Mantle had a disease that he didn't want known by the Yankees' front office.[11]

Recovering in the hospital, the stoic but weakened Mantle saw the rest of his team's games on television. He would try to play in the World Series, but his painful hip made it tough.

Tigers Roar Again

The Tigers, after splitting with the Yankees in the middle of September, were determined to finish the season on a high note. "We'll keep bearing down and win all we can," observed Bob Scheffing. Detroit's all-time record of 101 victories came when the Tigers of 1934 won the American League pennant, though the St. Louis Cardinals won the World Series.[12]

Revitalized, the Bengals won ten of their final 12 games, the first six in a row, starting with Detroit's last two home contests, both against the eighth-place Angels. In the opener on Tuesday, September 19, Don Mossi polished off the visitors with a four-hitter, 6–2. LA's runs came on bases-empty homers by Eddie Yost and Steve Bilko. Detroit scored four runs in the first inning off big Ken McBride and his tough sinker, and the fourth run came when catcher Ed Sadowski tried to pick off Cash at third base, but threw the ball away. The Bengals took a 6–2 lead in the sixth on RBI singles by Bubba Morton, pinch-hitting for Dick McAuliffe, and Billy Bruton.

On Wednesday afternoon, fastballing Ron Kline boosted his record to 8–8 (5–2 with Detroit) by scattering seven hits, and the Tigers won, 6–3. In the fourth inning, Cash, following Rocky Colavito's double, slugged homer number 38, a two-run shot into the upper deck in right, and ex–Tiger George Thomas tied it at 2–2 with his 13th home run in the sixth. Detroit won by scoring four times in the seventh, capped by Kaline's RBI single. The Tigers improved to 93–59, but still trailed the Yankees (104–50) by ten games, so few folks cared about the standings.

Detroit's personnel flew to the West Coast on Thursday for their final series with Los Angeles, three games that opened on Friday, September 22, with a night encounter at Wrigley Field. Frank Lary won his 22nd game against nine losses, 6–4, and on Saturday Jim Bunning won his 17th (and final) game against 11 losses, thanks to relief help from Terry Fox, who notched his 11th save.

The biggest show came on Sunday afternoon when the Bengals and the Angels, remarked Joe Falls, played "picnic-style baseball." The Tigers collected 14 hits and won, 7–5, in ten innings, as Bob Scheffing used 22 players, including seven pitchers. The Tigers made two errors, and the Angels committed three. Foytack started, and Scheffing paraded Regan, Staley, Aguirre, and Fox to the mound, until Ron Nischwitz, the former Ohio State ace, came in and fanned Lee Thomas to end the seventh inning with the teams tied at 4–4. Two singles and two wild pitches gave the Tigers a run in the eighth, but Ken Hunt tied the game at 5–5 with his 23rd home run, a leadoff blast off Nischwitz in the Angels' eighth. Rookie right-hander Howie Koplitz, called up from Birmingham of the Southern Association after compiling a 23–3 record with a 2.11 ERA, made his third appearance for Detroit, pitching two innings of scoreless relief to get his first major league victory. Prospects looked dim for Detroit in the tenth as Maxwell, playing right field, fanned and Colavito grounded out. Art Fowler, displaying shaky control in his three-inning stint, walked Cash and Boros. Wood lifted a fly to right that Hunt dropped for a two-base error, allowing the winning runs to score. When the stocky, 5'10" Koplitz allowed just a leadoff single to Lee Thomas in the Angels' tenth, the Tigers walked off with a sweep of the series.[13]

Arriving in Kansas City in the wee hours of the morning, the Tigers opened the last week of the season with an exhausting twi-night doubleheader on Monday. Scheffing was still using his regulars, but he was also working younger players into the lineup. The Bengals split the twin bill, winning the opener, 6–4, by amassing 15 hits off four Kansas City pitchers. Hank Aguirre, who pitched the seventh inning before his teammates scored five runs in the eighth for a 6–3 lead, squared his mark at 4–4 in relief of Don Mossi, and sinkerballer-turned-knuckler Gerry Staley earned his fourth save, the second for Detroit, with two frames of relief. The victory allowed Detroit to clinch second place, which meant about $1,500 for each Tiger.

The A's won the nightcap, 6–3, as Bob Shaw (12–13) flirted with a no-hitter for eight innings before giving up three hits in the ninth, and Ron Kline's mark fell to 8–9. The Tigers scored all three runs in the ninth, starting when McAuliffe reached base on shortstop Dick Howser's throwing error. Morton ended the no-hitter with a single to center. Maxwell, who again started in place of Kaline, was hitless in three previous trips. "Ol' Paw Paw," quietly displeased with his reserve status, grounded out to first base unassisted. George Alusik, batting just .143, hit a sacrifice fly to right to score McAuliffe. Bo Osborne, playing first base for Cash, slugged a two-run homer for the final tally of 6–3.[14]

Detroit split the last two games with Kansas City, losing on Tuesday, 8–5, and winning on Wednesday, 10–2. Tuesday's contest marked the debut of Bill Freehan, the 19-year-old rookie catcher signed off the campus of the

University of Michigan for a reported bonus of $100,000. Freehan, a 6'3",
200-pounder, had starred on the gridiron for Michigan and in Wolverines
baseball during the spring of 1961 led the Big Ten with a then-record .585
average. The Tigers' All-Star catcher of the future was called up from Class
A Knoxville, where he batted .289. The Detroit native, smart, big, and
rugged, met the Tigers in New York on September 1, but Bob Scheffing
indicated Freehan would not play against the Yankees. "He said, 'I'd love to
put you in a game, but we're going for first place still, and there's money
involved for each of these guys. I can't put you in until we clinch either first
or second place.' That made sense to me," Freehan recalled. "I wasn't ready
to play in the major leagues. The more I could learn, the more acclimated
you became to the major leagues, the better off you're going to be."[15]

Neither game was exciting. On Tuesday, before a small crowd of 3,262
at Municipal Stadium, southpaw Ron Nischwitz made his first major league
start, but he suffered his first loss by coughing up six runs on seven hits in
2⅓ innings. Aguirre and Foytack worked well in relief, but too late. Freehan,
who handled himself well behind the plate, singled to center in the second
inning, scoring Colavito, who walked and advanced on McAuliffe's single.
But the A's added three more runs in the second for a 5–1 lead, and Nischwitz departed after shortstop Dick Howser's one-out RBI double in the
third. Altogether, the Tigers totaled 12 hits, three of them singles by Boros.
Colavito, the only regular besides Wood in the lineup, slammed his 44th
home run, a solo blast in the eighth, but the Bengals couldn't overcome the
early deficit, losing 8–5.[16]

On Wednesday the Tigers' big news was that Lary started and, though
he was injured in the eighth inning, won his 23rd, and final game of 1961,
10–2. Morton and Colavito hammered back-to-back, 400-foot solo home
runs in the sixth, number two for Morton and for "the Rock," number 45,
a career best. Lary was forced to leave the game in the top of the eighth
when, batting against reliever Dave Wickersham, he was struck in the right
(pitching) hand, suffering, the Tigers later said, a bruise. Cash, still going
strong with a .355 mark, belted homer number 39, a three-run, tape-
measure drive in the seventh that nearly went into orbit, carrying more
than 420 feet before hitting the ballpark's 40-foot outer wall atop the
embankment in right field. Cash's homer raised the Bengals' bulge to 9–2.
Next to Lary's injury, the worst news was that Wood fanned for the 138th
time, tying Jim Lemon's major league record. None of the Tigers were
excited afterward, even though they had unloaded 13 hits.[17]

Once again a chartered jet carried the Tigers to another league city,
this time to Minneapolis and the final series of the season. At that point,
however, Frank Lary was given permission to go home for the year, and he

left for Alabama on a passenger flight. Also, Kaline was on limited duty. He had bruised his knee sliding into third base on Sunday, September 17, in Detroit's final game against New York. He aggravated the knee the following Saturday against Los Angeles. Kaline didn't start against the Angels on Sunday, and, as it developed, he was used only for pinch-hitting during the remainder of 1961. At the time he was pulled from the lineup, Kaline had 189 hits and lost his hope for a second 200-hit season, the first coming in 1955 when the Tigers' icon totaled 200 hits and won his only batting title with a .340 average.[18]

On September 29, a cold and dreary Friday afternoon at Metropolitan Stadium, following a day off for the Tigers, Bob Scheffing again nearly filled a scorecard, using 19 players. The Tigers wanted 100 victories in the worst way. Bunning, however, couldn't win his 18th game, which would have been his best total since his league-leading 20–8 mark in 1957, and he departed after yielding four runs on four hits in four innings. Kline, Aguirre, and Fox pitched two shutout innings apiece in relief, and Fox lifted his mark to 5–2 by working the ninth and tenth frames. Leading off the fifth inning against curveballing Camilo Pascual, an All-Star and the league's strikeout leader, Cash walloped home run number 40. Boros singled, and Brown doubled to cut the Twins' early lead to 4–2. The Bengals tied the game with two runs in the ninth, when Maxwell, pinch-hitting for Hank Aguirre, dribbled a bases-loaded infield hit to Pascual, who couldn't handle it. Kaline, batting for Dick McAuliffe, grounded out to Pascual, scoring Wood. Detroit won in the extra inning when Wood ripped a bases-loaded single for the final lead of 6–4. Fox gave up a two-out single to reserve catcher Hal Naragon, but he got Bill Tuttle on a pop to first base to clinch Detroit's win number 99.[19]

On Saturday morning, in a contest that began at 10:25 to avoid a conflict with the University of Minnesota's football game against the visiting 11 from the University of Missouri, the Tigers won, 6–4, racking up the 100th victory for the third time in franchise history. Detroit first won 100 games in 1915 with a team led by manager Hughie Jennings and the immortal Ty Cobb, who won 11 AL batting titles in his 24-year Hall of Fame career.[20] Mickey Cochrane's 1934 Tigers won 101 times, sparked by Hall of Famers Hank Greenberg and Charlie Gehringer.

On this Saturday, a 42-degree temperature and a chilling rain ended play after six innings before a hardy crowd of 3,151 (although 8,668 tickets were sold). Chico Fernandez, wearing batting gloves to protect both hands, enjoyed a 3-for-3 day, raising his mark to .248, and Morton and Colavito each contributed two hits. The Tigers leaped ahead with three runs in the first inning. Wood capped the rally with a two-run single, and when the speedster's hit bounced past the center fielder, he tried to race around and score, but was thrown out at home on a quick relay by shortstop Jose Valdivielso. The Tigers started Howie Koplitz, voted Minor League Player of the Year after his 23–3 season at Birmingham. The Twins scored four times in the first inning to take a 4–2 lead, but Koplitz settled down and gave up no further runs. The Bengals took a 6–4 edge in the third on RBI singles by Bruton and Colavito and Freehan's bases-loaded walk off Jim Kaat. The rain came, Koplitz smiled about his 2–0 record, and Kaat finished his season at 9–17.[21]

Sunday dawned sunny and cold as the Tigers, packing in advance for the post-game flight back to Detroit, prepared to wrap up their once-glowing season with a winning finale against the Twins.

Maris Looks for Number 61

After Maris hit number 60 on September 26, the papers were full of his latest feat. For example, the *Detroit Free Press* headlined the *Associated Press* story on the sports page, "LATE, BUT … MARIS HIT 60TH."[22] Regardless, the headlines and stories were misleading. Ford Frick's 154-game deadline had made the attempt to tie or break Ruth's record almost more important on the printed page than in reality. Maris' recent biographers, Tom Clavin and Danny Peary, pointed out that Ruth, who hit 60 homers in a 154-game season in 1927, actually hit the 60th in the 153rd game, before going 0-for-3 with one walk in the Yankees' final game, a 4–3 victory over the Washington Nationals. When Ruth hit number 60, he did so in 687 total *plate appearances*. When Maris hit number 60 against the Orioles in the Yankees' 158th game (not counting the tie on April 22), he did so in his 684th plate appearance. In other words, Maris took five more games, but three fewer plate appearances. Maris topped Ruth's single-season mark, but in 1961, most sportswriters, Maris critics, and Bambino followers chose to focus on the number of games.

Further, the Yankees' front office, which favored Mantle over Maris, did not publicize his home-run chase after the 154th game, which in effect said to baseball fans everywhere that Frick's pronouncement that a home run hit after game 154 didn't really count was correct.[23] Of course the home runs counted, and Maris, dedicated and determined but anxious and worried, remained positive and focused enough to continue the relentless pursuit of his own record.

Maris, however, was worn out, and he decided not to play in the game against the Orioles on Wednesday. Only 7,594 paid to see the game, more than might have attended if they realized Maris was taking his long-awaited day off. The Yankees lost, 3–2, and Jim Gentile, Baltimore's most prolific slugger, connected for his 46th, and final, home run, a long drive into the left field seats off Bill Stafford in the first inning. Yogi Berra banged his 22nd, and last, home run, but left fielder Boog Powell hit an RBI single in the third inning that gave Baltimore the eventual winning run.

Maris started out the day by sitting in the Yankees' clubhouse and reading his mail, much of which was congratulatory, rather than the usual critical letters. Later, co-owner Dan Topping summoned Maris to his office upstairs and suggested he ask Houk for permission to leave, and take the day completely off. Houk agreed. Maris showered, dressed fashionably, and took Pat for a day out on the town. "It was just a wonderful day and evening," Maris recalled. "I hadn't felt this relaxed and at ease since the season started." Further, there was no game scheduled for Thursday, so the next day he was able to take his wife and do some of the things she wanted to do.[24]

On Friday Maris, his nerves still on edge despite what he may have said later, returned to the lineup as the Red Sox came to the Bronx for the final three-game series. The Yankees won all three, but the biggest question was whether Maris could hit number 61. A crowd of 21,485 showed up. Most of the seats in left field were empty, but the stands in right were packed, because fans knew about the $5,000 reward offered to the person who caught Maris' number 61. Bill Monbouquette was the opposing pitcher, and he permitted five hits through eight innings, pitching away from Maris each time. Maris wrote, "I never saw a decent pitch."

Neither team scored until the fourth inning when, with two outs, Blanchard clouted his 21st home run, a long drive into the right field seats. Whitey Ford started, but he gave way to Luis Arroyo after six innings. Little Luis gave up the tying run on Chuck Schilling's RBI single in the seventh. By the ninth, Maris had walked, popped to the shortstop, and fouled out to first base. "I began swinging at bad balls ... and popping up,"[25] he said later.

Monbouquette didn't want to be the pitcher who gave up the 61st homer, and when Maris led off the ninth, "Monbo" walked him. Rollie Sheldon batted next, because he had come in for Arroyo, who was subbed into Berra's slot. Sheldon bounced to Don Gile, and the Red Sox first baseman threw badly to second, leaving both runners safe. Blanchard singled to right to drive home the winning run, marking the 12th time he tied or won a game with a late-inning hit. Next to Maris and Mantle, Blanchard enjoyed the most amazing Yankees season with the bat in 1961.

On Saturday, designated "Youth Day," it was the same story at the cavernous stadium: the right fields stands were full, though the crowd numbered 19,061. Again folks were rooting for Maris to connect for a home run, but he didn't. Don Schwall pitched for the Bosox, and the rookie scattered seven hits over eight innings, but the Yankees made those hits count for a 3–1 victory. Nobody on either team homered, and Howard knocked in the final run with a sacrifice fly in the eighth inning, following a double by Lopez and Maris' base hit. Plenty of kids were wearing baseball gloves in right field, but once again Maris saw no good pitches. "I managed a cheap little single," he said, "but not one of the pitches I swung at would have been a strike."[26]

The Yankees improved their record to 108–53, leaving them eight games ahead of the second-place Tigers. Ralph Terry won, finishing his season at 16–3, and Bud Daley and Jim Coates combined for three innings of scoreless relief. All that remained was for Maris to have one more shot at an all-time home run record, and, of course, the World Series against Cincinnati.

Home Runs and Heroes

On October 1, a sunny 40-degree Sunday at Metropolitan Stadium in Bloomington, a suburb just south of the twin cities of Minneapolis and St. Paul, the once promising but still erratic Paul Foytack lifted his ledger to 11–10 with an eight-hit performance, and the Tigers finished their season in style, winning 8–3. Minnesota's journeyman right-hander Al Schroll lasted through two outs in the first inning, giving up five runs on four hits and one error, before Pedro Ramos came on to give the season-ending crowd of 15,723 some relief. McAuliffe started the contest by bouncing out to Schroll. Bruton doubled to right, and the hot-hitting Cash, batting third in place of Kaline (who later pinch-hit a single to finish his season at .324), drew a walk. Colavito singled for one run, Morton was safe on an error by Bill Tuttle, the ex–Bengals center fielder who was playing third base, and another run scored. Boros walked on a wild pitch, and Colavito scored the third run. Wood singled to advance the runners, and when Freehan, who finished with two singles and a .400 mark, hit into a force play at second, Morton scored. Foytack singled to center for a 5–0 lead, and manager Sam Mele called to the pen for Ramos. In the end, the Tigers collected ten hits, two each by Freehan, Cash, and Colavito.

For the Twins, Ramos, the "Cuban Cowboy" who liked wearing Western duds, poled his third home run off Foytack in the third, and Tuttle socked number five off Foytack in the fourth. The club's big belter, Harmon Killebrew, the gentle star who three days earlier clubbed his 46th home run in a 12–5 loss to the visiting Indians, had a quiet day. "The Killer" walked once, was hit by the pitcher, grounded to third base, and finished his fine season by flying to right field.

Leading off Detroit's ninth against right-hander Don Lee, "Stormin' Norman Cash," displaying another burst of infectious enthusiasm for the game he loved, capped his memorable season by smashing a long home run, number 41, into the right field seats. Cash's 193rd safety also gave him the AL hits title, one more than Baltimore's Brooks Robinson. As Cash circled the bases, his teammates gave him a warm ovation. The Twins scored one run in the ninth on three singles and a double play grounder by Julio Becquer, but Foytack ended Detroit's franchise record-tying 101st victory by retiring Lenny Green on a roller to first base. Fittingly, Cash, who scored the Tigers' final run, made the play to end the Bengals' final game in their historic 1961 season.[27]

Back in New York, the Marises spent Saturday night at the Queens apartment with "Big Julie" Isaacson, a friend who had located the summer rental for Maris, Cerv, and, later, Mantle. Maris purchased 100 World Series tickets, and he and Julie were putting the special tickets into envelopes marked to be given to several of Maris' relatives and friends. The Rajah also provided tickets for many who helped him in 1961, such as Max and Hymie Asner, who owned his favorite eatery, the Stage Deli, and for the deli's waitresses, busboys, and cooks. Early on Sunday, Isaacson picked up Maris at the apartment, and they ate breakfast at the Stage. One more time Maris enjoyed his favorite, eggs and fried baloney. Maris, nervous, was quiet as the two men rode to the Bronx for the game. Later, Pat Maris would take a taxi to the ballpark.[28]

On October 1, a cool, clear Sunday, 23,154 turned out at Yankee Stadium to see if Maris, finishing one of baseball's most memorable seasons ever, could hit the historic 61st home run, an achievement seen as unthinkable a few months earlier. Again the stands in right field, particularly the lower deck, were full of excited spectators hoping for the chance to see, or maybe catch, a unique baseball.

Dozens of writers were on hand, but what would they see? "Sometime during the 1961 season a rampant negativity virus had infected the press," Tom Clavin and Danny Peary observed. "Quite clearly, the Roger Maris/ Babe Ruth story was a turning point in the history of American sports journalism because for the first time failure was an even more important theme than success."[29]

"Between the writers and Frick," Whitey Ford said later, "they tried to make it out to be some kind of fluke, like the whole thing was phony. I remember thinking that day, even if Roger breaks it [Ruth's record] he won't get the recognition he deserves because of all the garbage that had been in the papers. The man was making history, and a lot of people wanted to turn the other way."[30]

Mantle and Cerv watched on TV from the hospital as the Yankees started Bill Stafford, the right-hander from upstate New York, and the Red Sox started Tracy Stallard, a hard-throwing but often wild right-hander who had a brief look from Boston in 1960, but posted no decisions in four appearances. Bill Kinnamon, a good umpire, was behind home plate. Unlike Detroit, there were no cameramen on the field, because that wasn't allowed at Yankee Stadium.

The contest turned into a pitchers' duel, with Stafford striking out the side in the top of the first inning, and Stallard also pitching shutout ball. Richardson led off the Yankees' first with a bouncer to the mound, and Stallard tossed him out at first. Next up, Kubek singled to center. As Maris, batting third as usual, walked from the on-deck circle to the batter's box, all eyes were watching him. Stallard fooled Maris on a changeup, and he lifted a fly ball to left, where Carl Yastrzemski made the catch. Facing Berra, Stallard bounced a fastball past the catcher, Russ Nixon, and Kubek took second. On the next pitch Berra popped up to second, and the inning was over.

The hurlers' duel continued into the bottom of the fourth, when Kubek fanned leading off. Maris, up for his second try, took the first pitch high for ball one. Stallard's second pitch was in the dirt, and the fans booed loudly, because they didn't want to see Maris walk. Stallard wound up and delivered a fastball just above the knees and out over the plate, and Maris, getting the eighth of an inch he loved, turned on the pitch and drove a liner toward the right field stands.

"As soon as I hit it," Maris recalled, "I knew it was number sixty-one.... It was the only time the number of the homer ever flashed into my mind as I hit it. Then I heard the tremendous roar from the crowd. I could see them all standing, and my mind went blank again."

Roger Maris, pictured on one of the happiest days of his life, holds up Yankees jersey number 61 to signify hitting his 61st home run off Tracy Stallard of the Red Sox on October 1, the final day of the regular season (National Baseball Hall of Fame, Cooperstown, New York).

Trotting around the bases in his customary head-down style, as he had done on 60 previous occasions in 1961, but this time following in the path of the Babe, Maris crossed home plate to one of the season's great ovations. As he continued to the dugout, the Rajah kept getting greetings, congratulations, and slaps on the back from excited teammates,[31] many of whom later gave their memories to Tony Kubek for his book *Sixty-One*.

The stadium scoreboard flashed, MARIS 61 HOMERS BREAK RUTH'S 1927 RECORD FOR A SEASON. Maris, pushed up to the top step of the dugout more than once, smiled and waved his cap for a few seconds each time, and he tried to duck inside as the cheering, clapping, and stomping continued. Curtain calls, after all, were not the order of the day in those times.

Presently the game moved ahead, but the happiest fan was Sal Durante, a 19-year-old delivery guy for an auto parts store in Brooklyn who caught Maris' historic home run in the lower right field seats from a box in Section 33, about 360 feet from home plate. According to the UPI, the ball "landed close to the spot where the immortal Babe hit his 60th on September 30, 1927."[32]

Ushers hustled Durante to the Yankees' clubhouse a few minutes later, and Maris met him. The young fan, who became a lifetime friend of the Maris family, offered Maris the ball. The Yankees slugger refused, telling Durante he should collect the $5,000, the equivalent of a year's salary for many people in the early 1960s, offered by a restaurateur in Sacramento. Durante gave the ball to a Yankees official for safekeeping, returning to his seat and his girl friend, Rosemary Calabrese.[33]

Maris went back to the dugout, and in the fifth inning he returned to center. He remembered little about the rest of the game. Stallard gave up no more runs, and Stafford, for six innings, Hal Reniff for one, and Luis Arroyo for the last two frames hurled a 1–0 shutout. "I was as happy as it is possible for anyone to be," Maris said in *Roger Maris at Bat*. Indeed, it was his greatest thrill in baseball, and the pressure, the anxiety, and the excitement were finally over.[34]

Maris was gracious to everyone afterward. Proud but humble, he praised Durante for wanting to give him the ball. "He plans to get married, and he can use the money," the slugger said, "but he still wanted to give the ball to me for nothing. It shows there's some good people left in this world after all." Maris also praised the Red Sox pitcher: "I appreciate the fact that Stallard was man enough to pitch to me." Stallard, surrounded by writers in the visitors' clubhouse, tried to shake it off, knowing his name would be forever linked to Maris' number 61. "I'm not going to lose any sleep over it," Stallard remarked. "After all, he hit 60 homers off some other guys, and it was a fast ball ... a good pitch ... and he hit the hell out of it."[35]

That evening Roger and Pat, along with Julie and Selma Isaacson, enjoyed a nice dinner together at the Spindletop in Manhattan. The menu for the couples included shrimp cocktail, salad, steak, baked potato, cheesecake, and coffee, and Roger had two glasses of wine. Afterward, he fulfilled a promise by visiting Mantle and Cerv in the hospital. When the new record-holder entered the room, Mantle laughed and shouted, "I hate your guts!" All three ballplayers smiled over their summer joke about Maris and Mantle "feuding," and Mantle called Maris' 61st homer "the greatest feat in sports history."[36]

So the first 162-game regular season ended with a monumental finish for Maris and New York. In many ways, the World Series was anticlimactic for the greatest Yankees team ever. After it was over, Ralph Houk called the 1961 Yankees "the best all-around team" he had ever seen.[37]

Yankees Win World Series

The biggest questions about the World Series were not about who would win, the Yankees or the Cincinnati Reds, but whether Mickey Mantle could play and whether Roger Maris would continue his home run bombardment. The fall classic opened in the Bronx on Wednesday, October 4, and Maris was worn out, physically and emotionally, from his season. The Yankees wanted to win for several reasons: to come back from the loss to the Pirates in the 1960 fall classic, to prove Ralph Houk was the better choice to manage, not Casey Stengel, and to show that the 1961 Yankees were the best team ever, better even than the 1927 Yankees.

The surprising Reds, managed by Fred Hutchinson, who had piloted the Tigers in 1953 and 1954, but left when Detroit's front office wouldn't give him more than another one-year contract, fielded an excellent team. Cincinnati fashioned a 93–61 record (the NL played its last 154-game season in 1961), following a sixth-place finish in 1960. Cincy featured right fielder Frank Robinson, an intimidating right-handed batter who crowded the plate and hit with power. Robinson, the best of four black players with the Reds, won the league's MVP Award for his .323 average with 37 home runs and 124 RBI. Another star was Vada Pinson, a standout trumpeter and center fielder who grew up in Oakland, California, who hit .343 with 16 homers and 87 RBI that season. Other major figures were first baseman Gordy Coleman, who hit .287 with 26 homers and 87 RBI, and third baseman Gene Freese, who batted .277 with 26 homers and 87 RBI. Wally Post, the veteran left fielder, hit .294 with 20 homers and 57 RBI, and the Reds as a team averaged .270.

For pitching Cincinnati relied on Joey Jay, the former Braves right-hander who went 21–10 with a 3.53 ERA, tying Milwaukee lefty Warren Spahn for the NL lead with 21 wins. The Reds' rotation also starred left-hander Jim O'Toole, who was 19–9 with a 3.10 ERA, and Bob Purkey, the ex–Pirate who had a 16–12 mark with a 3.73 ERA. Jay and Purkey were All-Stars along with Robinson and Eddie Kasko, the slick-fielding shortstop who batted .271.

True, the Reds' total of 158 home runs fell well below the Yankees' record of 240 four-baggers, but typically, several writers, perhaps due to anti–Yankees sentiments, favored Cincinnati. Detroit's Joe Falls argued that the Reds would win, first, because they had "the psychology (and Wally Post) going for them," and that the short best-of-seven series helped Cincy. Falls' other reasons concerned Mantle and Maris: Mantle had been sick, and Maris was "bushed."[38] Regardless, Oscar Kahan, citing a poll of 18 correspondents who wrote for *The Sporting News*, found 13 of the writers favored New York on "the basis that the power of Roger Maris, Mickey Mantle, & Co. will prevail over the pitching of Joey Jay, Bob Purkey and Jim O'Toole."[39]

Mantle, released from the hospital on Monday, October 2, went to the Stadium for treatment. The wound had to be drained and bandaged over and over, and Mantle, a specialist in locker-room humor and the ultimate macho man, joked about it. The day before the opener, Mantle took five batting practice swings and told Houk he couldn't play. That evening he and Merlyn went to the Harwyn Club for dinner, but Mantle couldn't sit long enough to eat. The couple left.[40]

The Reds faced their season's greatest challenge in the star-studded lineup of the World Series–tested Yankees, whether or not Maris or Mantle made big impacts. At batting practice before the first game on Wednesday, October 4, Maris knew his swing was off. He was still going for the fences. "My normal swing was gone," he said. "I was completely off stride."[41]

That overcast afternoon, Houk started the league's biggest winner, Whitey Ford, soon to win the Major Leagues' Cy Young Award. The 32-year-old, 25-game-winning lefty, mixing his pitches well and cutting the corners, blanked the Reds on two harmless singles, a blooper by Kasko, the number two hitter, and a solid hit by Post, fifth in the lineup. Six-foot Jim O'Toole pitched well, keeping his slider in tight and his fastball away. The lefty spaced six hits, but two were solo home runs, one in the fourth inning by Ellie Howard, batting cleanup, and another in the sixth by Moose Skowron, the fifth batter. Maris patrolled center, and he moved to right field in the ninth when Hector Lopez's defensive standby, Jack Reed, entered the game. Maris went 0-for-4, and he hit nothing to the outfield, but O'Toole gave the slugger no good pitches. A crowd of 62,397 jammed the stadium to root for their heroes, but Maris was hitless and Mantle couldn't play.

More important, Ford, yet another hero in pinstripes, completed his third straight World Series shutout, making 27 consecutive scoreless innings starting with his 10–0 and 12–0 victories over Pittsburgh in 1960. In Cincinnati, Ford would go after another remarkable but lesser-known Ruth record, the Babe's mark of 29 consecutive scoreless innings in World Series play set in 1918 when the southpaw was still pitching—as well as playing the outfield—for the Red Sox.

On Thursday Houk came back with 16-game winner Ralph Terry, and "Hutch" used his ace, Joey Jay. Cincinnati won, 6–2, as Jay stifled the Bronx Bombers on four hits. Maris led off with a walk in the fourth inning, and Berra golfed a two-run home run to the right field seats, tying the score at 2–2, but that was it for the Yankees. Gordy Coleman, a fun guy who often kept his teammates laughing, belted a two-run homer in the fourth, and the Reds took the lead on two singles and Howard's passed ball in the fifth. Catcher Johnny Edwards added a run-scoring single in the sixth, and two innings later, the Reds scored two more, the second on Edwards' RBI dou-

The Yankees' John Blanchard shows his home run form. In the eighth inning of Game Three of the 1961 World Series, Blanchard homered off Cincinnati's Bob Purkey to lift New York into a 2–2 tie. In the ninth, Roger Maris followed with another solo home run, giving the Yankees a 3–2 edge that Luis Arroyo preserved (National Baseball Hall of Fame, Cooperstown, New York).

ble. Maris, hitless, had walked and scored on Berra's home run. The teams were tied at one game each, the Reds flew home in a hopeful mood, while the Yankees rode a special train to Cincinnati for Game Three.

On Friday during early batting practice (the visitors take their swings first) at 30,000-seat Crosley Field, Mantle, determined to play, stepped to the plate with people several rows deep watching from behind the batting cage. Maybe 2,000 early arrivals saw the workout. On the first swing, Mantle winced and bent over with pain. Pounding his bat on the plate, he regained his composure. He slugged several balls into the stands, including a few over the center field fence. Houk didn't think playing was a good idea, but Mantle, with his hip bandaged, padded, and cushioned, insisted. The doctors told the manager Mantle would feel pain, but he wouldn't hurt himself more. When the Yankees took the field, Mantle was cheered, but Maris was jeered.

Saturday's game saw Bill Stafford square off against the Reds' junkballing Bob Purkey, and the contest was a thriller, but the Yankees, winners for so many Octobers since 1923, won, 3–2, boosted by Maris. The gutsy, limping Mantle went hitless, but he played. Frank Robinson opened the scoring with an RBI double in the third inning, Yogi Berra tied it with a run-scoring single in the seventh, and Eddie Kasko gave the Reds' a 2–1 edge with his RBI single in the Reds' seventh.

In the Yankees' eighth, Blanchard, the catcher who swung an explosive bat, spoke to Mantle about Purkey before batting with two outs and the score tied. Mantle told John, "He's going to throw you a slider first pitch for a strike. Then he's gonna come back with knuckleballs." Blanchard, looking for the slider, homered into the right field seats to tie the game at 2–2. Afterward, Mantle joked, "Hey, Blanch. You owe me a six-pack!" Blanchard, who also loved the Yankees' camaraderie and the clubhouse fun, recalled, "I bought him a case."[42]

Batting in the top of the ninth, Maris, hitless in ten trips for the fall classic and not having hit a single ball over the fence in batting practice, was still his usual focused self. Like Blanchard, he swung on Purkey's first pitch, also a slider, felt that special crack of the bat as he pulled the pitch, and drove the ball more than 360 feet over the right field fence. Arroyo, who could be reached on occasion, came out of the pen. The clutch-hurling screwball specialist fanned Gene Freese to start the bottom of the ninth, and surrendered a long drive to left-center by Leo Cardenas, a second-year Cuban flychaser, but the ball hit the scoreboard and bounced back, just missing a home run.[43] Arroyo, unfazed, retired pinch-hitters Dick Gernert and Gus Bell on a pair of infield grounders. The excitement was over, the Yankees led two games to one, and Mantle and Maris had both contributed, making Game Three a fitting victory for the aptly-nicknamed Bombers.

Talking about Maris' homer, number 62 in 1961, Fred Hutchinson said, "It was the key hit of the Series. We were never the same after that."[44] Also, Maris' blast tied him with Ruth for the season and the post-season combined, as the Babe hit two homers to help the Yankees win the World Series of 1927, making a total of 62 each for Ruth and Maris.

New York's last two victories came easier. On Sunday, the Yankees won a 7–0 shutout behind Ford, fueled by three hits by Richardson and Skowron and a two-run single by Hector Lopez. The Yankees' newest October hero, Lopez, who went 3-for-9 against Reds pitching and drove in seven runs in four games, took over for the struggling Mantle. Also, Ford fouled a ball off his foot in the fifth inning. Hurting, the lefty gave up a single to one batter in the sixth and left the game with a new World Series record of 32 scoreless innings pitched, breaking Ruth's 1918 mark of 29⅔ scoreless innings[45] (Ford extended his World Series scoreless pitching record to 33⅔ innings in 1962). Jim Coates finished Ford's shutout, allowing one hit in four innings. Later, Ford, dubbed "Chairman of the Board" by Mantle, was voted the World Series MVP.

October Hero: Hector Lopez batted .333 and drove in seven runs in four games the 1961 World Series. The Panamanian hero helped win the deciding Game Five by hitting an RBI triple in the five-run first inning, and slugging a three-run homer to cap the five-run fourth and give the Yankees an 11–3 lead (author's collection).

On Monday the Yankees bombed Joey Jay, who lasted just two-thirds of an inning, and seven relievers for 15 hits and a 13–5 rout. The gray-uniformed visitors scored five times in the first inning, featuring Blanchard's two-run homer, Skowron's RBI single, Lopez's run-scoring triple off reliever Jim Maloney, and Boyer's RBI double. The Yankees scored five more in the fourth, boosted by Lopez's three-run homer, and suddenly the score was 11–3. The Reds totaled 11 hits, reaching Ralph Terry for three runs in 2⅓ innings, but another new October hero, Bud Daley, finished the afternoon and recorded the World Series–clinching victory.

Recalled Jim O'Toole, who won

Cincy's only World Series game, "I think the 1961 Yankees were the greatest team of the era." Reliever Jim Brosnan, the 6'4" right-hander who kept a candid diary about Cincinnati's 1961 season and turned it into a book, *Pennant Race,* observed, "We didn't belong on the field with the 1961 Yankees, one of the greatest teams of all time."[46]

Heroic Feats in 1961

The momentous 1961 season already had ended for the Tigers and Norm Cash, and now it was over for the World Champion Yankees and Roger Maris. Those two unlikely heroes both enjoyed individually unique seasons that thrilled countless fans. Along with their ball clubs, the Tigers and the Yankees, respectively, they represented the best of baseball in 1961.

For the Tigers, the 1961 season showed how far Bob Scheffing, a shrewd, down-to-earth, and innovative manager who handled all kinds of players

Tigers Heroes: The Tigers' big three sluggers didn't match the home run heroics of the Yankees in 1961, but Rocky Colavito, Al Kaline, and Norm Cash were three of Detroit's most popular stars (National Baseball Hall of Fame, Cooperstown, New York).

well, could secure the best out of a combination of established stars, talented veterans, and new players, including rookies. As the season progressed, Scheffing worked on the diamond and in the clubhouse with the likes of Al Kaline, the face of Detroit's franchise, who averaged .324; Rocky Colavito, who produced his greatest single season with a .290 average, 45 home runs; and 140 RBI, Norm Cash, named first baseman on *The Sporting News'* All-Star team; Frank Lary, the tough right-hander who was known for beating the Yankees, who produced a career-best 23 wins; Don Mossi, the tough-luck southpaw who won 15 games; Jim Bunning, the intense competitor who won 17 games; and Billy Bruton, the onetime Braves' center fielder who provided spark, speed, and leadership.

Further, Scheffing worked with many newcomers, notably rookie Jake Wood, who started 160 games (and played two more) at second base and led the league in triples; Steve Boros, who made important contributions at third base and at the plate; Phil Regan, an inexperienced right-hander who was 0–4 in 1960 but contributed ten wins in 1961; Terry Fox, the Braves castoff who became the Bengals' best bullpen stopper in years; Charlie Maxwell, a Tigers slugging hero since 1956 who delivered several timely hits as a reserve; Dick Brown, the journeyman catcher who socked 16 homers in his best season ever; Mike Roarke, an untested rookie catcher who shored up the pitching staff after Brown was injured; Chico Fernandez, the veteran shortstop who kept improving as the year progressed; Dick McAuliffe, a timely-hitting rookie who would become a Tigers' fixture in the future; and Bo Osborne, a minor league slugger who helped the team's camaraderie and performance with his bat, his glove, and his upbeat personality.

Through it all the Tigers played consistently well, until they reached New York on September 1, when they couldn't stop the Yankees' juggernaut in three crucial games. After stumbling to eight straight losses, the Bengals, determined to roar again, won 12 of the last 15 games, the franchise's best season since a second-place finish in 1950. On the closing day, Cash, one of Detroit's most popular stars, went 2-for-3 and slugged his 41st home run in his last at-bat, ending his season with a flourish and the promise of future stardom.

For the Yankees, Ralph Houk, a first-year leader who replaced the legendary Casey Stengel, pulled off an excellent job of managing a first-rate team of World Series–tested performers, including the pitching staff, boosted by the arrival of Bud Daley in mid–June. Houk, largely by encouraging, supporting, and backing his stable of stars and Mantle, his superstar, secured career-best seasons out of Roger Maris, Whitey Ford, John Blanchard, Ellie Howard, and Luis Arroyo, plus a splendid season out of Mantle.

Equally important, Houk coaxed very good seasons out of almost every Yankee, notably Yogi Berra, Bill Skowron, Bobby Richardson, Tony Kubek, and Clete Boyer. Even Bob Turley, suffering arm problems, helped read opposing pitchers for his teammates. Houk's job was at once tougher than Scheffing's, because of the higher expectations for the Yankees, and easier, because of the franchise's larger array of talented players. Still, the Major used his personal skills and his knowledge of the men to meld his team's togetherness, camaraderie, and pride, carrying on the Yankees' great tradition of winning pennants and the World Series.

Scheffing and Houk shared one important tactic. Scheffing persuaded the normally reserved Kaline to become the Tigers' on-field leader through the example of his All-Star performance, and Houk persuaded the reluctant Mantle to do likewise for the Yankees. While it is difficult to measure the value of such intangible leadership, Kaline's and Mantle's play surely inspired many of each superstar's teammates, especially the younger ones. Ironically, neither Kaline nor Mantle produced the most remarkable individual season for his team in 1961. Still, Scheffing and Houk deserve kudos for the seasons enjoyed by their respective teams.

In the end, baseball's first truly media-hyped season generated an unending supply of stories and interviews, particularly about Mantle and Maris and the exciting home run chase. The Yankees, off to a slower start, moved ahead of the faster-starting Tigers in late July, and the two teams waged a seesaw battle in August. But in September, the month crucial to any pennant race, the Yankees swept the season's biggest series with Detroit and went on to win 109 games and the flag, while the Tigers, who faltered in the Bronx, won 101 games and finished second.

When longtime fans and readers who love baseball remember the 1961 season, they think about the pennant-winning Yankees and the home run heroics of Maris and Mantle. Tigers fans recall the hitting and home run exploits of heroes like Cash, Colavito, and Kaline, but outside of Detroit and Michigan, fewer fans remember the Tigers' glorious season. Still, players as diverse as Mickey Mantle, Al Kaline, Elston Howard, Frank Lary, Whitey Ford, Mike Roarke, Bobby Richardson, Hector Lopez, and Jake Wood each inspired their share of fans by their daily performances.

In retrospect, the beauty of baseball is that Roger Maris might slug 61 homers or Norm Cash might hit .361, and such extraordinary feats can neither be predicted nor purchased. Of course, such skilled athletes shared a deep love of the game. Even if Maris and Cash rode the momentum of an unusual season to new heights and could never repeat their supreme achievement, they succeeded in 1961 against all odds. Regardless of those who would debunk them, Maris and Cash had seasons that would live forever in the records and, perhaps more importantly, in the lore of baseball and in the memories of their fans. Any big boy has a shot at enjoying such an excellent season, and those players good enough to wear the Yankees' pinstripes or the Tigers' white flannels were living the dream about that shining but elusive opportunity.

Chapter Notes

Chapter 1

1. Joe Falls, "Cash Clears the Roof! Norm Hits 3 Home Runs as Tigers Split with Nats," *Detroit Free Press* (hereafter cited as *DFP*), June 12, 1961, 1–2.

2. Watson Spoelstra, "Motor City Wheels Out Snappy Twin-Engine Job," *The Sporting News* (hereafter cited as *TSN*), June 21, 1961, 6.

3. Falls, "Cash Is Disrupting Life on the Home Front, Too," *DFP*, June 13, 1961, 29.

4. Dick Schaap, "On the Spot in 62: Norm Cash and Vada Pinson," *Sport*, April 1962, 23.

5. Peter Golenbock, *Dynasty: The New York Yankees, 1949–1964* (Mineola, NY: Dover Publications, 1975, 2010), 512–513.

6. Editorial, "Doesn't Anybody Just Play Ball Any More?" *TSN*, April 5, 1961, 10.

7. Detailed analysis by the Society for American Baseball Research, or SABR, found that Maris was incorrectly credited with an RBI in a game on July 5, 1961, for a run that scored on an error. As a result, Gentile, who produced 141 RBI, actually tied for the AL lead with Maris, now credited with 141, but listed with 142 in 1961 records. See Tyler Kepner, "For Jim Gentile, a Long-Awaited Bonus," July 6, 2010: http://bats.blogs.Nytimes.com/2010/08/06/for-jim-gentile-a-long-awaited-bonus/?_r=0.

8. Berry Stainback, "Jim Gentile: Baltimore Bomber," in Ray Robinson, ed., *Baseball Stars of 1962* (New York: Pyramid Books, March 1962), 81–88.

9. "Harmon Killebrew," by National Baseball Hall of Fame: http://baseballhall.org/hof/killebrew-harmon.

10. Danny Peary, ed., *We Played the Game: 65 Players Remember Baseball's Greatest Era, 1947–1964* (New York: Hyperion, 1994), 528.

11. Dick Kaplan, "Whitey Ford and Luis Arroyo: Me and My Caddy," in *Baseball Stars of 1962*, 37–43.

12. Tom Clavin and Danny Peary, *Roger Maris: Baseball's Reluctant Hero* (New York: Simon & Schuster, 2010), 159–161.

13. Clavin and Peary, *Roger Maris*, 159.

14. Arnold Hano, "How the Home Run Is Breaking Up the Game," *Sport*, May 1962, 30–33, 35, 84–85.

15. Harold Rosenthal, "Rocky Colavito and Norm Cash: Tiger Terrors," in *Baseball Stars of 1962*, 69–73.

16. Hal Middlesworth, "Kaline's Circus Catch Saves Sweep of Yanks," *DFP*, July 19, 1956, 23.

17. Donald A. Carter, U.S. Army Center of Military History, "The U.S. Military Response to the 1960–1962 Berlin Crisis"; see: http://www.foia.cia.gov/sites/default/files/document_conversions/16/USMilitaryResponse.pdf.

18. Fred Olmstead, "GM Sales and Earnings Zoom in Second Quarter: 3-Month Income Is $252 Million," *DFP*, July 27, 1961, 3.

Chapter 2

1. Tony Kubek and Terry Pluto, *Sixty-One: The Team, the Record, the Men* (New York: Macmillan, 1987), 71.

2. Hal Butler, *Al Kaline and the Detroit Tigers* (Chicago: Henry Regnery, 1973), 102–104.

3. *1961: Detroit Tigers, Official Yearbook* (Detroit: Detroit Baseball Co., 1961), 3.

4. Kerrie Ferrell, *Rick Ferrell, Knuckleball Catcher: A Hall of Famer's Life Behind the Plate and in the Front Office* (Jefferson, NC: McFarland, 2010), 184–186.

5. Interview with Jake Wood, May 5, 2013.

6. Patrick Harrigan, *The Detroit Tigers: Club and Community, 1945–1995* (Toronto: University of Toronto Press, 1997), 109–111.

7. Interview with Jim Proctor, August 29, 2013.

8. *Ibid.*

9. Larry Moffi and Jonathan Kronstadt, *Crossing the Line: Black Major Leaguers, 1947–1959* (Lincoln, NE: University of Nebraska Press, 2006 ed.), v, 10, 229–235.

10. Interview with Jake Wood, June 30, 2014.

11. J. G. Taylor Spink, comp., *Baseball Register: 1962 Edition* (St. Louis, Missouri: C. C. Spink & Son, Publishers, 1962), 46.

12. Bill Furlong, "A Negro Ballplayer's Life Today," *Sport*, May 1962, 91–92.

13. Larry Moffi, *This Side of Cooperstown: An Oral History of Major League Baseball in the 1950s* (Iowa City, IA: University of Iowa Press, 1996), 100–101.

14. Richard Goldstein, "Vic Power, First Baseman with a Flair, Is Dead at 78," *New York Times*, November 30, 2005.

15. Kubek and Pluto, *Sixty-One*, 77–78.

16. Kubek and Pluto, *Sixty-One*, 213.

17. Hal Butler, *Stormin' Norman Cash* (New York: Julian Messner, 1968), 54–57.

18. Watson Spoelstra, "Ol' Paw Paw Socking Hero of Tiger Fans," *The Sporting News*, January 18, 1961, 22.

19. Jim Hawkins, *Al Kaline: The Biography of a Tigers Icon* (Chicago: Triumph Books, 2010), 112–115.

20. Butler, *Al Kaline*, 104–105.

21. Kubek and Pluto, *Sixty-One*, 168.

22. Arlene Howard with Ralph Wimbush, *Elston and Me: The Story of the First Black Yankee* (Columbia, MO: University of Missouri Press, 2001), 99–101.

23. Dan Daniel, "Yankees Likely to Move Camp to Fort Lauderdale," *TSN*, February 15, 1961, 5.

24. Lawrence Leonard, "Broward County Welcomes Vees [Richmond, Virginia, of International League], Hails Yankees," *TSN*, April 5, 1961, 16.

25. Daniel, "Houk Grips Yank Reins Like Born Leader," *TSN*, March 1, 1961, 2.

26. Daniel, "Handy-Man Kubek Lands Steady Job as Yank Shortstop," and "Bombers Begin Drills Without Single Holdout," *TSN*, March 8, 1961, 5.

27. Peter Golenbock, *Dynasty: The New York Yankees, 1949–1964* (Mineola, NY: Dover Publications, 1975, 2010), 501–502.

28. Til Ferdenzi, "Mick Gives Own Slant on 'Take-Charge' Role," *TSN*, March 29, 1961, 1–2.

29. Daniel, "Bombers Begin Drills Without a Single Holdout," *TSN*, March 8, 1961, 5.

30. Kubek and Pluto, *Sixty-One*, 74–75.

31. Ralph Houk and Robert W. Creamer,
Season of Glory (New York: Simon & Schuster, 1988), 50.

32. Frederick G. Lieb, "Dimag's No. 5 Brightens St. Pete Scene," *TSN*, March 22, 1961, 2.

33. Tom Meany, "From DiMaggio—To Mantle, *Sport*, September 1961, 26–27.

34. Daniel, "Pilot Houk Pegs Stafford Heavy-Duty Yankee Hurler," *TSN*, March 22, 1961; Ford and Luis Arroyo," in *Baseball Stars of 1962*, Ray Robinson, editor (New York: Pyramid Books, 1962), 37–44.

35. Dick Kaplan, "Whitey Ford and Luis Arroyo," in *Baseball Stars of 1962*, Ray Robinson, editor, 37–44.

36. Daniel, "Arroyo Fracture Climaxes Heavy Toll of Injuries," *TSN*, March 22, 1961, 6.

37. Ralph Houk, edited by Charles Dexter, *Ballplayers Are Human, Too* (New York: G.P. Putnam's Sons, 1962), 87.

38. Roger Maris and Jim Ogle, *Roger Maris at Bat* (New York: Duell, Sloan, and Pearce, 1962), xvii, 4–7.

39. Kubek and Pluto, *Sixty-One*, 75–76.

40. Lieb, "Lieb, Who Covered Yankees' First St. Pete Drill, Describes Finale," *TSN*, April 12, 1961, 17, 31.

41. Joe Falls, "Speed-Boy Bruton Labeled Cure for Bengals' Fadeouts," *TSN*, March 22, 1961, 17.

42. Falls, "Bubba's Torrid Bat Sets Off Fireworks in Bengals' Garden," *TSN*, April 5, 1961, 21.

43. Interview with Jake Wood, May 5, 2013.

44. Joe King, "Clouting 'Em," *TSN*, March 8, 1961, 15.

45. Falls, "Flash or Flop–Chico Gives Bengals Fits," *TSN*, April 12, 1961, 27.

46. Houk and Creamer, *Season of Glory*, 99.

47. Gordon Cobbledick, *Don't Knock the Rock: The Rocky Colavito Story* (Cleveland: World Publishing, 1966), 128–129.

48. "Scouting Reports—1961," *Sports Illustrated*, April 10, 1961, 72–73, 82–83.

49. Herbert Simons, "Scouting Reports: On 1961 Major League Rookies," *Baseball Digest*, March 1961, 92–94.

50. Simons, "Scouting Reports," 84–87.

51. J. G. Taylor Spink, "Swami Spink See Dodgers, Oriole Flags," *TSN*, April 12, 1961, 7.

Chapter 3

1. Players like Bill Bruton, the former Braves star, said umpires in the American

League called the strike zone higher than did arbiters in the National League. Having played in both leagues, Bruton concluded, "I Would Say About Eight to Ten Inches Higher." See Bill Furlong, "A Negro Ballplayer's Life Today," *Sport*, May 1962, 92–93.

2. Interview with Jake Wood, March 6, 2015.

3. Joe Falls, "Kids (Wood and Boros) Did Better than Anyone," *DFP*, April 13, 1961, 33.

4. Watson Spoelstra, "Bob Scheffing Lauds Tigers' Battling Kids," *TSN*, April 19, 1961, 17.

5. Tom Briere, "Twins Kick Up Quick Tango for Gay Pedro," *TSN*, April 19, 1961, 19.

6. Dan Daniel, "Rep as Clutch Crew Pins 'Favorites' Tag on Yanks," *TSN*, April 19, 1961, 8.

7. Spoelstra, "Lary Backs Scrivener's Decision That Shattered No-Hitter Hopes," *TSN*, April 26, 1961, 20.

8. Spoelstra, "Tigers Smack Lips Over Tasty Start of Former Tepee Trio," *TSN*, April 26, 1961, 20.

9. Falls, "Tigers Find Diamond in Rough," *DFP*, April 24, 36, 37.

10. Falls, "League Leaders Clip Angels, 3–1, 3–2," *DFP*, April 24, 1961, 36, 37.

11. Falls, "Tigers Beat Yanks for 8th in Row," *DFP*, April 25, 1961, 1, 30.

12. George Puscas, "That Boros Has Just Been Near Perfect," *DFP*, April 25, 1961, 29, 30.

13. Spoelstra, "Joe E.'s Hot Quips Spark Charity Fete," *TSN*, May 3, 1961, 4; Spoelstra, "Dinner Is Most Successful," *Detroit News*, April 25, 1961, 2-B.

14. Falls, "Youthful Tigers Stir 'Old Al,'" *DFP*, April 26, 1961, 29, 31.

15. Falls, "Pow, Pow–Tigers Bow," *DFP*, April 27, 1961, 31, 32.

16. Interview with Jake Wood, March 6, 2015.

17. Spoelstra, "Rivals Scurry to Dodge Slashing Tigers," *TSN*, May 3, 1961, 3.

18. Daniel, "Yankees Spinning Wheels, Look to Maris for Push," *TSN*, May 3, 1961, 12.

19. *Baseball Register* (St. Louis: C .C. Spink & Son, Publishers, 1962), 107–108, published by *The Sporting News* before each season, listed Mantle at 6'0" and 200 pounds for 1962, but both figures were exaggerations released by the Yankees. See Baseball-reference.com: http://www.baseball-reference.com/players/m/mantlmi01.shtml.

20. Peter Golenbock, *Dynasty: The New York Yankees, 1949–1964* (Mineola, NY: Dover Publications, 1975, 2010), 306–307.

21. Golenbock, *Dynasty*, 351–358.

22. Louis Effrat in *The New York Times*, August 15, 1960, 27, indicated that Mantle trotted to first base, Casey Stengel replaced him, and Stengel afterward said, "If He Can't Run, He Should Tell Me." Effrat said Stengel did not mention a possible fine for Mantle, but the writer, not looking to embarrass the Yankees, made no mention of the booing.

23. Also see Jane Leavy, *The Last Boy: Mickey Mantle and the End of America's Childhood* (New York: HarperCollins Books, 2010), 186–197.

24. Golenbock, *Dynasty*, 465–467.

25. George Rekela, "Johnny Blanchard, on SABR's Bio-Project: http://Sabr.Org/Bioproj/Person/92bd6f3l.

26. Leavy, the *Last Boy: Mickey Mantle*, 198–204.

27. Dick Schaap, "Mickey Mantle: Wunderkind Grows Up," in Ray Robinson, ed., *Baseball Stars of 1961* (New York: Pyramid Books, March 1961), 38–44.

28. "Mickey Signs Up for Life," *TSN*, January 2, 1952, 26.

29. Leavy, *The Last Boy: Mickey Mantle*, 28–29, 76–77, 216–219.

30. Daniel, "Rags to Riches–Magic Leap by Mantle, Mays," *TSN*, March 16, 1963,5.

31. Tom Clavin and Danny Peary, *Roger Maris: Baseball's Reluctant Hero* (New York: Simon & Schuster, 2010), 177–178.

32. Jim Hawkins, *Al Kaline: The Biography of a Tigers Icon* (Chicago: Triumph Books, 2010), 102–103.

33. Mike Klingaman, "Kaline Can Still Remember Days of Southern Hospitality," *Baltimore Sun*, June 21, 2004.

34. Interview with Merry Sue Roarke, October 25, 2013.

35. George Cantor, *The Tigers of '68: Baseball's Last Real Champions* (Dallas: Taylor, 1997), 158–160.

36. Joe King, "Houk Sees Yanks Mound Depth Collaring Fast-Starting Rivals," *TSN*, May 10, 1961, 18.

37. Tony Kubek and Terry Pluto, *Sixty-One: The Team, the Record, the Men* (New York: Macmillan, 1987), 80–81.

38. Spoelstra, "Bold Bengals Sharpening Teeth Behind Quartet of Vet Twirlers," *TSN*, May 10, 1961, 17.

Chapter 4

1. Kubek and Terry Pluto, *Sixty-One: The Team, the Record, the Men* (New York: Macmil-

lan, 1987), 32–33. Kubek called Ogle "The Sportswriter Covering the Yankees Whom Roger Trusted the Most."

2. Joe King, "Houk Sees Red at Maris' Trip to Eye Doctor," *TSN*, May 31, 1961, 13.

3. Roger Maris and Jim Ogle, *Roger Maris at Bat* (New York: Duell, Sloan and Pearce, 1962), 12–15.

4. King, "Houk Steams and Seethes as Yanks Play Jekyll-Hyde," *TSN*, May 31, 1961, 13.

5. Tom Clavin and Roger Peary, *Roger Maris: Baseball's Reluctant Hero* (New York: Simon & Schuster, 2010), 153, offered useful insights into New York's writers in 1961, notably which ones liked to rip Maris.

6. King, "Colavito Rockets into Stands in Answering the Call of the Clan," *TSN*, May 24, 1961, 11.

7. Interview with Jake Wood, June 30, 2014.

8. Clavin and Peary, *Roger Maris*, 5, 23, 65–55.

9. Clavin and Peary, *Roger Maris*, 38.

10. Clavin and Peary, *Roger Maris*, 72.

11. Clavin and Peary, *Roger Maris*, especially 19–73.

12. Kubek and Pluto, *Sixty-One*, 84–87.

13. The best source on Colavito, especially for his Cleveland years, is the biography by local sportswriter Gordon Cobbledick, *Don't Knock the Rock: The Rocky Colavito Story* (Cleveland: World Publishing, 1966), 32–82.

14. Spoelstra, "Tigers Tip Topper to Braves for Early Spurt," *TSN*, May 17, 1961, 7.

15. Spoelstra, "Lary Unlocks Triple Fury as Yankee Tamer," *TSN*, May 24, 1961, 25.

16. King, "Tigers Flouting Forecasts of Crackup/Earn Respect of Yanks with Stout Rallies," *TSN*, May 24, 1961, 1–2.

17. "Three Homers-In-Row Record Tied Second Time This Year," *TSN*, May 31, 1961, 7.

18. Braven Dyer, "Angels Croon Sweet June Melody, Here Comes McBride," *TSN*, June 7, 1961, 7.

19. Joe Falls, "Roaring Tigers Unpack for a Holiday at Home," *Detroit Free Press*, May 30, 1961, 11.

Chapter 5

1. Hal Butler, *Stormin' Norman Cash* (New York: Julian Messner, 1968), 67–68.

2. Steve Wolf, "Tricks of the Trade," *Sports Illustrated*, April 13, 1981, 98 (see SI Vault).

Also see "Norm Cash Awards" on Baseball Almanac: http://www.baseball-almanac.com/players/awards.php?p=cashno01.

3. Butler, *Stormin' Norman Cash*, 67.

4. Norman Cash on Baseball-reference: http://www.baseball-reference.com/players/c/cashno01.shtml?redir.

5. Joe Williams, "Homer Hero Cash Draws Coolie Wage," *New York World Telegram & Sun*, June 13, 1961, copy in Cash File, Baseball Hall of Fame Library (hereafter cited as BB HOF), Cooperstown, New York.

6. Lyall Smith, "Tiger D-Day Near: To Trade … Or Not?" *DFP*, June 4, 1961, 4-F.

7. Joe Falls, "Indians: Surprise of 1961," *DFP*, June 8, 1961, 33.

8. Neal Shine, "Fans Flip as Bengals Split," *DFP*, June 9, 1961, 1–2.

9. Falls, "Tigers Split 2 Dillies with Indians," *DFP*, June 9, 1961, 51, 57.

10. "As of Today," *DFP*, June 13, 1961, 29, 31.

11. Falls, "Cash Bashes Two More–Tigers Win, 7–1," *DFP*, June 14, 1961, 1, 31–32.

12. Falls, "Thanks, Bosox!–Tigers Win, 4–2," *DFP*, June 15, 1961, 37–38.

13. Falls, "Grand Slam Knocks Tigers Off Top," *DFP*, June 16, 1961, 47, 49.

14. Judd Arnett, "Tiger Fans Swing Between Gloom and Joy as Yankees Bow," *DFP* June 17, 1961, 1–2; Falls, "Tigers Beat Yankees to Tie for First Place," and "Who's Mad? Norm Cash, Everybody?" *DFP*, June 17, 1961, 11.

15. Falls, "Tigers Stagger by Yanks, 12–10," *DFP*, June 18, 1961, D1, D3.

16. Bob Pille, "Ford Driving for 20-Win Season," *DFP*, June 19, 1961, 31.

17. Falls, "Yanks Rout Tigers and Lary, 9–0," *DFP*, June 19, 1961, 1, 31.

18. Whitey Ford, with Phil Pepe, *Slick: My Life in and Around Baseball* (New York: William Morrow, 1987), 17–49.

19. Peter Golenbock, *Dynasty: The New York Yankees, 1949–1964* (Mineola, NY: Dover Publications, 1975, 2010), 246–252.

20. Ford, with Pepe, *Slick*, 11.

21. Tony Kubek and Terry Pluto, *Sixty-One: The Team, the Record, the Players* (New York: Macmillan, 1987), 220–228.

22. Sam Greene, "Lary Credits Knuckle Ball as Tigers Blank Cleveland," *Detroit News*, August 16, 1956, 57; Hal Middlesworth, "Lary Started Soaring on Butterfly Ball," *TSN*, September 21, 1956, 5.

23. Arthur Richman, "Even Lary Can't Explain How He Hex-Rays the Yanks," *Baseball Digest*, June 1959, 57–58.

24. Furman Bisher, "How Frank Lary Learned," *Sport*, August 1961, 28, 58–59.

25. Interview with Bob "Red" Wilson, June 26, 2007.

26. Robert H. Boyle, "Taters Keeps the Tigers Up There," *Sports Illustrated*, September 4, 1961, 16–17.

27. Roger Maris and Jim Ogle, *Roger Maris at Bat* (New York: Duell, Sloan, and Pearce, 1962), 28–29.

28. Kubek and Pluto, *Sixty-One*, 88.

29. Falls, "Managers Stall Before Making Pitch," *DFP*, July 4, 1961, 11, 13.

30. "Rookie Makes Line-Up Pronto," *DFP*, June 23, 1961, 47.

31. Falls, "LARY BEATS YANKS, GIVES TIGERS SPLIT" headlined the *Free Press'* issue of July 5, 1961, 1, 27; Pille, "Lary and Chico Use Their Noggins," *Ibid.*, 27, 31.

32. Maris and Ogle, *Roger Maris at Bat*, 39–41.

33. Winn Pennant, "Meet Winn … He's on Job for Tiger Pennant Push," *DFP*, July 6, 1961, 1.

Chapter 6

1. Yogi Berra, *The Yogi Book: "I Really Didn't Say Everything I Said"* (New York: Workman, 1998), 9.

2. I used the term dynasty to refer to the years covered by Peter Golenbock's *Dynasty: The New York Yankees, 1949–1964* (Mineola, NY: Dover Publications, 1975, 2010), ix–xix.

3. Jim Sargent, "Hector Lopez": http://sabr.org/bioproj/person/048dfeef.

4. Yogi Berra and Ed Fitzgerald, *Yogi: The Autobiography of a Professional Baseball Player* (New York: Doubleday, 1961), 55–56.

5. Interview with Yogi Berra, August 15, 2002.

6. Golenbock, *Dynasty*, 310–322.

7. Tony Kubek and Terry Pluto, *Sixty-One: The Team, the Record, the Men* (New York: Macmillan, 1987), 161–165.

8. Allen Barra, *Yogi Berra: Eternal Yankee* (New York: W.W. Norton, 2009), 283.

9. "July 6, 1933: Major League Baseball's First All-Star Game Is Held": http://www.history.com/this-day-in-history/major-league-baseballs-first-all-star-game-is-held.

10. "Scriveners Choose Own All-Star Line-ups," *TSN*, July 5, 1961, 7.

11. Jim Hawkins, *Al Kaline: The Biography of a Tigers Icon* (Chicago: Triumph Books, 2010), 65.

12. Hal Butler, *Stormin' Norman Cash* (New York: Julian Messner, 1968), 78.

13. Interview with Terry Fox, July 11, 2013.

14. Roger Maris and Jim Ogle, *Roger Maris at Bat* (New York: Duell, Sloan and Pearce, 1962), 33–35.

15. *Detroit Tigers: 1961 Guide: Press, TV, Radio* (Detroit: Detroit Baseball Company, 1961), 20–21.

16. Interview with Mike and Merry Sue Roarke, October 25, 2013.

17. Maris and Ogle, *Roger Maris at Bat*, 53–54.

18. "Mantle, Maris Spark Gate Boom," *TSN*, July 26, 1961, 1, 8.

19. Tom Clavin and Danny Peary, *Roger Maris: Baseball's Reluctant Hero* (New York: Simon & Schuster, 2010), 171–175.

20. Allen Barra, "Roger Maris' Misunderstood Quest to Break the Home Run Record," *The Atlantic*, July 27, 2011. See: http://www.theatlantic.com/entertainment/archive/2011/07/roger-mariss-misunderstood-quest-to-break-the-home-run-record/242586/.

21. Maris and Ogle, *Roger Maris at Bat*, 38–39.

22. Clavin and Peary, *Roger Maris*, 166–170.

23. Kubek and Pluto, *Sixty-One*, 175.

24. Bobby Richardson, *The Bobby Richardson Story* (Westwood, NJ: Fleming H. Revell, 1965), 103–111.

25. Len Pasculli, "Bobby Richardson": http://sabr.org/bioproj/person/47363efd.

26. Jim Sargent, "Jake Wood": http://sabr.org/bioproj/person/0801bd7e.

27. Interview with Jake Wood, statement included in Foreword, March 6, 2015.

28. Tom Gage, "Tigers Trail Blazers Still Are Standing Tall Today," *Detroit News*, March 2, 2010; also see: http://www.motownsports.com/forums/archive/index.php/t-80085.html.

29. Joe Falls, "Red Sox Salvage 'Cap, 8–3," *DFP*, July 6, 1961, 37, 38.

30. Bob Pille, "Tiger Pitching Shortage Shows," *DFP*, July 6, 37, 39.

31. Watson Spoelstra, "Scheffing Will Back Three Hill Aces in Pennant Poker," *TSN*, July 9, 1961, 4.

32. Interview with Mike Roarke, March 8, 2014.

33. Falls, "Hello, Pepe Montejo," *DFP*, July 25, 1961, 25.

34. Lyall Smith, "As of Today," *DFP*, July 25, 1961, 25, 27.

35. Spoelstra, "Drydocking of Boros Helps

Whet Tiger Flag Appetite," *TSN*, August 2, 1961, 11.

36. Bob Addie, "Bob Addie's Atoms," *TSN*, August 2, 1961, 18.

Chapter 7

1. Hy Hurwitz, "Aparicio Failure to Charge Kasko Dribbler Key to Tie," *TSN*, August 9, 1961, 1–2.

2. Lyall Smith, "Tiger Stars Shine Through Rain, 1–1," *DFP*, August 1, 1961, 25, 28.

3. Roger Maris and Jim Ogle, *Roger Maris at Bat* (New York: Duell, Sloan and Pearce, 1962), 77–87.

4. Joe Falls, "Tigers Lose–Fall 2 Behind the Yankees," *DFP*, July 30, 1961, D1, D3.

5. Interview with Terry Fox, August 22, 2014.

6. Falls, "Tiger Lose Again, Still Gain Ground," *DFP*, July 31, 1961, 29, 32.

7. Smith, "Tigers Eye Trade," *DFP*, July 31, 1961, 29, 30.

8. Winn Pennant, "Tigers' Top Fan Still Confident," *DFP*, July 31, 1961, 1.

9. Interview with Jake Wood, June 30, 2014.

10. Watson Spoelstra, "Bengals' Big Three Facing Tall Order–60 Wins for Season," *TSN*, August 16, 1961, 7.

11. Maris and Ogle, *Roger Maris*, 88–89.

12. Tom Clavin and Danny Peary, *Roger Maris: Baseball's Reluctant Hero* (New York: Simon & Schuster, 2010), 182–183.

13. Maris and Ogle, *Roger Maris*, 88–94.

14. *The Baseball Register for 1962* (St. Louis: C.C. Spink & Son, 1962), 104, mistakenly listed Lopez's birth year as 1932, but Lopez didn't correct the error at the time; interview with Hector Lopez, June 18, 2003.

15. Jim Sargent, "Hector Lopez," SABR's Bio-Project: http://sabr.org/bioproj/person/048dfeef.

16. Maury Allen, "Hector Lopez," in *Yankees: Where Have You Gone?* (New York: Sports Publishing, 2004), 182–186.

17. Interview with Sandra Osborne, September 22, 2014.

18. George Rekela, "Johnny Blanchard, on SABR's Bio-Project": http://Sabr.Org/Bioproj/Person/92bd6f31.

19. Tony Kubek and Terry Pluto, *Sixty-One: The Team, the Record, the Men* (New York: Macmillan, 1987), 210–211.

20. Allen, "Johnny Blanchard," in *Yankees: Where Have You Gone?* 98–102.

21. Jim Sargent, "Mike Roarke," on SABR's Bio-Project: http://sabr.org/bioproj/person/9e00e4ce.

22. Maris and Ogle, *Roger Maris*, 124–131.

23. Interview with Paul Foytack, June 12, 2007.

24. Dan Daniel, "Blasé Broadway Buzzing Over Maris, Mantle, Hrs," *TSN*, August 23, 1961, 7.

Chapter 8

1. Joe Falls, "Tigers Line Up Big 3 for Yanks," *DFP*, August 25, 1961, 72.

2. Watson Spoelstra, "Tigers Tap Flag Beat to 20-Win Tempo of Lary-Bunning Duet," *TSN*, September 6, 1961, 4.

3. Falls, "Tigers Line Up Big 3 for Yanks," 72.

4. Alex Remington, "Happy Birthday Boy! Don 'The Sphinx' Mossi Turns 82," Big League Stew, January 11, 2011: http://sports.yahoo.com/mlb/blog/big_league_stew/post/Happy-Birthday-Boy-Don-The-Sphinx-Mossi-turns?urn=mlb-306085.

5. Falls, "Colavito Slams 4 Homers," *DFP*, August 28, 1961, 1, 31.

6. Interview with Terry Fox, July 11, 2013.

7. Lyall Smith, "Newest Craze: Twisting and Squirming at Plate," *DFP*, August 29, 1961, 25, 26.

8. Falls, "Tigers Lose Again; Fall 2½ Back," *DFP*, August 31, 1968, 41, 42.

9. Falls, "It's Tigers' Turn to Win," *DFP*, September 1, 1961, 41, 44.

10. Falls, "Tigers Confident They Won't Blow Up," *DFP*, September 1, 1961, 1, 2.

11. Philip J. Lowry, *Green Cathedrals: The Ultimate Celebration of Major League and Negro League Ballparks* (New York: Walker, 2006), 159–163.

12. Joe King, "Phenoms Sheldon and Stafford Steady Yanks' Shaky Staff," *TSN*, June 14, 1961, 11.

13. Harold Rosenthal, "Yanks Wonder About Their Pitching," *Ibid*.

14. Smith, "As of Today," *DFP*, August 31, 1961, 41, 45.

15. Tom Clavin and Danny Peary, *Roger Maris: Baseball's Reluctant Hero* (New York: Simon & Schuster, 2010), 183.

16. Tony Kubek and Terry Pluto, *Sixty-One: The Team, the Record, the Men* (New York: Macmillan, 1987), 102–103.

17. Kubek and Pluto, *Sixty-One*, 102–103.

18. Smith, "One Lousy Curve, Mutters Mossi," *DFP*, September 2, 1961, 11, 14.

19. Falls, "Mossi, Tigers Lose with 2 Out in 9th," *DFP*, September 2, 1961, 11, 13.

20. UPI, "Houk: 'It Was Our Toughest of Year,'" *DFP*, September 2, 1961, 13.

21. Jean Sharley, "Squeeze Play: Yankee Stadium Is Packed–With Tiger Friends," *DFP*, September 2, 1961, 1, 2.

22. Falls, "It's Roger: Over and Out, 7 to 2," *DFP*, September 3, 1961, 1, 3.

23. Smith, "No. 52 Gives Maris a Belt," *DFP*, September 3, 1961, 1, 10.

24. Falls, "'Play Me,' Says Mantle—He Plays, and HOW!" *DFP*, September 4, 1961, 13.

25. John Drebinger, "Mantle Makes It 49 and 50 and Yanks Make It Three Straight Over Tigers," *New York Times* (hereafter cited as *NYT*), September 4, 1961, 18.

26. Roger Maris and Jim Ogle, *Roger Maris at Bat* (New York: Duell, Sloan and Pearce, 1962), 144.

27. Smith, "New Theme Song: 'The Party's Over,'" *DFP*, September 4, 1961, 13, 14.

28. Sharley, "Damnyankees Beat Us Again," *DFP*, September 4, 1961, 1.

29. Winn Pennant, "Don't Panic, Fans, It CAN Be Done," *DFP*, September 4, 1961, 1.

30. Kubek and Pluto, *Sixty-One*, 106.

31. *Ibid.*

32. Maris and Ogle, *Roger Maris at Bat*, 146–147.

33. Clavin and Peary, *Roger Maris*, 195–198.

34. Maris and Ogle, *Roger Maris at Bat*, 157.

35. Maris and Ogle, *Roger Maris at Bat*, 167–168.

36. Maris and Ogle, *Roger Maris at Bat*, 172–173.

37. Smith, "It's the Blues at Birdland," *DFP*, September 5, 1961, 35, 39.

38. Falls, "…And 2nd [Loss] Drops Tigers 7½ Back," *DFP*, September 6, 1961, 33, 34.

39. Smith, "As of Today: That First Loss Took the Starch Out," *Ibid.*

40. Smith, "As of Today: Fairweather Friends of Tigers Off Base," *DFP*, September 7, 1961, 35, 36.

41. Spoelstra, "Loyal Fans Welcome Tigers Home After 1–9 Road Flop," *Ibid.*

42. Spoelstra, "September Mourn for Dodgers and Tigers," *TSN*, September 27, 1961, 7.

43. Falls, "Tigers Fall to KC, 5–2," *DFP*, September 15, 1961, 49, 51.

44. Falls, "Tigers Let a Smile Be Their Umbrella," *DFP*, September 7, 1961, 35, 36.

45. Louis Effrat, "Maris Sulks in Trainer's Room as Futile Night Changes Mood," *NYT*, September 16, 1961, 13.

46. Maris and Ogle, *Roger Maris at Bat*, 175–180.

47. Falls, "Yanks Don't Explode Any M-Bombs," *DFP*, September 16, 1961, 11, 13.

48. Smith, "They're Booing Maris!," *DFP*, September 17, 1961, 1D, 3D.

49. Kubek and Pluto, *Sixty-One*, 3–4.

50. Falls, "Greatest Thrill, He Says," under the headline, "Maris Slams 58th, Ties Foxx, Greenberg," *DFP*, September 18, 1961, 1, 6; Drebinger, "Maris' 58th Homer Gives Yanks Victory Over Tigers in 12th Before 44,219," *NYT*, September 18, 1961, 38.

51. Maris and Ogle, *Roger Maris at Bat*, 191.

52. News Wire Service, "Misses 60, Maris Glad It's Over," *Detroit News*, September 21, 1961, 1D, 6D.

53. Kubek and Pluto, *Sixty-One*, 115–117.

54. Maris and Ogle, *Roger Maris at Bat*, 192–197.

55. Jane Leavy, *The Last Boy: Mickey Mantle and the End of America's Childhood* (New York: HarperCollins, 2010), 224–225.

56. Maris and Ogle, *Roger Maris at Bat*, 199.

Chapter 9

1. Roger Maris and Jim Ogle, *Roger Maris at Bat* (New York: Duell, Sloan and Pearce, 1962), 200–201.

2. UPI, "Maris Still Looking for 60," *DFP*, September 25, 1961, 35.

3. Jane Leavy, *The Last Boy: Mickey Mantle and the End of America's Childhood* (New York: HarperCollins, 2010), 210–223.

4. Maris and Ogle, *Roger Maris at Bat*, 191.

5. Leavy, *The Last Boy*, 225–226.

6. Mickey Mantle with Herb Gluck, *The Mick* (Garden City, NY: Doubleday, 1985), 194–195.

7. Maris and Ogle, *Roger Maris at Bat*, 204–205.

8. Tom Clavin and Danny Peary, *Roger Maris: Baseball's Reluctant Hero* (New York: Simon & Schuster, 2010), 216–217.

9. Leavy, *The Last Boy*, 226.

10. Mantle with Gluck, *The Mick*, 195–196.

11. Leavy, *The Last Boy*, 225–228.

12. Watson Spoelstra, "Bengals Beefing Up Bench for Shot at Bombers in '62," *TSN*, September 20, 1961, 7.

13. Joe Falls, "Tigers Win 7–5 Farce," *DFP*, September 25, 1961, 35.

14. Falls, "Tigers Clinch Second," *DFP*, September 26, 1961, 31, 33.

15. Interview with Bill Freehan, April 21, 1999.

16. Falls, "Freehan Flashy in Tiger Debut," *DFP*, September 27, 1961, 33.

17. Falls, "Tiger Hrs Blast A's," *DFP*, September 28, 1961, 35, 36.

18. Falls, "He [Lary] May Skip Last 3 Games," *DFP*, September 29, 1961, 51.

19. Falls, "Tigers Pocket No. 99," *DFP*, September 30, 1961, 11, 13.

20. Dan Holmes, "How Many Batting Titles Does Ty Cobb Really Have," Detroit Athletic Company Blog, September 15, 2012: http://blog.detroitathletic.com/2012/09/15/how-many-batting-titles-does-ty-cobb-really-have/.

21. Falls, "Early Bird Tigers Win Their 100th," *DFP*, October 1, 1961, 1D, 4D.

22. "Late, But … Maris Hits 60th: Ties Babe's Record in 158 Games," *DFP*, September 27, 1961, 33–34.

23. Clavin and Peary, *Roger Maris*, 217–218.

24. Maris and Ogle, *Roger Maris at Bat*, 208.

25. Maris and Ogle, *Roger Maris at Bat*, 208–209.

26. Maris and Ogle, *Roger Maris at Bat*, 209–210.

27. Falls, "Tigers Bow Out a Winner," *DFP*, October 2, 1961, 33.

28. Tony Kubek and Terry Pluto, *Sixty-One: The Team, the Record, the Men* (New York: Macmillan, 1987), 125.

29. Clavin and Peary, *Roger Maris*, 220–221.

30. Kubek and Pluto, *Sixty-One*, 125.

31. Maris and Ogle, *Roger Maris at Bat*, 211–212.

32. UPI, "Yank Slugger Tops Ruth in Last Game," *DFP*, October 2, 1961, 3.

33. Clavin and Peary, *Roger Maris*, 222–227.

34. Maris and Ogle, *Roger Maris at Bat*, 213–215.

35. Free Press Wire Services, "Roger Hails 2 Others," *DFP*, October 2, 1961, 35.

36. Clavin and Peary, *Roger Maris*, 226–227.

37. Joseph M. Sheehan, "Jubilant Houk Calls 1961 Yanks Best All-Around Team He Has Ever Seen," *NYT*, October 10, 1961, 48.

38. Falls, "Reds Will Win in Five Games," *DFP*, October 3, 1961, 29.

39. Oscar Kahan, "Series Forecast Carbon Copy of Sizeup from 22 Years Ago," *TSN*, October 4, 1961, 1, 6.

40. Leavy, *The Last Boy*, 229–230.

41. Maris and Ogle, *Roger Maris at Bat*, 219.

42. Leavy, *The Last Boy*, 230–231.

43. Maris and Ogle, *Roger Maris at Bat*, 221–222.

44. Clavin and Peary, *Roger Maris*, 230.

45. Joseph M. Sheehan, "Ford Breaks Ruthian Pitching Marks and Says Maybe He'll Take Up Hitting," *NYT*, October 9, 1961, 45.

46. Danny Peary, ed., *We Played the Game: 65 Players Remember Baseball's Greatest Era, 1947–1964* (New York: Hyperion, 1994), 529–530.

Bibliography

Newspapers

Detroit Free Press
Detroit News
New York Times
The Sporting News

Magazine Articles

Barra, Allen. "Roger Maris' Misunderstood Quest to Break the Home Run Record." *The Atlantic*, July 27, 2011.

Bisher, Furman. "How Frank Lary Learned." *Sport*, August 1961.

Boyle, Robert H. "Taters Keeps the Tigers Up There." *Sports Illustrated*, September 4, 1961.

Furlong, Bill. "A Negro Ballplayer's Life Today." *Sport*, May 1962.

Hano, Arnold. "How the Home Run Is Breaking Up the Game." *Sport*, May 1962.

Meany, Tom. "From DiMaggio—To Mantle." *Sport*, September 1961.

Richman, Arthur. "Even Lary Can't Explain How He Hex-Rays the Yanks." *Baseball Digest*, June 1959.

Schaap, Dick. "On the Spot in '62: Norm Cash and Vada Pinson." *Sport*, April 1962.

"Scouting Reports—1961." *Sports Illustrated*, April 10, 1961.

Simons, Herbert. "Scouting Reports: On 1961 Major League Rookies." *Baseball Digest*, March 1961.

Wolf, Steve. "Tricks of the Trade." *Sports Illustrated*, April 13, 1981.

Books

Allen, Maury. *Yankees: Where Have You Gone?* New York: Sports Publishing, 2004.

Barra, Allen. *Yogi Berra: Eternal Yankee.* New York: W.W. Norton, 2009.

Baseball Register. St. Louis: C.C. Spink & Son, Publishers, 1962.

Berra, Yogi. *The Yogi Book: "I Really Didn't Say Everything I Said."* New York: Workman, 1998.

Berra, Yogi, and Ed Fitzgerald. *Yogi: The Autobiography of a Professional Baseball Player.* New York: Doubleday, 1961.

Butler, Hal. *Al Kaline and the Detroit Tigers.* Chicago: Henry Regnery, 1973.

_____. *Stormin' Norman Cash.* New York: Julian Messner, 1968.

Cantor, George. *The Tigers of '68: Baseball's Last Real Champions.* Dallas: Taylor, 1997.

Clavin, Tom, and Danny Peary. *Roger Maris: Baseball's Reluctant Hero.* New York: Simon & Schuster, 2010.

Cobbledick, Gordon. *Don't Knock the Rock: The Rocky Colavito Story.* Cleveland: World Publishing, 1966.

Detroit Baseball Company. *Detroit Tigers: 1961 Guide: Press, TV, Radio.* Detroit: Detroit Baseball, 1961.

_____. *1961: Detroit Tigers, Official Yearbook.* Detroit: Detroit Baseball, 1961.

Ferrell, Kerrie. *Rick Ferrell, Knuckleball Catcher: A Hall of Famer's Life Behind the Plate and in the Front Office.* Jefferson, NC: McFarland, 2010.

Ford, Whitey, with Phil Pepe. *Slick: My Life in and Around Baseball.* New York: William Morrow, 1987.

Golenbock, Peter. *Dynasty: The New York Yankees, 1949–1964*. Mineola, NY: Dover, 1975 and 2010.

Harrigan, Patrick. *The Detroit Tigers: Club and Community, 1945–1995*. Toronto: University of Toronto Press, 1997.

Hawkins, Jim. *Al Kaline: The Biography of a Tigers Icon*. Chicago: Triumph, 2010.

Howard, Arlene, with Ralph Wimbush. *Elston and Me: The Story of the First Black Yankee*. Columbia: University of Missouri Press, 2001.

Houk, Ralph, edited by Charles Dexter. *Ballplayers Are Human, Too*. New York: G. P. Putnam's Sons, 1962.

Houk, Ralph, and Robert W. Creamer. *Season of Glory*. New York: Simon & Schuster, 1988.

Kubek, Tony, and Terry Pluto. *Sixty-One: The Team, the Record, the Men*. New York: Macmillan, 1987.

Leavy, Jane. *The Last Boy: Mickey Mantle and the End of America's Childhood*. New York: HarperCollins, 2010.

Lowry, Philip J. *Green Cathedrals: The Ultimate Celebration of Major League and Negro League Ballparks*. New York: Walker, 2006.

Mantle, Mickey, with Herb Gluck. *The Mick*. Garden City, NY: Doubleday, 1985.

Maris, Roger, and Jim Ogle. *Roger Maris at Bat*. New York: Duell, Sloan, and Pearce, 1962.

Moffi, Larry. *This Side of Cooperstown: An Oral History of Major League Baseball in the 1950s*. Iowa City: University of Iowa Press, 1996.

Moffi, Larry, and Jonathan Kronstadt. *Crossing the Line: Black Major Leaguers, 1947–1959*. Jefferson, NC: McFarland, 1994 (repr., Lincoln: University of Nebraska Press, 2006).

Peary, Danny, ed. *We Played the Game: 65 Players Remember Baseball's Greatest Era, 1947–1964*. New York: Hyperion, 1994.

Richardson, Bobby. *The Bobby Richardson Story*. Westwood, NJ: Fleming H. Revell, 1965.

Spink, J. G. Taylor, comp. *Baseball Register: 1962 Edition*. St. Louis: C. C. Spink & Son, 1962.

Robinson, Ray, ed. *Baseball Stars of 1961*. New York: Pyramid Books, 1961.

_____. *Baseball Stars of 1962*. New York: Pyramid Books, 1962.

Index

Numbers in **_bold italics_** refer to pages with photographs.